Bergdorf Blondes

Bergdorf Blondes

Plum Sykes

VIKING
an imprint of
PENGUIN BOOKS

PENGUIN BOOKS

Published by the Penguin Group
Penguin Books Ltd, 80 Strand, London WC2R 0RL, England
Penguin Putnam Inc., 375 Hudson Street, New York, New York 10014, USA
Penguin Books Australia Ltd, 250 Camberwell Road, Camberwell, Victoria 3124, Australia
Penguin Books Canada Ltd, 10 Alcorn Avenue, Toronto, Ontario, Canada M4V 3B2
Penguin Books India (P) Ltd, 11 Community Centre, Panchsheel Park, New Delhi – 110 017, India
Penguin Books (NZ) Ltd, Cnr Rosedale and Airborne Roads, Albany, Auckland, New Zealand
Penguin Books (South Africa) (Pty) Ltd, 24 Sturdee Avenue, Rosebank 2196, South Africa

Penguin Books Ltd, Registered Offices: 80 Strand, London WC2R 0RL, England

www.penguin.com

First published in the United States of America by Hyperion Books 2004
First published in Great Britain by Viking 2004
4

Printed in England by Clays Ltd, St Ives plc

A CIP catalogue record for this book is available from the British Library

HARDBACK ISBN 0-670-91432-0
TRADE PAPERBACK ISBN 0-670-91433-9

Bergdorf Blondes

1

Bergdorf Blondes are a *thing*, you know, a New York craze. Absolutely everyone wants to be one, but it's actually *très* difficult. You wouldn't believe the dedication it takes to be a gorgeous, flaxen-haired, dermatologically perfect New York girl with a life that's fabulous beyond belief. Honestly, it all requires a level of commitment comparable to, say, learning Hebrew or quitting cigarettes.

Getting the hair color right is murder, for a start. It all began with my best friend, Julie Bergdorf. She's the ultimate New York girl, since glamorous, thin, blonde department-store heiresses are the chicest thing to be here. Someone heard she'd been going to Ariette at Bergdorf for her color since high school, because apparently she told her personal shopper at Calvin Klein who told all her clients. Anyway, it was rumored in certain circles that Julie got her blonde touched up every thirteen days exactly and suddenly everyone else wanted to be Thirteen-Day Blondes. The hair can't be yellow, it has to be very white, like Carolyn Bessette Kennedy's was. She's the icon, the hair to worship. It's beyond expensive. Ariette is like $450 a highlight, if you can get in with her, which obviously you can't.

Inevitably, Bergdorf Blondes are talked and gossiped about endlessly. Every time you open a magazine or newspaper there's another item about a BB's latest romantic drama or new obsession (right now it's fringed Missoni dresses). But sometimes gossip is by far the most reliable source of information about yourself and all your friends, especially in Manhattan. I always say why trust myself when gossip can tell *moi* the real truth about *moi*?

Anyway, according to gossip I'm this champagne bubble of a girl about town—New York being the only town that cares about having girls about it—living the perfect party-girl life, if that's what you think a perfect life is. I never tell a soul this, but sometimes before the parties I look in the mirror and see someone who looks like they are straight out of a movie like *Fargo*. I've heard that almost all Manhattan girls suffer from this debilitating condition. They never admit it either. Julie gets the Fargos so badly that she's never able to leave her apartment in The Pierre in time for anything she has to be in time for.

Everyone thinks the party-girl life is the best life you can lead here. The truth is that combined with work it's completely draining, but no one dares say that in case they look ungrateful. All anyone in New York ever says is "everything's fabulous!" even if they're on Zoloft for depression. Still, there are plenty of upsides. Like, you never have to pay for anything important like manis or pedis or highlights or blow-outs. The downside is that sometimes the freebies wreak havoc with your social life—believe me, if your dermatologist's kid can't get into Episcopal he'll be on the phone to you day and night.

To be specific, last Tuesday I went to my friend Mimi's townhouse on Sixty-third and Madison for her "super-duper-casual baby shower. Just the girls getting together," she'd said. There were three staff per guest, handmade pink cookies from Payard Patisserie on Lexington, and chocolate booties from Fauchon. It was about as casual as the inauguration. No one ate a thing, which is standard protocol at Upper East Side baby showers. I'd just walked through the door when my cell rang.

"Hello?" I said.

"You need highlights!" yelled a desperate voice. It was George, my hairdresser. I use George when I can't get in with Ariette which is almost all the time because she's permanently booked with Julie.

"Are you in Arizona?" I asked. ("Arizona" is what everyone says instead of "rehab." A lot of hairdressers in New York visit Arizona almost every month.)

"Just back," he replied. "If you don't go blonde you are going to be a very lonely girl," continued George tearfully.

Even though you'd think George, being a hairdresser, would know this already, I explained that a brunette like me can't go blonde.

"Can in New York," he said, choking up.

I ended up spending the present-opening ceremony in Mimi's library discussing addictive personality types with George and hearing all the one-liners he'd picked up in rehab, like "Say what you mean and mean what you say and don't be mean when you say it." Every time George goes into rehab he starts talking more and more like the Dalai Lama. Personally I think if hairdressers are going to offer deep insights they should be exclusively on the subject of hair. Anyway, no one thought George's behavior was odd because everyone in New York takes calls from their beauty experts at social occasions. It was lucky I was out of the room when Mimi opened my gift, which was a library of Beatrix Potter books. She totally freaked because it was more books than she'd ever read. Now I know why most girls give fashion from Bonpoint rather than controversial literature at baby showers.

Sometimes the hairdressers and their addictions and the parties and the blow-outs take up so much time it starts to feel like work and you can't focus on your real career. (And I do have a real career to think about—more of which later.) But that's what happens in Manhattan. Everything just kind of creeps up on you, and before you know it you're out every night, working like crazy and secretly waxing the hair on the inside of your nose like everyone else. It's not long before you start thinking that if you don't do the nose-hair-wax thing your whole world's going to fall apart.

Before I give you the rest of the goss from Mimi's shower, here are a few character traits you might want to know about me:

1. Fluent in French, intermittently. I'm really good at words like *moi* and *très,* which seem to take care of just about everything a girl needs. A few unkind people have pointed out that this does not make me exactly fluent, but I say, well, that's lucky because if I spoke *perfect* fluent French no one would like me, and no one likes a perfect girl, do they?
2. Always concerned for others' well-being. I mean, if a friendly billionaire offers you a ride from New York to Paris on his PJ (that's a quick NY way of

saying private jet), one is morally bound to say yes, because that means the person you would have been sitting next to on the commercial flight now has two seats to themself, which is a real luxury for them. And when you get tired you can go sleep in the bedroom, whereas however hard I look I have never found a bedroom on an American Airlines *767*. If someone else's comfort is at stake, I say, always take the private jet.

3. Tolerant. If a girl is wearing last season's Manolo Blahnik stilettos, I won't immediately rule her out as a friend. I mean, you never know if a super-duper-nice person is lurking in a past-it pair of shoes. (Some girls in New York are so ruthless they won't speak to a girl unless she's in next season's shoes, which is really asking a lot.)
4. Common sense. I really am fluent in it. You've got to recognize it when a day is a total waste of makeup.
5. English lit major. Everyone thinks it's unbelievable that a girl who is as obsessed with Chloé jeans as I am could have studied at Princeton but when I told one of the girls at the baby shower about school she said, "Oh my god! Ivy League! You're like the female Stephen Hawking." Listen, someone that brainy would never do something as crazy as spend $325 on a pair of Chloé jeans, but I just can't help it, like most New York girls. The reason I can just about afford the $325 jeans is because the aforementioned career consists of writing articles for a fashion magazine, which say that spending $325 on a pair of jeans will make you deliriously happy. (I've tried all the other jeans—Rogan, Seven, Earl, Juicy, Blue Cult—but I

always come back to the classic, Chloé. They just do something to your butt the others can't.) The other thing that helps fund my habit is if I don't pay my rent on my Perry Street apartment. I often don't, because my landlord seems to like being paid in other ways, like if I let him come up for a triple espresso he reduces my rent by over 100 percent. I always say, waste not, want not, which is a terrible cliché the British invented during the war to get kids to eat their whole-wheat bread, but when I say it I mean, waste not money on boring old rent when it can be unwasted on Chloé jeans.

6. Punctual. I am up every morning at 10:30 AM and not a minute earlier.
7. Thrifty. You can be frugal even if you have expensive tastes. Please don't tell a soul, because, you know, some girls get so jealous, but I hardly pay for a thing I wear. You see, fashion designers in New York love giving clothes away. Sometimes I wonder if fashion designers, who I consider to be geniuses, are actually thickos, like lots of mean people are always saying they are. Isn't giving something away for nothing when you could sell it for something a bit stupid? But there is something really, really clever about this particular form of stupidity because fashion designer–type people all seem to own at least four expensively decorated homes (St. Barths, Aspen, Biarritz, Paris), whereas all the clever people with regular jobs selling things for money only seem to own about one barely decorated house each. So I maintain that fashion designers are geniuses because it takes a genius to make money by giving things away.

Overall, I can safely say that my value system is intact, despite the temptations of New York, which, I regret to say, have made some girls into very spoiled little princesses.

❦

Talking of princesses, Mimi's shower was packed with the Park Avenue version. Everyone was there except—oddly—Julie, the biggest princess of them all. The most glamorous girls were all working the $325-Chloé-jeans look. They looked deliriously happy. Then there was another group who were working the Harry Winston engagement ring look and they seemed what I can only describe as beyond radiant. Jolene Morgan, Cari Phillips (who had the biggest ring, but then she'd gotten a deal because her mom was a Winston), and K.K. Adams were in this group. Soon they abandoned the main party for an engagement-ring summit in Mimi's bedroom, which is so big an entire dorm could sleep in it. Everything in there's upholstered in dove gray chintz, even the insides of her closets. When I finally got poor George sorted out and off my cell, I joined them. Jolene—who's curvacious and blonde and pale and worships Sophie Dahl because she heard she's never sunbathed in her life—has been engaged twice before. I wondered how she could be sure this latest fiancé was the right one.

"Oh, easy! I've got a new, watertight method of selection. If you use the same criteria to choose a man that you would when choosing a handbag, I guarantee you will find one that suits you perfectly," she explained.

Jolene's theory is that a man has many wonderful things in common with a handbag, like the fact that there's a wait list for the best ones. Some are two weeks (college boys and L.L. Bean totes), some are three years (funny men and alligator Hermès Birkin bags). Even if you are on the list for the whole three years, another woman with a superior claim can jump the line. Jolene says you have to hide a really sexy one or your best friend will borrow it without telling you. Her main concern is that without one, a girl looks underdressed.

". . . which makes it completely understandable that a girl may need to try out several styles of fiancé before she finds one that really suits her," concluded Jolene.

Maybe I had misjudged Jolene Morgan: I secretly used to think she was one of the shallowest girls in New York, but Jolene has hidden depths when it comes to relationships. Sometimes you go to a baby shower expecting nothing more than a conversation about the advantages of a scheduled C-section (you can pick your kid's birth sign), and come away having learned a lot about life. The minute I got home I e-mailed Julie.

To: JulieBergdorf@attglobal.net
From: Moi@moi.com
Re: Happiness

Just got back from Mimi's baby shower. Darling, where were you? Jolene, K. K., and Cari all engaged. Have detected glaring difference between Chloé jeans happiness and engagement ring happiness this afternoon. I mean, have you any idea how awesome your skin looks if you are engaged?

Julie Bergdorf has been my best friend since the minute I met her at her mother's corner apartment in The Pierre Hotel on Fifth and Sixty-first. She was an eleven-year-old department-store heiress. Her great-grandfather started Bergdorf Goodman and a whole chain of stores around America, which is why Julie says she always has at least $100 million in the bank "and not a dime more," as she puts it. Julie spent most of her teens shoplifting from Bergdorf's after getting out of Spence each day. She still finds it hard not to see Bergdorf's as her walk-in closet even though most of it was sold to Neiman Marcus years ago. The best thing she ever stole was a Fabergé egg encrusted with rubies that was once owned by Catherine the Great. Her excuse for her childhood hobby is that she "liked nice stuff. It must have been so icky being a Woolworth kid, I mean they used to have to shoplift, like, toilet cleaner, but I got to take really glam stuff, like handmade kid leather gloves."

Julie's favorite words are *icky* and *glam.* Julie once said she wished there was no ickiness in the world, and I said to her, if there was no ickiness there wouldn't be any glamour. You've got to have the ickiness just for contrast. She said, oh, like if there were no poor people then no one would be rich, and I said, well, what I actually mean is, if you were happy all the time, how would you know you were happy? She said, because you'd always be happy. I said, no, you have to have unhappiness to know what happiness is. Julie frowned and said, "Have you been reading *The New Yorker* again?" Julie thinks *The New Yorker* and PBS are completely evil and boring and that everyone should read *US Weekly* and watch the E! channel instead.

Our mothers were both mainline Philadelphia WASPs

who had been best friends in the seventies. I grew up in England because my dad's English and everything about England is "better" according to Mom, but you don't get department-store heiresses in England and Mom was very concerned that I should have one as a friend. Meanwhile, Julie's mom thought I would be a civilizing influence on her daughter. They made sure we met every summer and sent us to camp in Connecticut. I don't think they realized how amazingly convenient this was for taking the train straight back to New York the moment they dropped us off and went on to the Bergdorf family compound on Nantucket.

Back in New York, the young Julie and I sat around at The Pierre ordering the hotel's special hot orange cakes with chocolate sauce and maple syrup from room service. It was much more fun being an American little girl in New York than being an American little girl in England. New York girls like Julie got to be very spoiled and had Rollerblades and ice skates and makeup and facialists. They had wonderfully absent parents. Julie knew the geography of Barneys intimately by thirteen, and had actually shopped there. She was already a Bergdorf Blonde, even though we didn't know about them yet.

Thanks to Julie, I returned to England that summer addicted to *Vogue* magazine and MTV and bearing a much-improved American accent that I cultivated by watching *High Society* over and over. Mom was totally freaked out by it, which meant it was really working.

All I wanted to do was move to New York and get highlights that looked as awesome as Julie's. To that end I begged Mom and Dad for an American college education. Please don't tell a soul that I said this, but I honestly think the only reason I got the grades Princeton required was because throughout the algebra and the Latin and the Romantic poets, the thing that kept me going was the thought of the oxygen facials you could get in New York. When I got the place at Princeton, all Mom could say was, "But how could you leave England for America? How? *How?*"

She obviously had no idea about the oxygen facials.

❧

It turned out there was a good reason Julie didn't make it to Mimi's. She'd been arrested for shoplifting from Bergdorf Goodman. People called late that afternoon to deliver the hot news, but when I tried to reach Julie her cell phone went straight to voice mail. I wasn't surprised. Even though Julie swore to me she'd quit stealing when she'd come into her trust fund, it was the kind of crazy thing she'd do just because she was feeling bored for five minutes. Still, I was beginning to get a little worried when Julie herself called just after 7 PM.

"Hey boo! It's really funny, I've been arrested. Can you come get me? Bail me out? I'm sending my driver to pick you up right now."

When I arrived at the 17th Precinct on East Fifty-first Street forty-five minutes later, Julie was sitting in the shabby waiting area looking impossibly chic. She was dressed for the chilly October day in skinny white cashmere pants, a casual fox fur jacket, and huge sunglasses. She looked ridiculously sophisticated for a girl in her mid-twenties, but all the Park Avenue Princesses are. An adoring cop was just handing her a Starbucks latte that he'd clearly gone out to collect on her behalf. I sat down on the bench next to her.

"Julie, you're nuts," I said. "Why have you started stealing again?"

"Because, *duh,* I wanted that Hermès Birkin, you know the new ostrich one in baby pink with the white trim? I felt so depressed not having it," she said, all *faux* innocence.

"Why didn't you just buy it? You could totally afford it."

"You can't 'just buy' a Birkin! There's a three-year wait list, unless you're Renée Zellweger, and even then you might not get one. I'm already on the wait list anyway for the baby blue suede and it's killing me."

"But Julie, it's *stealing* and you're kind of stealing from yourself."

"Isn't that neat!"

"You've got to stop. You're going to be all over the newspapers."

"Isn't it *great*?"

Julie and I must have been there for at least an hour before Julie's lawyer appeared and told us that he had managed to get the police to drop the charges. He'd told them that Julie always intended to buy the goods, she just never usually pays in the store, the bills go straight to her apartment. This was simply an embarrassing mix-up.

Julie was really very cheerful about the whole episode. She seemed almost reluctant to finally leave the precinct that night. Clearly she had loved the attention she got from the cops. She had charmed Detective Owen—who was obviously 100 percent in love with her the minute he arrested her—into letting her call in hair and makeup for the mug shot. I guess she was right to treat it like a fashion shoot. I mean, that picture could be reproduced for years to come.

The media went a bit nuts about Julie after the arrest. When she left The Pierre (where Daddy had generously bought Julie the other corner apartment) the next morning to go to the gym, she was faced by hordes of photographers. Julie ran back inside and telephoned me, wailing, "Oh my god! They're all out there! Paparazzi, press, and they got my picture! Ugh! I can't handle it."

Julie was crying hysterically, but this happens all the time so no one did anything dramatic like call 911 or anything. I told her that no one would look at the pictures, or even remember what had happened the next day. Really, it didn't matter if she was all over the papers.

"It's not being in the papers that I mind," she moaned, "it's that they got me in sweatpants! I can never be seen on the corner of Madison and Seventy-sixth Street again! Please come over?"

Sometimes, when Julie says things like that, I think, well, it's lucky she's my best friend because if she wasn't I wouldn't like her *at all*.

When I arrived at her apartment, the housekeeper sent me straight through to Julie. Hair and makeup were on standby, hovering in terrified silence in the bedroom, which is painted pale jade, Julie's favorite color. Two antique Chinese mother-of-pearl chests sit on either side of the fireplace. The upholstered sleigh bed is an heirloom from Julie's grandmother. Julie won't get into it unless it's just been made with sheets monogrammed with her initials in pale pistachio silk. I found Julie red-faced in the dressing room, frantically raking through the closets. As fast as she tossed clothes out and into a mountainous pile on the thick white rug, her maid put them back in the closet, so that the pile never increased or decreased significantly. Finally Julie dug out an understated black Chanel dress of her mother's, kitten heels, and very large sunglasses. She was totally channeling CBK, as usual. An hour later, blown out and made up beyond belief, she strolled out of The Pierre, a confident smile on her face, and gave an interview to the waiting press in which she explained about the "mix-up."

The next Sunday a fabulously glamorous picture of Julie appeared on the cover of the *New York Times* Style section, with the headline BEAUTIFUL BERGDORF INNOCENT and an accompanying article by the *Times*'s fashion critic. Julie was thrilled. So was her dad. She called me the following Monday to say that an antique bracelet had arrived from him with a note reading, "Thank you darling daughter. D."

"He's *pleased*?" I asked.

"I'm so happy," said Julie. "I've never been in Dad's good books like this before. All that shoplifting heiress stuff, it's been like the greatest PR for the store; sales have gone through the roof, especially of the sunglasses I was wearing. He's recommended the board make me marketing director. I just hope I don't have to work too hard."

After that, Julie couldn't go anywhere without having her picture taken, all in the cause, she said, of raising Bergdorf's profile, which she did, along with her own. She thought the publicity was very good for her self-esteem and was helping with her issues—issues being the hip term for the glamorous psychological problems of the type that afflict those living in New York and Los Angeles.

Julie has issues with the receptionist at Bliss Spa who won't book her vitamin C skin injections with Simonetta, the top facialist there. She is encouraged by her doctors to explore her "childhood issues" and is "in a lot of pain" over the fact that her parents used to fly her business class to Gstaad every Christmas, when everyone else's parents flew their kids first. Naturally, she has a catalog of "food issues" and once followed Dr. Perricone's Wrinkle Cure Diet, which led to her acquiring "issues with potatoes and wheat." She has issues about having too much money and she has issues about not having as much money as some of the other Park Avenue Princesses. She previously had issues about being a Jewish WASP, which she recovered from when her licensed psychologist told her that Gwyneth Paltrow also suffered from this affliction, being the product of a Jewish father and WASPy mother. After this issue was resolved, Julie then got another issue about her psychologist charging her $250 for information she could have gotten from *Vanity Fair* at a cost of $3.50, which, it transpired, was the place where the licensed psychologist learned of Gwyneth's ethnic roots. When anyone disagrees with Julie it means they have issues, and when Julie disagrees with her shrink it's because he's the one with the real issues.

When I once suggested to Julie that maybe her issues would eventually be resolved she replied, "God, I hope not. I'd be so uninteresting if I was just rich and not screwed up about it." Without her issues, she said, "I'd be a personality-free zone."

Luckily it's *très* chic to be neurotic in New York, which means that Julie and I fit in perfectly.

You can imagine Julie's reaction to the e-mail about the glaring difference between our kind of Chloé jeans happiness and Jolene's and K.K.'s and Cari's fiancé happiness. We were having brunch a few days later at Joe's, this super-unhealthy diner on the corner of Sullivan and Houston. Julie was way overdressed in that tiny new Mendel mink jacket that everyone's gone nuts about. But then Park Avenue Princesses overdress for everything, even ordering in. I would too if I had that many new clothes every week. She was basking in her shoplifting triumph but frowned when I reminded her about Mimi's shower.

"Are you trying to give me another issue? Eew! How could you! It's beyond!" she cried tearfully.

"How could I what?" I said, pouring maple syrup onto a silver dollar pancake.

"E-mail me that whole thing about, like, everyone but me having a fiancé. It's so unfair. I'm happy but I'm not *beyond* happy like K.K. and Jolene. You've got to be in love for that."

"You don't have to be in love to be happy," I said.

"You only think that because you've never been in love. God, I feel so unhappy and so un-*chic*! I heard they all look *amazing* now that they're engaged."

Underneath all the issues and the drama and the clothes and the vitamin C injections, Julie is hopelessly romantic.

She claims to have been in love more than fifty-four times. She started young—acquiring her first boyfriend at seven—"but that was before the oral sex epidemic hit," she always says. She actually *believes* love songs. Like she really does think that love lifts you up where you belong and seriously fell for the Beatles' crazy idea that all you need is love. Most of her love-type problems have been caused by Dolly Parton, who inspired her so much with "I Will Always Love You" that Julie says she genuinely loves all her exes, "even the ones I really hate," which her shrink says is a "*huge* issue." She thinks "Heartbreak Hotel" refers to the Four Seasons Hotel on Fifty-seventh Street where she checks in every time she rows with a boyfriend. If I could afford a suite at that divine place, I'd break up with a man every two weeks, too. Julie was convinced the only way she could be happy was to be in love and have a fiancé on her arm like everyone else.

"I have all the Vuitton bags Marc Jacobs ever made, but what's the point if my other arm doesn't have a fiancé supporting it? And look!" she gasped, pointing at my legs under the table. "You're wearing fishnets! Are fishnets in, too? *Why didn't anyone tell me?*"

Julie flopped her head dramatically onto the table and wiped her tears on her mink, which I thought was a really spoiled princessy way to behave, but this is totally in keeping with her personality so I shouldn't be too shocked, I suppose. After a few minutes she calmed down and her face suddenly lit up. Julie's mood swings are so unpredictable, sometimes I think she's schizophrenic.

"I've got an idea. Let's go fishnet-stocking and fiancé shopping together!" she said excitedly.

Julie honestly thinks fiancés are as easy to come by as hose.

"Julie, why on earth would you want to get married now?" I said.

"Eew! I don't. I said I wanted a fiancé! I'm not necessarily going to *marry* him right away. Ooh, I can hardly wait. We are going Prospective Husband hunting," she continued.

"We?!" I exclaimed. "Isn't America supposed to be a modern country where career girls don't need things like fiancés?"

"Everyone wants to fall in love eventually. Fiancés are *so glam*! Tell me this, who was CBK before JFK Jr.?"

"Julie, you can't get engaged just to look glamorous, that would be selfish," I said.

"Really?" exclaimed Julie, her face growing brighter. (Every week Julie's therapist tells her she'll be happier if she's more selfish, not less. Judging by most people's behavior, everyone's therapist in New York must be saying this.) "I'm so excited! Okay, I gotta go home and not eat. I'm putting on weight just looking at the napkins in this place," said Julie.

Before she left, Julie made me promise to help her out with her "PH campaign"—her way of referring to the Prospective Husband hunt. She would acquire the fiancé just as easily as the fishnet stockings. I was sure of it. Julie is a shining example of the Park Avenue Princess ethic at work. She doesn't let anything stand in her way.

Julie headed back uptown and I rushed off to a work appointment. God, I thought in the cab, Julie's PH hunt could be stressful. Sometimes the perfect party-girl life is as exhausting as boot camp. Sometimes, I thought, I could be doing something less exhausting, like living the perfect non-party-girl life somewhere relaxing like the British country-side. Okay, so I wouldn't have any nice shoes, but there *are* other benefits to living in a Manolo-free zone. None came to mind right away, but I was sure I would think of something positive.

Then Mom called.

2

I let voice mail pick up.

The sound of Mom's voice always reminds me that there are very good reasons why I am living the party-girl life here, and not living the non-party-girl life over there.

Four reasons to leave England, in ascending order of importance:

1. *Mom*

Migraine-prone. Migraines caused by such terrifying prospects as driving into multi-story carpark at Heathrow Airport; taking a holiday abroad because she might have to drive into multi-story carpark to get plane because planes leave from airports, which generally include multi-story carparks; remembering she's an American; sending a fax; sending a postcard; thinking about the idea of learning how to send an e-mail; living at our house in rural Northamptonshire; living in London. In other words, *everything*.

The result is that Mom, who always calls herself "Mummy, because it's more British," is obsessed with controlling her only daughter's life. A Professional Mom and a stunningly unembarrassed snob, she's fixated on the British aristocracy, their interior decorating style, and the brand of Wellington boots they wear (*Le Chameau,* leather lined). Her ambition was to marry me off to someone British and aristocratic. (A career wasn't part of her plan, but it was part of mine.) The ideal candidate was "the Boy Next Door," the son of the local peer, the Earl of Swyre. Julie could never understand why I hated Mom's idea so much. She always says she'd do anything to marry a guy with an English castle. But then, she has no idea how damp they get in winter.

Our house sits on the border of the twenty-five-thousand-acre estate of Swyre Castle. "Next door" for the English upper classes means a twenty-minute drive. Ever since I can remember, every time we motored by the castle gates Mom would exclaim, as though she'd just that minute thought of it, "Little Earl is just your age! He's the most eligible man in Northamptonshire!" (She was describing our six-year-old neighbor, whom I'd never actually met.)

"Mom, I'm five and a half. You have to be sixteen to get married," I said.

"Start young! You are going to be the most beautiful girl and you are going to marry Little Earl next door and live in the pretty castle, which is much grander than any of your relations' castles."

"Mom—"

"It's 'Mummy.' Stop saying 'Mom' and talking in that unflattering American accent or no one will ever marry you."

My accent was a replica of Mom's. I couldn't change it, just like she couldn't. The difference was, I didn't want to. I wanted a *more* American accent, even at five and a half.

"Mummy, why do you always say that all our relations live in castles when only one of them does?"

"Because the others died, darling."

"When?"

"Very recently, in the Wars of the Roses."

One of our relations did have a castle near Aberdeen. We visited the Hon. William Courtenay, my father's aging great-uncle, every Christmas. His grandsons, Archie and Ralph (pronounced, inexplicably, "Rafe" in England), were also on Mom's shortlist of future husbands, their considerable inheritances making up for their lack of titles.

Mom told me that everyone in America wished they got to go to a real Scottish castle for Christmas vacation. I never quite believed her. I mean, who wants to spend five days in a house colder than the North Pole when they could be at Disney World? After six arctic Christmases I developed a phobia of country houses that I doubt will ever leave me. Most of the time I fantasized about being Jewish so we could forget the whole Christmas thing altogether.

Mom's marital ambitions for me came up in almost every childhood conversation I can remember, the way other parents go on at their kids about getting into college or not taking drugs. I remember being about ten years old when we had a very tense talk over breakfast.

"Darling, when are you going to go round to Swyre Castle and have tea with Little Earl? I hear he's very handsome. He'd fall in love with you if he met you," said Mom.

"Mom, you know that no one's seen the Swyres since Daddy sold the Earl of Swyre those chairs," I replied.

"Sshhh!!! All that was a long time ago. I'm sure the Earl and Countess have forgotten all about it."

"Anyway, Mom, everyone says they've moved away. No one's seen them for years," I said, exasperated.

"Well, I'm sure they visit! How could anyone abandon a house that beautiful? That dome! Those Capability Brown grounds. Next time they're here let's call . . ."

"Can we not, please?" I replied, even though I was secretly a little curious about the castle and its owners.

Mom was in complete denial about two rather significant facts: first, that the Swyres had divorced about four years before—the mysterious Countess was famous for her affairs—and the Earl and his little boy seemed to have vanished; second, that ever since my father, who was always chasing a new "bargain," sold the Earl four Chippendale chairs that turned out to be fakes, the two families had been on non-speaks. The Chair Affair—as it was dubbed by the local newspaper—was a typical English village feud destined never to be resolved. Although the chairs were returned, and my father repaid the money and apologized in writing to the furious Earl, saying that he had been duped by his suppliers, the Earl refused to believe him. He let it be known that he distrusted Dad and wanted nothing to do with him. The Countess, naturally, sided with her husband. Mom, naturally, sided with Dad. Everyone in the village, naturally, sided with the Swyres, as was tradition, thereby increasing their chances of being invited to the big house for dinner.

Mom, desperate to be friends with them, tried to make

amends with the Swyres. However, when she invited them to her annual summer drinks party, they declined. When Christmas came around, there was no invitation to the castle for Boxing Day lunch. At church, the Countess publicly snubbed Mom by moving pews when Mom sat at the end of hers.

Mom found the whole affair so socially embarrassing that she eventually started pretending it had never happened. Mom always hoped everything would be forgotten, but the village thrived on the story and wouldn't let it go. Honestly, in small English villages people have lifelong feuds over the dumbest stuff, like the size of their cabbages, or what kind of tree their neighbors planted on the boundary (oaks are acceptable, conifers will precipitate legal proceedings). It's tradition. I think it keeps them going through the long winter nights.

After the divorce, the castle was run as a conference center, although the family kept a wing for themselves. The Earl was rumored to occasionally appear, alone, and then vanish.

The older I got, the more Mom's attitudes annoyed me. When I said, "I'm going to have a career and marry for love, if I do. You married Dad for love," she replied, without missing a beat, "Exactly. Don't do anything as silly as that."

To be fair to Mom, she had tried to stick to her principles and *not* marry for love. Before she was a Professional Mom, she was a Professional Brown Signer.

A Brown Signer is a woman who is interested exclusively in British men with houses that have brown signs outside. I'll explain: The only way the British aristocracy can afford to go on living in their huge beautiful houses is if they open them to the public. A sign that is generally brown with white lettering is placed on the closest highway to direct the public to the house. The brown signs often have a cute little icon of a stately home on them. Only very large houses have brown signs, because if your house is small, you can afford the repairs and upkeep yourself, but if your roof is sixteen square acres, financial aid is required every time a tile comes loose. So quite ironically, although a brown sign is an indication of too little money to mend a roof, it is also a reverse status symbol. Because if you don't have enough money to mend your roof that means you must have a vast roof and we all know what's underneath a vast roof: a vast house.

You'd be surprised how many girls want a man with a brown sign. Brown Signers are cunning, leggy, international beauties from Manhattan, Paris, and London, who pose as uncunning things like handbag designers, actresses, and artists. It's perfect cover because no one would ever imagine that a fabulous girl with a modern career would swap it for something as retro as a brown sign. It makes no sense at all—I mean, it would be the moral equivalent of swapping the new Prada shoe for last season's.

Before a date, Brown Signers do their homework. They look up the man in *Debrett's Peerage & Baronetage*, a British guidebook that lists Brits of high birth, plus their addresses. If the house has a "The" in front of it—e.g., "The Priory" or "The Manor"—it is more than likely to have over twenty rooms and a brown sign. Regardless of his looks, mind, hair quantity, or neck measurement, the Brown Signer is in love with the proprietor of the brown sign before she has closed her *Debrett's* and curled her eyelashes.

Mom was an American Brown Signer posing as a student. It was the seventies and she couldn't get out of the Upper East Side quick enough. Her destination: London's Chelsea College of Art, the perfect hunting ground.

Mom thought she was getting The Manor-at-Ashby-Under-Little-Sleightholmdale by marrying Dad, which she did practically the day after he'd taken her to dinner at Annabel's in Berkeley Square and driven her home in his Jaguar XJS (which was apparently a very cool car back then). After the wedding she discovered that although he has aristocratic roots, Dad was about thirteenth in line for The Manor-at-Ashby-Under-Little-Sleightholmdale. The Jaguar was borrowed. Mom blamed the confusion on her being an American, because Americans trust guidebooks like *Debrett's* as much as they trust the *Michelin Blue Guide*.

That's when the migraines started. Mom realized that not only was she married to a not very rich man, she was in love with him, too. It wasn't what she wanted.

I say, complain not when you've saved yourself a life sentence like writing out The Manor-at-Ashby-Under-Little-Sleightholmdale every time you want to send a letter. I don't think Mom agrees. She renamed our house, which was originally called Vicarage Cottage, The Old Rectory at Stibbly-on-the-Wold, which is a very grand title for a four-bedroom house that isn't exactly old. Whenever I ask Mom why everyone else calls the village just "Stibbly" she says its because no one in the village knows their correct address.

Speaking of long names, this reminds me:

2. *Toffs*

The main reason to *avoid* a brown sign is because it comes with an aristocrat, known fondly as a "toff" in Britain. Toffs call their palaces "dumps," wear sweaters with holes in them darned by their ancient nannies whom they love more than any other women in their lives, and really do call sex "shagging" *à la* Austin Powers. Amazingly a lot of English girls tolerate The toff in return for The House and The Title. Personally I think it would be beyond exhausting to have a title like The Marchioness of Dufferin and Ava, or Alice, Duchess of Drumllandrig. It's bad enough signing checks with a name with two parts, let alone five or six. But to some women, a six-part name and a toff are worth all the sacrifices—like absolutely no central heating allowed, ever.

Seriously, the British aristocracy actually think heating is low class. I have always thought this is unfair to people like me who just get cold easily. Mom often said when I was a kid that she'd be happier if I died of pneumonia in a historic four-poster bed at twenty-nine than if I lived to be eighty-five in a centrally heated house. That's one of the reasons I was allergic to Mom's idea of the Boy Next Door: I just didn't know if, being an American designed to thrive in balmy, artificial heat, my fragile constitution would survive the low temperatures associated with a toff marriage.

3. *Dad*

Dad describes himself as an "antiques entrepreneur," but he's so entrepreneurial that he's totally gullible about any bargain, including those fake Chippendales he sold to the Earl. He was so cross about the whole affair that we could never mention it. In fact, no one in the house really spoke about chairs of any type when they were around Dad.

4. Brazilians

When I first moved to New York after college, this cute guy, a twenty-seven-year-old movie director (who'd never actually directed a movie) told me I "needed a Brazilian here." Considering the position of his head at the time, which I'm way too polite to reveal, I thought it was *très* peculiar that he was proposing that a man of Latin origin should put his head in the same place.

"Chad!" I said. "Why would you want a Brazilian here as well as you?" (I mean, not to be racist or anything, but one foreigner at a time.)

"There's too much hair down here for a New Yorker like me."

"Would a Brazilian be more suited to this than you?" I asked.

"You don't know what a Brazilian is, do you?"

"It's a person like Ricky Martin."

"Duh! Ricky Martin's French. A Brazilian's a wax. You need one real bad."

Chad insisted I visit the J. Sisters the next morning at 35 West Fifty-seventh Street, which is where I discovered the true meaning of the word *Brazilian.* It's a bikini wax that involves waxing virtually everything off the place where Chad had had his head. On the pain scale, it's right up there with unfriendly things like cervical biopsies, so *entre nous,* next time I will get an epidural first.

Chad was thrilled with the new Brazilian. Most men are, I've subsequently discovered. Ironically it was to be the cause of our breakup. He wanted his head to be near it constantly, which got a bit much after a while. Then he started doing creepola things like spontaneously booking appointments for me with the J. Sisters and getting overly upset if I cancelled. (No one has the pain threshold to tolerate a Brazilian every week. No one.) That's when I started to suspect that I don't have quite as good taste in men as I do in shoes. A man whose affections are swayed by the shallow charms of a bikini wax wasn't exactly what I wanted. I had to end it.

"Only a really superficial person would break up over a fuckin' fifty-five-dollar wax," said Chad when I told him.

"Chad, its fuckin-*g*," I said. Chad was totally not into Received Pronunciation, which is the one British habit this American girl never kicked. I thought the way he spoke was cute actually, but I couldn't help correcting him.

"There's fuck*in'* noth*in'* more fuck*in'* annoy*in'* than go*in'* out with ya."

"Well then you must be happy I'm leav-*ing* you," I said, trying not to get upset. "A girl's more than the sum of her parts, Chad."

Even though there were things I missed about Chad (the Brazilian was the start of many useful beauty tips), I was relieved it was over. I mean, he wasn't exactly an honest person. Ricky Martin is actually from Puerto Rico, not France as Chad insisted he was, and if you look at the globe you'll see Puerto Rico is much closer to Brazil than to France. Still, the one gift Chad gave me was the Brazilian. I couldn't survive without it now. Apparently it's the secret weapon of the most glamorous women in the world. And I would *never* tell Chad this, after everything that happened, but if I were a man I probably wouldn't want to date a woman who hadn't had a Brazilian either. So, although I didn't know about Brazilians until after I had left the English countryside, had I known about them before I decided to leave, it would definitely have made me go. Therefore, retrospectively, I can add Brazilians to my list of reasons to move to Manhattan.

Manhattan Shorthand: A Translation

1. Chip's—Harry Cipriani on Fifth and Fifty-ninth Street.

2. Ana—to the Park Avenue Princesses, ana = anorexic = thin = perfection.

3. Beyond—not somewhere far away. It's a substitute superlative replacing words like *fabulous/stunning/gorgeous*. E.g., "That eyebrow wax is beyond."

4. A Wollman—diamond the size of an ice rink.

5. A.T.M.—rich boyfriend.

6. M.I.T.—Mogul in Training (more desirable than an A.T.M.).

7. M.T.M.—Married to Mogul (better than both of previous).

8. Llamas on Madison—insanely glamorous South American girls who gallop up Madison in ponchos and pearls.

9. Fake Bake—tan acquired at Portofino Sun Soho Spa on West Broadway.

10. Eew!—mini-scream designed to show surprise/horror, as in "Eew! *She* got the new Bottega boots before *me*?" Used exclusively by Manhattan girls under twenty-seven and female stars of NBC sitcoms.

11. On the d-l—on the down low, from the low down, which means same as on the q-t.

12. Clinical—depressed, as in clinical depression.

13. The Fritz—abbreviation for "the fucking Ritz," as in The Ritz Hotel, Paris.

3

"The only sexually transmitted disease I wanna contract," said Julie, "is fiancé fever."

I could see why Julie wanted a Prospective Husband. American men are wonderful, buff creatures with unique talents. I mean, if you squint enough, they *all* look like JFK Jr., I swear it. For someone with attention deficit disorder, which has afflicted Julie and most of the other Park Avenue Princesses since childhood (although it doesn't seem to afflict them when shopping), her new ability to focus was miraculous. She had this crazy idea that if she selected exactly the right party, one that was the equivalent of attending six gallery openings, four museum benefits, three dinners, and two major movie premieres all in one night, she would be guaranteed to leave at the end of the evening with a Prospective Husband on her arm for sure. Julie said this was a project she didn't want to waste too much time on when, as she puts it, "I could waste my time doing other things, like getting eyebrow waxes."

Julie's attitude toward her imminent engagement was a

little disturbing. She honestly believed that when she got the perfect fiancé, if she hadn't had time to get her eyebrows shaped—which is, in her opinion, the most important facial procedure performed by the doctors at the Bergdorf Goodman salon—she would be so gutted, there would be no point in the fiancé anyway.

When Julie puts her mind to something, she can be surprisingly efficient. She selected the New York Conservatory Ball, a charity benefit, as the most promising hunting ground. Having bought a table, she called the honorary chairwoman, Mrs. E. Henry Steinway Zigler III, to "discuss strategy." Julie wanted to check the seating plan in advance. Mrs. Zigler invited us to tea at her marble mansion overlooking Central Park on Fifth Avenue and Eighty-second Street. She loves to play cupid.

"Call me Muffy, girls," she said warmly when we arrived.

Muffy was wearing a fringed Oscar de la Renta poncho, lime green cigarette pants, and enough jewels to empty a diamond mine. She said she was channeling Elizabeth Taylor in *The Sandpiper*. Everyone in New York is always channeling someone else. Her poncho swinging dramatically from side to side as she trotted ahead, she led us through the echoing atrium and into the drawing room. Grander than Versailles, it's hung with huge gilt mirrors and Italian oil paintings, and dotted with elegant antique sofas and chairs that Muffy bulk buys whenever she's close to a Sotheby's. Muffy tells people her home is decorated, "to look exactly like Oscar's. I went there, I saw his place, I couldn't stand it. I had to have it. I cloned his apartment!"

Muffy always says that "being rich is a life sentence that is mainly enjoyable, and I should know." Almost every

Upper East Side wife I have met is called Muffy. Apparently it was once a very popular name in Connecticut, where most Muffys were born, roughly in the middle of the last century. This Muffy, like all her neighborhood Muffys, says, "Ralph Lauren is my drug of choice." She's addicted to Botox injections and tells everyone she's "thirty-eight." She's an F.O.G.—Friend of George—and when Bill Clinton was in power, she was an F.O.B. She donates millions to the Republicans and millions more to the Democrats, because she still has a "special relationship" with Bill. All the other Muffys have special relationships with Bill too, but I don't think she knows that.

We sat in a little group on Muffy's matching Victorian Knole sofas. (Knole sofas are very, very in on the Upper East Side right now, especially if you can get one upholstered in seventeenth-century verdure tapestry, which of course is almost impossible.) A uniformed maid brought tea on a silver tray. With her party imminent, Muffy was as hyperactive as a Japanese tourist in a Louis Vuitton outlet store. She couldn't stop tugging at the tassels on the sofa cushions.

"Oh Lord! The party's tomorrow! I've secured *super-duper* princes, millionaires, movie producers, heirs, architects, politicians! Bill might be coming!" she exclaimed. "Everyone in New York will be here tomorrow night."

"Which charity is this party in aid of, Muffy?" I asked.

"Oh, Save Something or Other. Save Venice, Save the Met, Save the Ballet! Who knows? I'm on so many committees—Mr. Zigler just adores those tax breaks—that I just call them all the same thing, 'Save Whatever.' Isn't that *brilliant*! If only someone would save *me* from the ladies on the committees. If you don't donate a mil it's death by stiletto. I think this one is saving flowers of some kind. Charity is a *glorious* American institution because ultimately someone or other who needs it gets pots of money, and we all get to dress up in *super-duper* Michael Kors frocks. Now, business," she said, more seriously. "A little birdie tells me you want a fiancé, Julie. How marvelous! Do tell! What sort of man do you want?"

"Someone smart, and fun, who's going to make me laugh. And who I can moan and whine at for hours and they'll still adore me. Just don't hook me up with a creative type. I got those out of my system in high school. No actors, artists, or musicians for me, thank you," said Julie.

I hadn't realized Julie was so mature. Mind you, when you've had fifty-four boyfriends you should know what you want.

"There's no fear of that on the Upper East Side, dear," said Muffy. "There are no creative types up here, oh no! The mayor doesn't let them past Union Square."

"Oh, and I know this is going to sound totally spoiled and superficial, but I do like it if my boyfriends believe in drivers. I blame Dad. He ruined me for life by having me chauffeured to school every day in a Jaguar. That's just the way I am. I can't change myself, can I?" said Julie, blushing a little.

"No, dear," cooed Muffy soothingly. "If you don't like walking, you don't like walking and that's it. Look at me, I have *three* drivers! We have one at the house in Palm Beach, one in Aspen, and one here. There's nothing wrong with expressing your needs, Julie."

There's extravagant and there's extravagant. Even among her own set Muffy takes the word to new heights.

"I just want to fall in love, Muffy, like all the other girls, and have radiant skin without having to get Vitamin C injections," said Julie, her eyes looking watery. "I get really lonesome sometimes."

Muffy is an exceptionally mathematical socialite whose *placement* equations are as complex as chess. She has a system she uses whenever her "merging" services are required. She always makes sure she has one table of thirteen, with one too many men. Every guest has a number in the seating plan. Julie was number four and her seat would be second from the end of the rectangular table, which had the advantage of being accessible for conversation by four men. To Julie's left and right would be an Italian prince and a record producer, opposite would be a real estate mogul, and at the head of the table would be the thirteenth, the "extra" man, who would be told by the hostess she was terribly sorry she had to sit him next to two other men, "but there's just too many of you boys tonight!"

I don't know anyone else in New York who could avail a girl of four eligible dinner partners at one sitting. The only time Muffy's math fails her is when it comes to budgeting for the florist(s).

The next night Julie's smile was bigger than Africa. So were her diamond earrings. Sometimes, even someone as happy for her friend's good fortune as me goes a bit off-yellow with envy when I see Julie's Cartier "loot" as she calls it. Still, the nice thing about Julie is she shares everything and had loaned me her diamond hoops for the night. She'd also enlisted the Bergdorf beauty team to do our hair and makeup at her apartment.

When I arrived Julie was sitting on the chaise longue in her drawing room. It's a very elegant *salon*, painted duck-egg blue, with tall windows, thick cornicing, and an outrageous Guy Bourdin nude hanging over the fireplace just to mix things up. All Julie's furniture is that wonderful thirties Hollywood stuff she adores, reupholstered in pale velvet to match the walls. Still, I couldn't see much of anything wonderful because every surface was covered in some kind of cosmetic instrument. Davide, the makeup artist, had literally turned the room into his personal makeup studio. He was dabbing blush on Julie's cheeks, Raquel was ironing Julie's hair, and Irinia, the Polish pedicurist, was buffing Julie's toenails. This is nothing. I've heard that some girls in New York don't leave their apartment before a party without their dermatologist checking their epidermis for blemishes first.

"Do I look happy? Does my smile look, like, real?" asked Julie as I walked in.

Davide said her smile was as real as her Cartier loot, which I thought was a very appropriate metaphor.

"It's *totally* fake. Isn't it *beyond*?" said Julie.

"Ohmygoditsbey-ooond!" said Davide.

"I went to my dermatologist this afternoon, and you know those little muscles around your mouth, the platysma? You probably don't because most people don't think about them. Well, after like twenty-three, they start drooping, but there's this genius way of fixing them and giving you back your smile. Your derm injects a tiny bit of Botox to paralyze them, and the corners of your mouth turn instantly upward. Once you've got the Botox Smile, you can be smiling all night without actually smiling, which makes the smiling much less tiring," said Julie, as if she were making total sense.

The dress code for Muffy's party was black tie. As soon as Julie's hair and makeup were done she threw on a thigh-skimming, black silk minidress. (Chanel. Couture. FedExed from Paris.) While she disappeared into her dressing room to examine herself I sat down and took advantage of Davide and Raquel. There are certain parties in New York where you literally can't walk in the door without hair and makeup. Muffy's was one of them. The hair-makeup thing takes you up a notch. After a while you become convinced that you couldn't cope if you just swiped Maybelline mascara on yourself, which would probably clog. Manhattan makeup artists actually comb your eyelashes after they've applied eye makeup. Mascara clots are a federal crime here.

Just as Davide was patting gloss on my lips a loud cry came from the direction of Julie's bedroom. A fashion tantrum was brewing. I wasn't surprised. New York girls have one every time someone mentions clothes. I wandered into the bedroom and looked over Julie's shoulder at her in the mirror.

"It's totally and utterly wrong. I look . . . *conservative*!" she wailed dramatically, pulling at the hem of the little dress. "Look at me! I look like someone from that Broadway show with fat people. *Hairspray*. My future Prospective Husband is going to think I am a *troll*!"

The dress was gorgeous, 100 percent killer chic.

"Julie you look incredible. That dress is so short it's almost invisible. It's the inverse of conservative," I said, trying to reassure her.

"I'm freakin' out and you're saying things like *inverse* to me. Can everyone just go away," she cried, miserable.

Julie locked herself in the dressing room. She changed and changed and changed. She said through the door that she didn't want to go the party now because it would just be too much sartorial, intellectual, and sexual strain. Although I honestly didn't mind whether or not I went to some fabulous ball at Muffy's marble mansion, I had a gorgeous white chiffon dress on that I'd borrowed from the fashion closet at the office—a dress I am fully intending to return one day soon—and it would have been a terrible waste for it not to see the world.

"Julie, I don't care *in the slightest* whether we go," I said. I mean, I could wear the dress another time. "But it's going to be such a fun party."

"Parties in New York aren't fun. They're war," said Julie, unlocking the door and appearing in the killer Chanel again. "Davide, give me a Xanax. I always take a tranquilizer on a first date."

Davide dashed over to his makeup bag, which is filled with a variety of prescription drugs for just such occasions, and fished out a little package. Julie tore it open and popped this really cute baby blue pill in her mouth, which I thought was a very modern way to handle a war, and called her driver to take us to Muffy's.

I can safely say that I am almost definitely completely sure that I have no idea at all how I ended up with a Prospective Husband and Julie didn't. I mean, to be more precise, at the end of the night, the PH ended up with his head not at all close to the Brazilian region of Julie but in severely close proximity to that geographical zone on myself.

You see, this champagne bubble had sipped a few champagne bubbles herself, which makes it quite hard to remember exactly how things happened that night. But in the interest of correcting some rather nasty vicious Park Avenue Princess–type gossip, which is that I stole the PH from directly beneath my best friend's beautiful nose—which of course Julie doesn't believe, on principle—I feel bound to recount the events of the evening as far as I can almost definitely remember them.

We were an hour late for the party by the time we finally arrived at Muffy's. It was almost impossible to find our table because Muffy had bunches of white lilies and candles so densely packed in the room you could barely see a yard in front of you. (Flower-wise, the Lily Jungle is absolutely it right now in Manhattan despite the inherent navigational difficulties.)

There must have been 250 guests, with as many waiters, who were uniformed in white tuxes and gloves. The crowd was dazzling: Muffy always attracts the cream of Manhattan society to her soirees. Dress-wise, there was a major floral theme going on, which always happens at benefits for gardens. A lot of the girls were in Emanuel Ungaro because he does the best flowery dresses in the world, no argument. Jewel-wise, the younger girls had brought out their Asprey diamond daisies and the older women were weighed down with estate gems from the safe. Everyone was kissing everyone else hello and saying how thrilled they were to see one another, even if they weren't.

We were seated just as the starter of chilled mint soup was being served. Our table was right at the center of the room. Everyone else had already sat down. The four PHs Muffy had selected for Julie were *très* ethnically diverse. Julie barely had a moment to take a spoonful of soup before the Italian princeling, who was on her left, declared, "You more beautiful than Empire State Building!"

"You are charming," said Julie. Her smile was so dazzling that I think the Italian was encouraged and continued, "*Non-non-non*! You prettier than Rock-a Fell-a Cent-a."

The WASPy, blond-haired real estate heir on Julie's right interrupted to say, "Maurizio, forgive me, but I disagree. This woman is more beautiful than the Pentagon."

I've never heard a man compare a girl to a government building before. Julie must have been flattered because next she asked her key question.

"Do you believe in drivers?" she said, smiling beautifully at him.

It turned out everyone believed in drivers like they're a religion, including the record producer opposite, who was originally Polish, and the Thirteenth Man, who was an actor from LA by way of Minnesota. (I guess Muffy had relented and let one in after all.) It also seemed that everyone had pilots as well as drivers, because they all had private planes, except for the actor who "borrowed" the Warner Brothers jet "like totally like all the time. And you can totally like smoke Marlboro Reds on it, which is, like, genius."

The men started discussing altitudes and instruments and cigars and the Nasdaq, which must be much more fascinating subjects than they seem to an ignoramus like *moi* because men in New York seem to discuss almost nothing else. No one was talking to Julie, or yours truly, or any of the other girls at the table. Julie opened her gold clutch bag, pulled out a lip wand, and started glossing her mouth, a habit she always falls back on when she's extraordinarily bored, and said, "Why can't you guys be a bit more real?"

I thought this was a peculiar thing for Julie to say since she often says the only real thing she understands is a diamond. The record producer patted her on the hand, and said, "You don't get rich that way, babe."

"You're *so* interesting," said Julie sarcastically, but he didn't notice because he was back discussing cigars with the real estate guy.

Then the men carried on ignoring everyone but themselves and their jets and so Julie, who is very talented in the redirecting attention to herself department said, "I've got a hundred million dollars." The PHs went quiet. So Julie added, "All to myself," and suddenly they all started acting very interested in Julie's mind, whereupon she sweetly announced, "Excuse me. I have to go kill myself in the ladies' room."

While she was away, I explained that this is completely normal, it's just what Julie always does when she's really bored by the company and thinks people are interested in her only for her fortune and not for her sparkling personality. All the boys looked shamefully guilty so I said, "Don't feel bad! *Everyone* except me likes Julie for her money, it's nothing to be embarrassed about. She's completely used to it, I mean, even her friends in nursery school only played with her because their parents told them she was rich."

I think I managed to diffuse an abundantly awkward atmosphere because everyone looked very relieved and started asking me where Julie's wealth came from. Sometimes I feel pretty sorry for the Park Avenue Princesses: they only have to turn their backs for two seconds, and suddenly everyone's asking how much they're worth, or are going to be worth, as though they were a biotech stock or something. Naturally I said that I couldn't divulge anything as private as the source of the Bergdorf family fortune.

"She's a *Bergdorf*? No wonder her hair's the perfect blonde," said a dark-haired girl sitting opposite. "Do you think she'd get me in with Ariette?"

New York girls are always asking favors from complete strangers. They take the thing about the land of opportunity completely literally.

Anyway, while Julie was not really killing herself in the restroom, something amazing happened. I had a PH sighting. At a table in the far corner I glimpsed a potentially perfect man: tallish, leanish, with dark hair, and even darker eyes, he was wearing a suit but no black tie. (I worship a man who throws caution to the wind like that and doesn't wear a tie when he should.) But no, seriously, he was handsome beyond belief, I mean, he was totally giving Jude Law. I completely lost my appetite on the spot, exactly like I do when I hear Tchaikovsky's pas de deux from *Swan Lake.* Some things are just so romantic they make you feel like you'll never eat again. Humphrey Bogart only has to blink at Ingrid Bergman in *Casablanca* and I'm literally in danger of starvation unless I'm not careful.

Julie returned to the table and I pointed out the gorgeous PH to her, very discreetly, of course.

"Hmmm. He looks cute-*ish,* I guess," she said unenthusiastically. "But, you know, he looks a little, well, cool. You know what I mean, like maybe too cool to be engaged to me or anything trad like that."

"But maybe . . . I mean, you never know, he . . . he could

be dying to be someone's fiancé, just to . . ." I trailed off, mesmerized. "I mean, all fiancés are single until they're fiancés, right?"

Everyone at the table was staring at me like I was totally dumb. I wasn't making any sense. I remember getting very confused about what I was saying, which is the effect all Jude Law types have on me. You should have seen me after *The Talented Mr. Ripley*; I couldn't read or write for a week.

"You looking for 'usband?" said the Italian to Julie. "Surely this is not romantic, to be so, 'ow do you say eet? . . . *sistematico*."

"Maurizio, what's unromantic is all those girls who are looking for a husband but pretending they're not because they think it's politically correct. There's nothing *more* romantic than a girl who likes to be in love and is open about it," replied Julie. She paused and gazed at him flirtatiously. "Fiancés are beyond glamorous in this town. I think one would look really cute on my arm, don't you?"

Maurizio swallowed.

"'Ow can you treat a man like a fashion accessory?" he said.

"I'm an expert," sighed Julie. "I learned it from my boyfriends."

Completely on Julie's behalf I took it upon myself to perform a reconnaissance trip to the other side of the party. The closer I got, the more handsome Jude Law became, if that's possible. *God, what am I supposed to say?* I thought anxiously as I approached. I mean, I don't usually just go up to total strangers and start talking to them at parties.

"Excuse me, I don't mean to interrupt," I said shyly when

I reached his table. "But my friend over there has a question for you. Um, she wants to know if . . . well . . . if, you know . . . you believe in . . . drivers?"

Jude Law laughed, as though I had told the funniest joke in the world. This is always nice, even if secretly you have no idea you are making a joke.

"I take the subway actually," he answered.

God, how cute, I thought. I would have thought it was cute if he said he traveled by hedgehog, though. Everything's cute when you're as cute as he is.

"You're so original!!!" yelled a stunning brunette sitting opposite, too loudly. "Hi. I'm Adriana A? The model? I'm in the new Luca Luca ads? I don't think anyone introduced us yet. Hi! You're Zach Nicholson, the photographer, right?"

He nodded. Adriana was exotically beautiful, with bones like a Siamese cat's. She had on those professional smoky eyes models all wear for shoots. I made a note to myself to copy the eye makeup but not the personality.

"I mean, what's it like down there in those subways?" continued Adriana. She was so flirtatious I swear I could virtually see her eyelashes curling while she was talking. "I bet it's amazing. I bet you get so much inspiration for your work down there. You're a brilliant photographer!"

God, Muffy is *such* a liar sometimes. This man was 100 percent creative. Julie would be totally against the idea of a photographer as a fiancé.

"Thank you. But my inspiration is all in my mind. I just like to get from A to B the quickest way possible," replied Zach courteously.

I didn't think he was into Adriana. She was too much. God, he's cute, I found myself thinking again. And god, what a *crying shame* for Julie that Monsieur Cute here takes subways not drivers.

"I love love love the latest series. I went to MoMA to look. It's, like, genius to be at MoMA at twenty-nine!!!" said Adriana.

It really was bad luck for Julie. I mean, the photographer would have made a great fiancé, what with all that talent and charm. Suddenly he looked at me and whispered, "Save me from the Luca Luca model." Then he said louder, "Hey! Join us, I haven't seen you in so long," and pulled me into his lap. "Why don't you have some dessert," he said, offering me a plate piled high with profiteroles.

"I'd love to but I just developed an allergy to them," I said, pushing the plate away. "You wouldn't believe what a party like this does to your appetite."

Zach smiled and looked at me seductively.

"Are you the wittiest girl in New York? Or just the prettiest?" he asked.

"Neither," I said, blushing. Secretly I was flattered beyond belief.

"I think you might be both," he said.

I was completely, 150 percent charmed. I happily stayed put on Zach's knee. If someone needs me I can't say no. And god it was heaven to save someone this heavenly from a beautiful model. It did suddenly occur to me that it might take me at least another five minutes to disentangle myself from my reconnaissance duty, so I waved at Julie and made a thumbs-down sign, as if to say, what a drag, no PHs with drivers in this area.

At about 1 AM I was still saving Zach from Adriana. And even after she'd gone—not before telling us that we could see her on the billboard above the MTV building in

Times Square—I definitely got the impression that Zach still needed saving. And some time after that, somehow (and please don't ask me how because I am way too virginal to explain) Zach almost definitely ended up with his head pretty close to the aforementioned South American region of myself. And to all those gossips who gossiped that I stole a PH from under Julie's nose, the truth is Julie didn't want him anyway.

"Sounds way too creative to me. He'll never be anyone's fiancé," she warned me the next day about Zach.

This was fine. I mean, it was Julie who was looking for a fiancé, not me. I knew Julie was telling the truth when she said she wasn't upset about the photographer visiting my Latin zones and not hers, because the only remark she made about Muffy's party was "Well, that was a total waste of Paris couture."

4

Something happened to me the night I met Zach. Honestly, I never touched profiteroles again. I just went right off them, which is really saying something because they're literally my favorite food after the vanilla cupcakes at Magnolia Bakery.

I fell for Zach the minute I laid eyes on him. Something inside me went *ping!* and there I was, suddenly smack-dab in the middle of my own *coup de foudre,* just like the brother and sister falling for each other in *The Royal Tenenbaums*. I'm still not quite sure if it was Zach, or the Jude Law in him, but he was beyond romantic. I mean, get this. After we first met he rang me *every day* and asked me to have dinner alone with him each night. I said no exactly every other night because when a man looks like Jude Law and can have anyone he wants it's very important not to be too available. And it's a huge stress getting ready for dinner with Jude Law so I needed a whole forty-eight hours between each date for my lovelorn nerves—which were in total shreds—to recover.

Then, of course, there were other things about Zach that made me melt, like the fact that going to Brazil with him was better than with any of the other *very few* men I have gone with. I mean, he could find Rio absolutely every time, whereas most men only get as far as the suburbs before they want to go home. He seemed to adore everything about me, even the bad stuff. Like he thought it was charming when I offered to cook him dinner one night and ended up ordering in (being a New York girl at heart, the only thing I can cook properly is a twice-toasted bagel). He rewarded me by doing insanely romantic things, like one time he sent me a bunch of peonies (my favorite flower) every day for five days in a row with a note attached each time. The first note read "For." On the second was written "My." The next was "One." After that came two more notes, one saying "And," the other saying "Only." *For My One And Only.* It was too cute for words. I didn't eat a thing the whole week.

Zach was a spectacularly talented gift-giver. He always found things that I really wanted but didn't even know about until he gave them to me. On my birthday he surprised me with a beautiful black-and-white print of one of his photographs from the "Drowned" series he'd done a few years back. (The photo is of a burned-out truck, half submerged in a lake. I know it sounds like a weird birthday gift, but I was overwhelmed.) Here's the pick of the other gifts: leather-bound first edition of my personal bible, *Gentlemen Prefer Blondes*; *galuchat* jewel case from Asprey (that's a dead stingray by the way); baby pink monogrammed stationery from Mrs. John L. Strong that takes weeks to order unless you're someone like Zach and can charm them into doing it in a day;

fringed antique Peruvian shawl from the flea market in Lima.

Zach loved to take me for dinner at out-of-the-way, dreamy little restaurants. Of all of them, Jo Jo, on East Sixty-fourth Street, was my favorite. It's right off Madison Avenue, with a little paned window that you can glimpse twinkling candles and chandeliers through. You sit on slouchy velvet banquettes at little black lacquer tables. The walls are painted a faded old blue and antique screens separate the tables upstairs. Honestly, you can go there and feel like you are the only pair of sweethearts in the world. The night we went there—on an indulgent date celebrating our two-month anniversary—I think Zach wrapped his ankles round mine all night, as though he never wanted to let go. We just giggled and laughed and kissed all through dinner, at stupid things like how awesome the French fries were (the secret is they cook them in truffle oil or something crazy like that).

The only thing that slightly freaked me out in the first few months was Adriana A. A few times when I was over at Zach's loft in Chinatown, the phone rang and Zach didn't pick up. Adriana's voice came on the answering machine, asking Zach for lunch or dinner or drinks, to discuss work. Anyway, it turned out I was worrying about nothing. After a while she stopped calling.

The only person who wasn't delighted by my romance was Mom. It wasn't that I shared all the details of my Manhattan love life with her, but she'd read about it in a gossip column and called to check whether or not it was true.

"Darling, I heard Little Earl might be coming home for Christmas"—it was late December—"and I do think you two are meant for each other."

I took a deep breath.

"Mom, I'm sure Little Earl would loathe me on sight. And I have no intention of spending my life in a drafty castle looking at sheep. Anyway, I'm sure you and Dad would like Zach."

"Who are his parents, darling?"

"I've no idea. He comes from Ohio, he's a successful photographer."

It was true that I actually knew very little about Zach—apart from the fact that he was very handsome, lived in Chinatown in a huge loft, and never went to bed without drinking an espresso first. He took his career very seriously and sometimes would disappear for days without warning. He could be very mysterious and elusive when he wanted—which of course I adored.

Julie always says she can pack a bag for a weekend in St. Barths "in a heartbeat." This is an outright lie. She actually takes about a week to pack for a trip, but the point I'm trying to make is that when you're as madly in love as I was, everything seems to happen in a heartbeat. After what seemed like fifteen seconds—but in real time must have been six months, around the middle of March—Zach asked me to marry him. Can you imagine? We'd been having such fun it felt like no time at all had passed.

The only trouble was that the proposal meant that *moi* and not Julie would be the one with the PH, which was somewhat of a conflict of interest. But even if I was secretly freaked that Julie was going to be beyond mad at me about it, I couldn't say no. I was madly, madly in love. Zach was the perfect PH in every way. Despite the fact that sometimes his work binges meant that he vanished into a black hole for a whole week and didn't return my phone calls, he'd always emerge with a fabulous dinner invitation and thrill me all over again.

Julie was surprisingly relaxed when I told her I was engaged. She approved of Zach, recognizing that he was way too arty for her. She didn't seem to mind as much as you'd think that I'd snagged my PH first, saying, "Your wedding will be my dress rehearsal—I'll learn from your mistakes."

You can imagine Mom's reaction when I told her I was marrying Zach. First she threatened to die of a headache and then she insisted on throwing the wedding at Swyre Castle, which you can hire for functions. Even if it wasn't exactly my first choice of venue, I was so happy I decided to let Mom do whatever she wanted. She had the church, flowers, hors d'oeuvres, cake, scheduling, and even the particular type of confetti (freeze-dried rose petals from Covent Garden Market) mapped out in immaculate detail within hours of hearing my news. I guess Mom had been planning my wedding since the day I turned sixteen and had decided to put a brave face on the fact that I was marrying an American photographer rather than a British Earl.

After the engagement I felt like the most popular kid in high school or something. Everyone in New York was as addicted to Zach as I was. We were invited everywhere together, and everyone wanted to know about the wedding plans. Even the girls at my office were in love with Zach. They're all smitten with Jude Law, too. And my skin had never looked better.

You can imagine how delighted I was when my editor asked if I wanted to go out to LA for a few days to interview a famous actress. She sweetly insisted I take the gorgeous fiancé and booked us into a four-room penthouse suite at the Chateau Marmont, the famous one with a grand piano. People are so nice to you when you're engaged it's crazy. A whole four days with Zach sounded like bliss: in fact, it would be the longest time we'd spent together since we'd met. I couldn't wait.

When my friend Daphne Klingerman, who is an actress-turned-professional-wife of a brilliant agent-turned-producer-turned-studio-head, heard I was coming to LA, she e-mailed me from her Blackberry, saying,

Can't talk am in yoga class can I throw you party in beverly hills?

I can't imagine what yoga position you can send an e-mail from, but Daphne has been practicing Ashtanga yoga every day since her last role so I guess she's an expert because her last role was more than two years ago.

Spring is the best time to be in LA and I totally worship the Chateau Marmont, like everyone else in Hollywood. It always makes me think of Rapunzel's castle, perched like that just above Sunset Boulevard, with its little turrets peeking serenely above the craziness on the ground. By the time we arrived that night, it was very late. Even so, the lobby was buzzing with the usual super-cool Hollywood kids that favor the Chateau. I wasn't tempted by the scene: all I wanted to do was get Zach upstairs and take him on a very, very risqué trip somewhere south of the equator.

Our suite was totally sick, in a good way. The sitting room was huge and had two long modern sofas at one end, the grand piano at the other, a huge Art Deco mirror, and a slick, 1950s Italian coffee table in the center of the room. On top of it was an ice bucket containing a bottle of vintage champagne. The bedroom had nothing but a very inviting bed, two silver lamps, miles of stereo equipment, and a wall of floor-to-ceiling windows, which opened onto a terrace. While Zach tipped the bellboy I stepped out into the evening air, and looked into the Los Angeles night. The view was electric with its millions of lights stretching from Hollywood to the valley. Even though I was exhausted, the suite was so sexy I thought Zach would have no problem going to Brazil all over it and maybe even exploring as far as the Amazonian jungle immediately.

"Zach! Do you want to . . . hit the rainforest?" I called coyly from the balcony. He was unpacking in the bedroom.

"I'm busy."

"Hey, come on!" I giggled. "Stop being so boring."

"Stop being so needy," he replied, without turning around from the closet.

"Darling, Sting and Trudy visit the rainforest *all the time* and no one thinks they're needy," I said.

Zach didn't say a thing. He didn't get the joke at all. He always giggled with me about my silly jokes, but tonight he was different. He said he just wanted me to leave him alone so he could check his e-mails on the Internet, which is a real waste of a four-room suite at the Chateau if you ask me.

By 1 AM Zach still showed no sign of getting into bed. He was frantically typing at his keyboard in the sitting room, with a hostile look on his face. It was like he hadn't even noticed the view or anything. And as far as I know, men just don't turn down sex with women, period. When I finally mentioned this to Zach, he turned away from his laptop and looked very annoyed.

"Can you please let me get on with my work for one second?" he huffed.

I suddenly felt shamefully guilty for demanding his attention all night when he was so busy. "I'm sorry. What are you working on?"

"New ad campaign. It's a lot of money and the pressure's really on."

"That's great," I said. "Which campaign?"

"Luca Luca. They want a whole new approach."

"Is Adriana A in it?"

"Yeah. She's a drag. Can I get on now?"

Zach went back to his computer and I went into the bedroom and slumped on the bed. I felt disappointed. I lay there and stared out through the windows. Suddenly the view seemed bleak as hell. It was depressing. I felt like I'd woken up and found myself slap-bang in the middle of a Paul Thomas Anderson movie.

I was beyond embarrassed when I called Daphne two nights later. How could I tell her that Zach had barely said a word to me since we'd arrived? I know he was under a lot of pressure, but as far as going to Brazil and all that was concerned, well, I hadn't left the Arctic Circle once since we checked into the Chateau. I mean, I'm not saying Luca L. isn't a big deal, but Zach was acting as though he was about to paint the Sistine Chapel. Honestly, he'd barely let me near him. Whenever I even mentioned sex he'd just say, "Stop harassing me," or something really mean like that. It reminded me of a couple of times in the past few weeks when I'd suggested sex and he'd complained he was too tired or had a backache or something incredibly tiresome like that. I'd believed him, but maybe he secretly hadn't wanted to make love. The truth was we hadn't gone anywhere near Rio for over two weeks. Still, I'd never seen him like this before. He wouldn't do a thing. When I suggested a drive up South Topanga Canyon to my favorite thrift store, Hidden Treasures (you *have* to check it out, I swear, you just have to), he refused and went back to working on his ideas for the Luca Luca campaign, which is exactly how he'd spent the last forty-eight hours.

Where had Jude Law gone? This was like being engaged to a different person. The only thing that had stopped me from freaking out was knowing that I had to keep myself together to interview the actress, which I'd done yesterday.

"Daphne!" I wailed when she picked up.

"Get out!" she said. Daphne starts every sentence with "get out." "What is it?"

"It's Zach. He's in this horrible mood. All he'll do is watch CNN and send e-mails. He's barely spoken to me since we got here, all because he's shooting the new Luca Luca campaign with Adriana A. Maybe we should cancel?"

"Get out! You can't cancel! Bradley's flown in Le Cirque on the studio's plane to do the food! Look, about the not talking to you, don't worry! Bradley *hardly ever* talks to me. Men are so sexy when they're brooding and laconic," said Daphne. "You gotta come tonight, there's going to be a lot of people who want to know you and you are going to want to know them."

Zach eventually agreed to go to the party, but only after Daphne called him personally and told him there were going to be a lot of Hollywood mogul types there with "serious" photography collections. Strictly on the q-t, I think Daphne exaggerated a little. She has exactly one friend who collects photography. But then Daphne exaggerates everything, especially her age which she claims is twenty-nine but is closer to thirty-nine. As I got ready that night, I tried to be positive. I mean, one of the brilliant things about a virtually silent fiancé is that you have hours to get dressed, so I wore a terribly complicated Azzedine Alaia hook-and-eye number that takes forever to do up. Even my misgivings about Zach's sudden personality change couldn't stop me from being thrilled by the Alaia: there are killer dresses and there are killer dresses by Alaia, which are so killer they're homicidal. At the last minute Zach threw on a white shirt, jeans, and a beaten-up leather jacket, which completely ruined my appetite in advance. He looked so delicious that I knew Le Cirque's Symphony of Desserts wouldn't tempt me at all.

Daphne lives in Beverly Hills in a sprawling Spanish-style house set in grounds that sprawl almost as far as the Hotel Bel-Air. The driveway was lit with flares and as usual Daphne had gone way overboard with the flowers. There were huge vases filled with jasmine flowers and branches absolutely everywhere you looked, even in the restrooms. She'd gone completely over the top with the staff, too. Daphne likes to have about fifteen butlers per guest, which makes for a very crowded party. When we arrived, the drawing room was so full that guests were already spilling out onto the terrace towards the pool. The whole garden was lit with lanterns Daphne had picked up on one of her shopping trips to Morocco, and loungey tapestried rugs and cushions were spread out on the lawn. I'd barely had a chance to take in the scene before Zach veered off in the direction of Daphne's collector friends, leaving me standing alone in the center of the party.

Daphne suddenly grabbed my arm and introduced me to a young actress, Betthina Evans, who'd just won a Golden Globe. Betthina was an immaculate size zero; you know, how actresses are: tiny, petite, perfect. She had long, gleaming, honey-colored hair and was dressed in a yellow satin slip dress and strappy silver sandals. She was totally channeling Kate Hudson, which is what everyone is doing in LA right now. She was wearing a sparkling engagement ring the size of Manhattan.

"Oh, I'm engaged, too," I said.

"Where's your ring?" said Betthina examining my left hand.

"My fiancé hasn't got it yet."

It was true. Zach kept saying he was going to get me a ring, but somehow he never got around to it. I don't mean to sound superficial, but it was bugging the hell out of me. I mean, an engagement with no ring is like Elvis without the rhinestones, or a Bellini without the peach juice. I didn't care what kind of ring it was, but I wanted one. Zach had it easy with me. I'd made no specific demands regarding the ring, whereas Jolene had told her husband-to-be before he proposed that anything less than a D-flawless, five-carat diamond would be unacceptable.

"Eew!" shrieked Betthina. "There is no way I would have agreed to marry Tommy if he hadn't given me a ring bigger than California when he asked me."

"I'd feel terrible if someone got me a huge ring," I said.

This isn't quite true, actually. Secretly, I wanted a ring that was bigger than the planet but that isn't the kind of thing you should admit, so I never do.

"No matter how big a ring starts out, it shrinks when you wear it. And, okay, so this ring was, like, a quarter of a million, but when you look at it from the point of view of what Tommy's getting—*me*—it makes it seem cheap, because I am priceless," said Betthina conclusively.

"Oh," I said. Starlets must be exceptionally good at figures because I could never have come up with that equation.

"Is it true, what I read in Liz Smith? That he gave you the *Drowned Truck*? How romantic! And listen, even if there wasn't a ring, I'd agree to an engagement with the hottest photographer in New York. What a fabulous career move! And you'll get so much press when you break up with him, but just make sure you end it before anyone thinks you're really gonna go through with it."

I must have looked beyond upset, because Betthina suddenly put her arm around my shoulder. She patted me, as though I needed comforting.

"God! I'm sorry! I say the worst things! But . . . you're really going to marry a . . . *photographer*? It's just everyone gets engaged here all the time and they don't really mean it, especially with really creative people like your fiancé," she gasped, embarrassed. "I mean, there's *no way* I'm marrying Tommy. Eew, *gross*! Shall we go and talk to your guy? God, look at him! He's *unbelievably* cute."

Betthina started walking toward Zach. I held her back and whispered, "Actually, um . . . do you mind? It's just, we're not getting on brilliantly tonight. I mean, actually . . . he's not really speaking to me. He's real stressed about work." I was pink with shame.

"Hey, don't worry about it! My first two husbands hardly ever spoke to me. It's very common. Don't be upset. You know what they say, the only important thing about a husband is to have one!" She giggled.

"Oh, I'm not *upset*," I said, suddenly bursting into tears. "I'm just, you know, madly in love and, you know, being in love makes you cry almost all the time, doesn't it? I'm going to the restroom. Nice to meet you."

I was completely freaked out. The minute I was out of earshot of the party, I called Julie from my cell. I wanted to kill some time while I tried to calm down.

"Hi, Julie-shmoolie," I said. "I'm having a really fun time."

"Is that why you're crying like a Balenciaga bag that lost its buckle?" she replied. "Is something wrong?"

I told Julie that I was happier than I'd ever been in my life, that there were apple martinis everywhere you looked, and that Le Cirque's Symphony of Desserts was just delicious. I was just calling to say I wished she could have been at the party.

"Honey, when you're drinking martinis and your martini glass is full of tears, you gotta ask yourself, is the Universe trying to tell me something?" said Julie.

Oh god, when Julie starts talking about the Universe I worry about her. It means she's been reading an unhealthy amount of horoscope books again. But maybe she had a point, even if she was getting her information from *Moon Magic: How to Cast a Natal Horoscope*.

"Zach's acting weird, but I can't explain now. I gotta go," I said.

"Okay, feel better. Call me the minute you get back. Love-you-mean-it-later!"

A few minutes later Daphne found me sitting miserably on a bench outside the restroom. When she saw my tear-stained face she said, "Oh my god, what happened? Has Bradley been mean to you?"

"No, no. It's Zach, he never gave me a ring, and Betthina started asking me where it is and . . . I don't know, I feel terrible," I sobbed.

"Get out!!! If anyone else asks you about the *frigging* engagement ring, tell them you got the *Drowned Truck* instead, which would buy *six* engagement rings, okay? When a man gives you something personal like that, well, that's *real* love. Listen, Bradley went to Neil Lane for my ring, but so does *everyone* in Hollywood. Doesn't mean a thing. Julia Roberts has like fifteen rings from there and look what happens to all her fiancés. You know how I know Bradley really loves me? When he brings me tea in bed when I'm sick with something really catching like SARS. It's the small things that count. Now, can I see a smile? Hey, that's better," said Daphne as I grinned hopelessly at her. "You gotta *look* radiantly happy and in love if you want to *feel* radiantly happy and in love. Here."

"Thanks," I said, taking a Kleenex from her and wiping my eyes.

I guess I was totally in mood-swing central that night because as I walked back into the party I was overcome by a spontaneous feeling of giddy happiness. Daphne was right, a *Drowned Truck* is much more significant love-wise than a ring. It's just a bit of a drag you can't wear it on your ring finger so that everyone else knows about the significant love, too. I thought of all the adorable things Zach had done when we first met, and I sort of hypnotized myself into a wonderful smiling paralysis that lasted the rest of the night. I felt my appetite disappearing again, which was a relief: I was definitely still in love.

Daphne led me back into the sitting room, which was now a blur of pastel dresses. The room was crowded with a million girls dressed exactly like Betthina. They were all frantically dissecting some movie that hadn't even come out yet starring Keira Knightley, who they'd all be channeling when they were done with Kate Hudson. All the boyfriends and husbands were hanging on to their beautiful girls as though if they let go they'd never see them again, which was probably *très* smart of them. I didn't feel at all Kate Hudson-ish either, which was definitely a handicap in the current surroundings. My murderous dress was totally wrong for tonight—way too New York. What was I thinking wearing black in Los Angeles? I just wanted to go home.

"Oooh! Mmmm! There's Charlie Dunlain," said Daphne, dragging me toward a young guy sitting alone on one of her huge white sofas. Then she added in a whisper, "He's so cute and he's a *genius* young movie director. Well, that's what Bradley says, I haven't actually seen any of his movies but *don't tell him that* because Bradley's trying to sign him. Can you go talk to him while I check on the chef?"

Daphne introduced me and then disappeared to obsess about the canapés or something. Even if Charlie was as cute as Daphne thought, I didn't notice: no one was as cute as my personal Jude Law, speaking of whom, I couldn't see anywhere. Hopefully Zach was having a wonderful time with the mogul types elsewhere in the party, even though it was freaking me out that he was being so utterly evasive tonight.

"Are you okay?" was the first thing Charlie said to me when I sat down. He looked concerned. Was I that transparent? My paralytic smile was obviously *très* unconvincing.

"Yes, I . . ." I couldn't think what to say.

"What's wrong?" he said.

People can be really rude sometimes, can't they? I mean I hardly know this guy three seconds and already he's asking personal questions. It's hideous, absolutely hideous.

"Nothing's wrong," I said, collecting myself. "I'm having a *wonderful* time. I'm so happy tonight I can't eat a thing!"

"Not even Daphne's incredible desserts? Are you *sure* you're all right? You don't look very happy."

"I am *fine.* One hundred and fifty percent totally great, fine," I said, attempting to close that particular line of inquiry.

"So, how's New York?" said Charlie, getting the hint.

"How do you know I live in New York?"

"The dress. It's pretty serious."

"Actually, I call it my Homicide Dress because it's so *dangerous,*" I teased, perking up a little. "Thank god for Azzedine Alaia!"

"As in *Clueless*?" asked Charlie, chuckling.

"Totally!" I laughed. (One of my favorite movie moments is when Alicia Silverstone freaks out in *Clueless* about her Alaia dress getting dirty.) "How do you know about that?" I asked.

"I'm a movie geek. Everyone in the movie business worships *Clueless*. You have to study that film if you work here, I'm not kidding."

Maybe Charlie was kind of cute. I mean, he knew about Azzedine Alaia, which is a major plus. Don't get me wrong, he wasn't a patch on Jude Law, but you couldn't deny he had a great smile. His dark hair was sort of messy, he had unusually blue eyes, and he dressed kind of untidily, in jeans and a rock'n'roll T-shirt and old sneaks, but he sort of looked cool with it, like most LA boys do. Then he had these funny schoolteacher glasses on that he occasionally pushed up on his head. He was a little tan, as though he'd been surfing or something in Malibu. He seemed disarmingly frank and open. Of course, I like something rather more complicated, like Zach, I reminded myself.

"You wanna see something dumb and clueless for real?" said Charlie, grinning.

"Sure," I said, relieved that my mood was lifting.

"Okay, so here's what happened the last time I met a girl as pretty and happy and underfed as you. I took a sip of my drink like this"—he sipped his Coke through a straw—"and what happened was this." Somehow, the straw bounced out of the glass, hurtled through the air spraying Coca-Cola on the gorgeous white sofa, and lodged, miraculously, in the side of Charlie's glasses, sticking out at a right angle. I laughed and he said, "And that's why I am officially the Biggest Loser Ever when it comes to women."

Coca-Cola dripped drop by drop from the straw down his cheek. Charlie made a face as if to say, "See."

"But you're funny," I said, giggling. "Funny's funny and that's that."

I mean, even if I secretly thought it was *incredibly* rude of him to have pointed out that I possibly wasn't radiantly happy when we first met, he was definitely amusing.

"Girls can't resist a sense of humor. And then you're a director, too. I bet you have some really beautiful actress girlfriend," I said.

"Nope. No girlfriend right now."

"Well, do you want one?"

"I never think about it like that," said Charlie. "Girlfriends are one of the few things you get less of the more you want one. But yeah, it would be nice. Everyone wants to fall in love when it comes down to it, don't they?"

Suddenly, I thought *Julie*. She's desperate to fall in love. If he tried really hard not to do the straw trick in front of her, Charlie might be the perfect PH for her, especially since he knew about important fashion icons like Azzedine Alaia. I know she'd said she didn't want a creative type, but maybe she needed to broaden her horizons.

"How about if I set you up with one of my friends? What kind of girls do you like?"

"Happy ones, who can't eat a thing," he said flirtatiously.

"Oh, I'm taken, I'm engaged to him," I said coyly, gesturing at Zach. He had come into the room and was now standing in a far corner with his back to us. He turned momentarily but didn't see us.

"Handsome guy."

"Look, I can hook you up with a girlfriend of mine. But you've got to be more specific; *exactly* what kind of girl do you want to date?"

Charlie paused for what seemed like forever before he answered me. Then he looked me straight in the eye and said, "Someone *exactly* like you," which was slightly uncomfortable for someone as radiantly happy with her fiancé as *moi*.

I shook the ice around in the bottom of my glass while I thought of something to say.

"I'm in New York a lot for work right now," said Charlie, breaking the silence.

"Cool. I'll set you up at my engagement party," I said.

"I thought this *was* your engagement party."

"This is my Los Angeles engagement party. But my friend Muffy's throwing one for me in New York. Everyone's so nice to you when you get engaged, it's completely impossible! Would I have seen any of your movies?"

"I doubt it," he said. "They're an acquired taste."

"Are they art house?" I asked.

"No, comedies!" he exclaimed. "The trouble is, I think they're funny but no one else does. Most people find my work depressing, but I say there's no comedy without tragedy. Unfortunately, the studio heads don't agree with me. Now, would you like to see the straw trick again?"

❧

I was pretty happy driving home after the party. Seriously, after Daphne had rescued me, I'd laughed all night. Everything was going to be okay with Zach again soon, I was sure of it. I tried to talk to him as we drove along Sunset toward the Chateau. It was only eleven o'clock and I guess I wanted to smooth the way for some Latin American activity when we got back.

"Darling, even though I'm radiantly happy, I'm . . . *très, très* depressed," I said quietly.

Oh god, that came out all wrong. I hadn't meant to say that at all.

"Are you gonna hassle me about sex *again*?" said Zach, without taking his eyes off the road. "You're obsessed. It's so fuckin' weird."

Finally, Zach was talking to me. It was a breakthrough of sorts after the last few days. Did he have to be so gruesome though? Sometimes New Yorkers can be a little too direct for a demure girl like me, even one who's realized she's probably more sluttish than demure-ish.

"Sweetpea, I wish you wouldn't say that. It's not very romantic," I replied, half-joking and half-trying not to weep, which was all I really felt like doing.

"You are so fuckin' superficial. You think a relationship is all about sex. And it's fuckin' not, it's a lot fuckin' deeper than that."

Zach was really upsetting me now. Still, I tried to keep it together and be sweet: I didn't want this to become an issue.

"But darling, we're not best friends. I mean, most people make love with their fiancé—"

"I'm not 'most people.' That's why you're with me. I'm a *photographer.* I don't live by other people's rules. I am what I am. You're so selfish. You need to get a decent value system."

Zach jammed on the brakes and stared into the blackness of Stone Canyon. He looked furious. What had I done?

"It's all you you you and whether or not you're gettin' laid. Stop goin' on about the same fuckin' thing."

Zach was freaking me out even more than Patrick Bateman in *American Psycho*, and I found that book so freaky that I only read the first twelve pages, so I don't even know the half of it. I guess I was so shocked by what he'd said that I couldn't say a thing in reply. Finally he started the car again, and we drove back to the Chateau in silence. Hopefully everything would be okay again when we got back to New York, once the Luca Luca shoot was out of the way in a couple of weeks' time. And, I reminded myself, no one's perfect all the time, especially me, so I couldn't really complain. Even if Zach had been cool toward me tonight, I was still nuts about him. I then started wondering what, *in theory,* it would be like being engaged to someone warmer but less handsome, like that funny movie director. Of course, I put the thought out of my mind almost immediately, so I think of it as a thought that doesn't really count.

"Eeew! A movie director? Are you kidding me? Way, way too creative."

Julie's reaction when I told her I wanted to set her up with Charlie was exactly as expected. We were at Bergdorf's a week or so later for a painted highlight, which is the in highlight now that foiling is over, according to Ariette, who can be completely trusted regarding serious hair-related issues. The reason everyone is obsessed with the Bergdorf salon, which covers the entire ninth floor of the store, is because it's so relaxing in there you can totally forget icky things, like the fact that your fiancé has barely conversed with you for the last week. The place is just bliss actually. The floor has been divided up into three airy salons—a huge reception area, which always has the most incredible vase of cherry blossoms on the table, a cutting room, and a color room, which is where Julie and I were hanging out. There are mirrors, makeup tables, and manicure and pedicure stations everywhere you look. Assistants dressed in matching lilac blouses bustle back and forth bringing you iced lattes and apple sorbets, and there's even a whole person—Cherylee—devoted to eyebrow shaping, which has actually become a profession in itself. The entire place is painted pale violet and from the windows that wrap around the floor you can see all the way down Fifth Avenue in one direction and right across Central Park in the other. Who wouldn't forget they hadn't had sex in three weeks at the Bergdorf salon? That place *is* sex.

"Julie, it's only a suggestion, but maybe you should think about more diverse possibilities. I mean you could be missing out on some really wonderful men," I said. "And this guy I want you to meet is funny and sweet. I mean, if I wasn't with my PH I might want him as a PH."

This wasn't true at all, of course—I was mad about Zach despite everything. But I was trying to reform Julie's narrow horizons.

"If you like this guy Charlie, you gotta finish it with Zach."

"I don't 'like' like him Julie, I just like him, but what I am saying is if I weren't engaged—which I *very* much am—he's the kind of man I might 'like.' And he's just so funny and adorable. I'm going to seat you next to him at the party."

"Is he cute?"

"Daphne says he's unbelievably cute."

"Well what do *you* think?

"I don't know," I said.

Honestly, I had no idea whether Charlie was cute or not now. The only man I could think about with any clarity was Zach. All the others were just a blur.

"So, tell me everything," said Julie, as Ariette painted the dye onto her locks. "You sounded terrible when you called me from Daphne's. What happened after the party?"

"Oh, nothing," I said, casually flipping through the new

Vogue. (They always have next month's *Vogue* in the salon way before it's come out.)

"Yeah, right," said Julie sarcastically.

Julie knows me too well for me to hide anything from her. I told her about the hideous conversation in the car, selectively skimming over some of the details.

"Eew! How could he *say* those things?! What a total See You Next Tuesday. You can't marry this guy, honey. A marriage without sex would be very disappointing. You're in complete denial," said Julie.

I had no idea what she was talking about.

"That's the problem with people who are in denial," continued Julie. "If they're in it, they have no idea they're in it."

Sometimes Julie makes zero sense.

"But I love him," I said. Even just thinking about Zach made me feel like I was going to drop six pounds then and there.

"The only person you're in love with is Jude Law. You're in love with the idea of being in love," said Julie. "You're a hopeless romantic."

I thought this was a bit much coming from the original hopeless romantic herself. I mean, Julie admits she's totally in love with Jude Law too, so I would have thought she'd really understand. And Julie didn't know a thing about relationships anyway. I mean, she's had tons and none of them has ever worked out.

"But maybe Zach's right, maybe I am really superficial," I said.

"You are *not* superficial, you just seem like you are sometimes because of your Chloé jeans obsession. He's the superficial one, turning all the problems into your fault. Now, do you think it's chicer to be a single-process blonde or a double-process blonde?" said Julie, tipping her head back into the sink to have the color rinsed out of her hair.

"Single. Do you think if I gave up Chloé jeans he'd sleep with me?"

"I've got one word for you. Postpone."

Julie was absolutely, completely, and utterly deluded. I couldn't postpone! I couldn't even contemplate thinking about not marrying Zach. It was like I'd drunk the Kool-Aid: there was no going back now. And anyway, Muffy was twenty-four hours away from throwing me this divine engagement party. She'd gone even more overboard than Daphne and hired Lexington Kinnicut to do the flowers. He is New York's uncontested king of the Rose Jungle (the in jungle after Lily Jungles). The wait list for Lexington Kinnicut is comparable only to the wait list for the YSL horn bags. If I called off my engagement and Muffy had to cancel Lexington, she'd die on the spot, literally. The other thing was, I'd planned to introduce Julie and Charlie at the party: if I postponed there'd be no party and no introduction.

Even though there was absolutely no way I was planning to postpone, the second I got home from Bergdorf's I did call Mom for a postponement consultation. I know that sounds like an oxymoron, because it is, but I was confused beyond belief. I guess I was starting to realize that rushing into marriage with Patrick Bateman wasn't nearly as appealing as rushing into marriage with Jude Law. I told Mom, in strictest confidence, that Zach and I had a few issues in the Brazilian department and that if I wasn't exactly considering a postponement, a mini-delay might be in the offing. I made her promise not to tell a soul, since our New York engagement party was the following night. Zach mustn't find out I had any doubts. After all, why spoil a fabulous party before (especially after Lexington had flown in 200 pink orchids from the Dominican Republic to make the Rose Jungle more exotic), when I could experience the really fabulous party and spoil it afterward?

I went out to run some errands and when I returned a few hours later, my voice mail was flashing like crazy. I knew all my girlfriends would be calling to ask what to wear that night. I listened to my messages:

"This is the manager at Swyre Castle Conference Center. So sorry about the cancellation; we'll be keeping the three-thousand-pound deposit."

"Hi, it's your dad. How terrible about the broken engagement. Mom told me today. Is it true you hadn't had sex in three months?"

God, why does my family always have to exaggerate everything so much? I'd told Mom it was three *weeks*.

"This is Debbie Stoddard, *Daily Mail* Diary, London. We're running an item tomorrow about your broken engagement. Could you call me back to confirm?"

❧

"Mom, how *could* you?" I cried when I got through to her. I was furious.

"Well, darling, it just would have been so inconvenient for the Swyres, and embarrassing for me in the village, if you cancelled last minute, so I just gave everyone a bit of advance warning—"

"The Swyres don't even live there now. It's a conference center, Mom, and what's so embarrassing about cancelling a conference center? I am never telling you a private secret again. I *haven't* cancelled. I was just thinking a mini-delay might be appropriate."

I put the phone down, furious. What on earth was I going to do now? I had to make sure Zach never found out about this. That minute, Julie called. She was very excited about meeting Charlie.

"I just Googled him. He's like the most amazing director, totally eligible—"

"You Googled him? Julie!" I said.

"Everyone Googles everyone in New York. It's an integral part of dating now," she explained.

Sometimes the things Julie says make me feel like dating in New York is worse than it is on *Sex and the City*. And I always used to think *Sex and the City* is as terrifying as dating can possibly get.

"Anyway, whatever. Charlie makes the best movies," added Julie.

"You've seen the movies?" I said, confused.

"Eew, nooo! They sound way too depressing. But the reviews in *The New Yorker* are killer. Can you bear it? I'm so totally in love with him already, I mean, apparently he's an *auteur* in the making."

"Julie, you're being so cynical."

"You say that like it's a bad thing! Now, do you think he's into double- or single-process blondes? Because I can always nip back to Bergdorf's quickly."

I spent the next day—the day of Muffy's party—secretly

un-cancelling everything Mom had cancelled. This was beyond traumatic because it meant I didn't have time for a fake bake or makeup or anything and the worry of everything had gotten inside my brain and turned my complexion whiter than an entire Lily Jungle. All that mattered was that Zach never found out what Mom had done behind his back.

The only good thing about the day of the party was that I got to spend it in my apartment, which, by the way, I adore. I couldn't believe it when I found it, it was a steal. It's deep in the West Village, on the corner of Perry Street and Washington Street, the whole top floor of a redbrick, prewar walk-up. I've got pretty windows on two sides and I can just glimpse the river sparkling in the distance through them. I've painted all the walls a pale azure to match the water. It's not very big—just a bedroom, sitting room with a fireplace, and an alcove study—but it's pretty as hell with my things in it. It's sort of vintagey, but not cluttered with junk like some girls' apartments can be in New York. Shoes everywhere is something I'm totally allergic to actually, and I can't really be friends with girls who are into having rails and rails of clothes instead of furniture. I'm into clean vintage, if you get my meaning. I mean, I have this beautiful chandelier I found in Paris in the sitting room, and old photographs and things on the wall, and a soft, pale blue sofa that I lie on and read books for hours, listening to music. And then everything in my bedroom is covered in antique white linen that Mom sends over from England, when she's not busy doing annoying things like cancelling my wedding without telling me. God! Mom! Nightmare.

Lexington Kinnicut is not Manhattan's king of the Rose Jungle for nothing. That night he transformed Muffy's dining room into a bower of pink roses and orchids that smelled so delicious it was like being inside a bottle of Fracas. The pink cotton tablecloths matched the flowers so exactly it was as though they'd been grown in the hothouse together. Somehow Lexington had even managed to find pink mother-of-pearl dishes to put on the tables, which were overflowing with fresh strawberries. No wonder everyone says he's a genius: I mean, as far as I knew until tonight, there was no such thing as pink mother-of-pearl.

Something must have happened since we got back from LA, because that night at the party Zach was beyond adorable. Smiling, kissing me affectionately as though we'd been to Brazil yesterday or something, holding my hand all night—he was a different person. Thank god! It was just as I thought: Zach was a total doll, with mood swings like everyone else I knew in New York. Just as everyone was arriving, he swept me off alone into a bedroom and gave me the most beautiful necklace of pink amethysts that he'd had specially made because he knew pink is my favorite color. What a relief I hadn't asked for a mini-delay after all.

Julie was the most radiant heiress at the party. She flirted with Charlie all night. He asked her out for dinner within minutes of meeting her. They left the party together. My fiancé and I left the party separately. Zach was leaving for a work trip to Philadelphia early the next morning and said he didn't want to be kept up late by me. I guess I was pretty upset, but I couldn't complain, after he'd been so sweet all night and given me the necklace and everything. But it was certainly confusing, having him do his vanishing act on me on that particular night. Still, I guess that was the point about Zach. You never knew what to expect.

A few days later it was Zach's birthday, which was when he started acting strange again. He always said he hated his birthday because his mom never remembered it when he was a kid. (The upside was that this was very good for his work because it made him depressed. All the amazingly pretty receptionists at Zach's agent's office used to tell him it was important to be as depressed as possible if he was going to take good pictures.) I'd told him I would take him for lunch at Harry's Bar as a treat. I'd even asked Cipriani to bake a cake covered in Zach's favorite candies. I called him that morning to figure out what time to pick him up from his studio in the East Village for lunch.

"Not comin'. I told you I fuckin' hate birthdays. Stop harassin' me."

"But this is so you don't hate your birthday anymore. So you're un-upset by it," I said, shocked.

"Don't you get it? I fuckin' like being upset. That's how I function. How would I make my work if I was fuckin' happy all the time?"

He slammed the phone down on me. I tried calling back a few times, but the line was constantly engaged. I had to get out of the apartment. Desperate to distract myself, I took a cab uptown and met Julie at the Bergdorf salon where she was installed in a huge leather armchair in the private room getting a French manicure. It takes hours—it's the fingernail equivalent of painting the *Mona Lisa*.

"Eew! I'm so like totally beyond excited!" she cried when I walked in. "Charlie is *so cute*. He sends me these totally brainy intellectual e-mails every day that I don't understand. Isn't that adorable! He's taking me on vacation to Italy. He says he's going to send me flowers every day when he's back in LA, where he knows, like, everyone. I mean, I think he might know Brad Pitt and you know how much I want to get Jennifer shopping at Bergdorf's. This relationship is very good for my career . . . Okay, so the kissing wasn't exactly *9½ Weeks* but you can't have everything in a perfect relationship, can you?" said Julie.

Then she asked me why I wasn't at the birthday lunch with Zach and I didn't really get time to explain because my face was drowning in tears before I could open my mouth.

Desperate to cheer me up, Julie asked me to come out with her and Charlie that night. She said Charlie was so well informed she never knew what he was talking about, and maybe I could lighten things up a bit. I said I wouldn't dream of crashing a romantic dinner. Hopefully I would be able to see Zach later. I hadn't seen him since Muffy's party. I was sure his moodiness would have evaporated by then.

That evening, Zach didn't call. Whenever I tried to reach him, voice mail picked up. After I'd left my third "Happy Birthday please call me" message, I collapsed into a tearful depression in front of the TV. Even *Access Hollywood* couldn't lift my mood. As the tears rained down, the lovely smoky eye makeup I'd done specially for Zach's birthday lunch started to streak down my cheeks. I was just on the point of not caring how much Bobbi Brown Black Ink Gel

Eyeliner I'd wasted (it's the best for smoky eyes, I totally recommend it) when Charlie called. Would I meet him for dinner, with Julie?

"I've got eye-makeup issues," I replied, wiping my eyes. "And if I come out they might get worse."

I regarded myself in the mirror. The kohl was now down by my mouth. It had formed two shadowy rivers running from my eyes, along the edges of my nose and down to my lips. My face resembled a crevasse. Not a good look, even on a really pretty girl like me.

"You sound terrible. I'm coming to pick you up. Julie's not ready. She'll meet us there."

The second we walked into Da Silvano on Sixth Avenue, I cheered up. There's something about the place that makes you feel comfortable, whatever nastiness has happened that day. You feel like you're in a local trattoria, except if you look around you always see someone insanely interesting like Patti Smith or Joan Didion or Calvin Klein just hanging as though they're in their own kitchens. Julie was already installed at the best corner table when we arrived. She was "way traumatized" and was waiting for a very important phone call from Mooki, her personal shopper at Bergdorf's. Would we mind if she took it at the table? Seriously, Julie has the worst manners of anyone I know. Luckily, Charlie thinks this is a hilarious character trait. Would Charlie mind, I then asked, if I touched up my smoky eyes over my langoustine? I mean, I looked like one of the corpses on *Six Feet Under*.

"Girls, I'd be honored." He laughed.

"Oh, hon-eeeey, I adore you. You're so easy," replied Julie, kissing him. "I totally get my own way with him all the time."

"Do I have a choice?" he said with a smile.

"Cute! God, you are such a gentleman! It's beyond. You know Charlie is secretly half-British, too, that's where the manners come from—"

Julie's phone rang. She leapt up and grabbed it, crying, "OH MY GOD! Mooki, is there some kind of sicko plot in operation to excommunicate me from the New York social scene? Or am I just paranoid . . . you cannot imagine the shame of walking into Lara's party last week in the Alice & Olivia bootcut pants *you* sold me . . . and finding that bootcuts are *over* . . . everyone's wearing Allegra Hicks's kaftans now . . ."

Julie went silent as Mooki tried to console her. Meanwhile I chatted with Charlie.

He seemed about as British as the White House. He explained that although he was born in England and his second name—Dunlain—has Scottish roots, he didn't consider himself a Brit. His English father had moved to the West Coast when Charlie was about six years old, fed up with British snobbery, British gossip, and the terrible British weather.

"I've spent my whole life here," said Charlie. "I barely remember England. Even my dad doesn't talk about it too much—he's pretty eccentric and secretive. Anyway, why did you leave England?"

"Well, my mom's American anyway and I just always wanted to be here. Plus Mom became totally obsessed with me marrying a blue-blooded Englishman. Ugh! I hate toffs!"

"They're pretty bad, aren't they?"

"Ghastly. I live in perpetual fear of ending up in some freezing castle married to an Earl."

"Doesn't sound so painful. But I can see why you'd prefer New York."

Meanwhile, Julie was turning the color of her NARS rose lip gloss.

"It was totally icky! I thought I was going to vom! I was so humiliated . . ." she cried. "I got even more nauseated when I saw the Vandonbilt twins' new crinkled hair. *No one* in this town gets new hair before me, Mooki, no one!"

"Sounds real nasty," said Charlie. "You girls have a tough life."

"You cannot imagine the trauma of being as glamorous as Julie," I said.

"Ah, but I can," replied Charlie with a half smile. "You see I had the pleasure tonight of witnessing one particular trauma concerning choosing the right pair of jeans for this restaurant. Julie assured me it was a task of a magnitude that could be compared, say, to climbing Kilimanjaro. Naturally I agreed, because if I hadn't it would have taken her *two* hours to leave her place instead of one."

"You understand women so well," I told him. Honestly, this man was a catch. Julie was a lucky girl.

"I wish. The only thing I understand about women is that if you agree with them about everything, then you 'understand' them. I remember once when I didn't understand a girlfriend who thought boyfriends were there to be used as human credit cards on Rodeo Drive; she dropped me."

I was shocked. To know that there are *still* women on the loose like this in LA did not warm my heart. I thought they went out with *Dynasty*.

I was having eye-makeup issues now for all the best reasons. I'd gotten the giggles. It was such a relief after the last few days. Meanwhile Julie was pacing around the table like an angry lioness.

"And then I got out my cell and everyone looked at me like I was an *alien!* The Vandy twins communicate with satellite pagers, they think phones are, like, totally *out.*"

Charlie looked at Julie fondly and murmured, "The somehow irresistible joys of dating a shopaholic!"

Charlie treated Julie with a mixture of awe and amusement. I think you could say he was rather taken by her unique personality, even if he'd had issues with shopping-addicted girlfriends in the past. Then I did something a little bit sneaky. I decided to pry into his mysterious family life—purely for Julie's sake of course—and asked him about his mother. He sighed, "Aah . . . she's rather a flighty one. She was known as The Bolter. She ran off with a friend of my father's and lives in Switzerland now."

"I'm sorry," I said.

See, you should never pry like this. You always bring up something too sad for words and then you can't go back.

"Anyway, I'm not really in touch with her. I call her now and then to say hi, but my dad remarried and he's happy now."

"And you see him in LA? He lives there, right?"

"He's got a place in Santa Monica. I see him sometimes. He's a bit of an eccentric, my dad, always disappearing off. We're all a bit rootless . . ." He trailed off, looking troubled.

Why do I pry? Why? I made a vow to myself not to pry so much with strangers in the future. And Charlie seemed so nice. I hoped Julie appreciated him.

Julie finally got off her little camouflage Nokia—which I still thought was very in, even if the Vandonbilt girls didn't—grabbed her bag and jacket as if to leave, and said,

"I gotta go collect something. Can you guys just carry on without me?" and swirled out the door.

I wasn't surprised at all. As I've already said, Julie has beyond bad manners and I'm always filling in for her. I explained to Charlie that she abandons dinner dates all the time for late-night shopping trips and that he shouldn't be offended. Charlie shrugged and tucked into a plate of tagliatelle with truffles. Luckily, he didn't take Julie's exit personally. He looked at me in a warm, fraternal sort of way. With Julie gone, the atmosphere changed and I felt relaxed for the first time in weeks.

"You know about my parents," he said, "now let's talk about something else. Tell me how you and Julie met . . ."

The next morning I met Julie at Portofino on West Broadway for a fake bake. She thinks tanning cures her depression, so she goes almost every week. She must have been giddy with love that day because I noticed she was only using SPF 8 while we were lying there. (They have these great private rooms there where you can tan with a friend.) She was wearing a red satin eye mask with the words DRAMA QUEEN embroidered on it in pink silk.

"Charlie is *really* cute," said Julie from underneath her mask. "My boyfriend thinks he's really good for me."

"Your boyfriend? He *is* your boyfriend, Julie," I said, rubbing SPF 30 onto my legs.

"He's *one* of my boyfriends. I hate to break this to you, darling, but a lot of women have a husband and several boyfriends, too. You can't put all your diamonds in one safe."

I wondered how Charlie would feel if he knew he was one of several diamonds in Julie's safe. A lot of New York girls date two or three guys simultaneously in case one doesn't work out. Julie had told Charlie she couldn't be "exclusive" with him, but she hadn't admitted she had two other boyfriends, which seemed hopelessly unromantic for a hopeless romantic like Julie. I guess I felt bad for Charlie, almost protective. We almost had a row about it.

"So, is he unexclusive with you, too?" I asked.

"God no! I said he could only date me if it was exclusive," replied Julie, astonished.

"Julie, you can't sleep with three men at once. It's unhygienic."

"Why should I deny myself while he's in LA? You can hardly talk, Miss I've-only-slept-with-three-men-ever-but-I'm-obviously-lying-so-you-think-I'm-more-virginal-than-I-am."

"Julie! I have slept with only three men."

This was not strictly true but since I'd always maintained it was true, I could hardly change my mind now.

The truth is I am all for being a complete slut, but in private, I thought as I lay there tanning my skin to the perfect shade—light latte. (There's nothing tackier than a too-tan face in the city.) When it comes to sexual politics, my view is that the liberated modern girl is better off acting like a virgin so that she can do all sorts of pornographic things with no fear of getting a reputation. Even if someone were unkind enough to spread nasty pornographic rumors about her, it wouldn't matter because no one would believe them anyway. So the moral is look like a virgin, behave however you like, and that way you will always get what you want.

Not that this is *anything*, honestly, to do with *moi*, but if

I were to want a lot of *rendezvous* requiring contraceptive devices in glamorous places like the Paris Ritz, this is exactly how I would go about it. Which suddenly made it occur to me that, as far as *rendezvous* were concerned, I hadn't had one for over a week with Zach, not even one *without* a contraceptive device.

New York Nervous Breakdown

I have:

1. an acupuncturist @ $99 for 90 minutes
2. an Ashtanga yoga teacher @ $70 for 60 minutes
3. an osteopath @ $150 for 25 minutes
4. a chiropractor @ $100 for 15 minutes
5. a healer from Gujarat, India, who charges nothing
6. an ob-gyn @ $350 for the words "might not be ovulating but can't be sure"
7. a hypnotherapist @ $150 for 60 minutes
8. a cognitive behavioral therapist @ $200 for 55 minutes
9. a psychotherapist @ $40 for 90 minutes (too cheap to work)
10. a psychic @ $250 for 60 minutes
11. a masseuse @ $125 for 40 minutes

I am not at Bliss Spa. I am having a New York nervous breakdown. It's expensive.

5

Even in my most imaginative nightmares I never dreamed a day could start with an invitation to the Chanel sample sale and end with a New York nervous breakdown.

"Don't tell her I said this or she'll think I'm a two-faced liar," whispered Julie conspiratorially one beautiful May morning over café au lait at Tartine, "but K. K.'s New York City Opera benefit, which is universally considered to be *the* benefit of benefits, is not even five percent as thrilling as the Chanel sample sale. Show me a Manhattan girl who'd rather watch Don Giovanni than shop Chanel at Target prices, and I'll renew my membership at Equinox Gym on Sixty-third Street and actually start going on a semi-regular basis."

According to Julie, the Chanel sample sale is *the* event of New York events: absolutely no one gets invited except "very few, very exclusive girls. But you're in," Julie said, handing me a white envelope. "I got you on the list."

Inside was a stiff white card from Chanel. I was beyond excited, which was *très* alarming actually. I adore Julie but her shopping habits are not exactly healthy. I didn't want to turn into a girl like her, whose hormone system is ruled by retail opportunities. But apparently everyone's estrogen skyrockets the first time they get this particular invitation, so there's no need to be freaked by it. It read,

Chanel Sample Sale
Tuesday, May 7, 7:15 a.m.
Park Lane Hotel
58th Street, btw. 6th and 7th
Bring photo ID
No admittance without this card.
This is your security pass.

Security at Chanel is tighter than at the Pentagon. The president should take tips from the PR girls there because the Chanel guards run a tighter ship than the Department of Homeland Security.

The annoying thing was, I couldn't go to the sample sale because of work. Careers are very unreliable things and you have to be attentive to them or they just disappear. NY girls who go to too many parties and sample sales tend to have disappearing-type careers and I didn't want to be one of them. I was booked to fly down to Palm Beach to do an interview with a society girl. She'd just inherited an Art Deco beach mansion. She lived there all alone like a millennial Doris Duke. It was sad, really, but very glamorous.

"*Fool,*" said Julie when I told her I wasn't coming. "You cannot miss this."

I knew I should do the interview, but I just couldn't resist the idea of shopping Chanel like it was the Gap. Occasionally my value system inexplicably abandons me, and I find myself doing things I never usually would. Feeling unbelievably guilty, I called the office and said that the Palm Beach heiress had cancelled due to "fatigue." My editor believed me: society girls are always backing out of things at the absolute last minute because they are "too tired after last night." When I'd spoken to the heiress she'd sounded extremely tired anyway, poor rich thing, so it wasn't really a lie at all, just a convenient delay for both of us.

That Monday I could barely concentrate on anything. Chanel's invite was so mesmerzing with the future promise of quilted purses for $150 instead of $2,000 (no wonder your estrogen goes nuts), that I actually physically forgot that there had been zero *rendezvous* with Zach for a seriously long time. I'd become used to the lack of intimate Brazilian encounters but now it was like he wasn't even prepared to see me for a cocktail. Whenever I'd called in the last few days, his assistant had just said, "He'll return," and hung up. This never used to happen: Zach always used to take my calls.

The hottest sample sales in New York are so fraught with danger they make the Gaza Strip look peaceful. Honestly, I once saw K. K. almost *murder* her own cousin at a TSE sample sale because they both wanted this great white cashmere peacoat and there was only one of them. It's no wonder that Jolene Morgan organizes all her "shopping attacks" in advance on such occasions. She called a pre-Chanel "strategy meeting" with Lara Lowell, Julie, and myself over lunch at the Four Seasons restaurant on East Fifty-second Street. Sometimes I worry about Jolene's mental state, I really do. The Four Seasons is the kind of place the mayor and media moguls lunch. It wasn't exactly the most obvious place for a fashion summit. But I guess Jolene wanted to be in the company of other brilliant strategists.

When I arrived Lara and Jolene were already analyzing the menu for hidden carbs. They'd gotten one of the great tables right by the fountain, with leather banquette seating. Among the sea of power-lunchers, they looked like two colorful birds: Jolene was in a sexy pale blue dress, nipped in at the waist to show off her pretty curves. Lara, who has two of the longest legs in Manhattan, was in a tiny white miniskirt and a scarlet sweater. Her long blonde hair was scooped up in a ponytail. She has a tomboyish style and totally gets away with it, which bugs the hell out of Jolene, even though they've been best friends forever. Sometimes I think Lara is mainly Jolene's best friend because she does absolutely everything Jolene tells her to.

I sat down and ordered a Pellegrino and a salad. Jolene was acting like a crazy person, which isn't all that different from usual actually: she was obsessed with getting the new pink quilt purse with a gilt chain from the Chanel resort collection. I warned her that since Reese Witherspoon had carried the exact same purse to the Oscars, everyone was going to try and snag that one first. I didn't want Jolene to be disappointed; I mean, the fallout would be horrible for all of us.

"It's not an issue," declared Jolene. "I got the floor plan and I know exactly where the pastel quilts are going to be located: at the far end of the ballroom behind the size thirty-eight cashmere twin sets." All New York girls illegally buy floor plans from fashion publicists before sample sales. It's the only way to get the best stuff.

Jolene and Lara were both exhausted. They had been

at a super-cool dinner the previous night at one of the Pink Floyd kids' lofts downtown. A waiter brought our drinks, but Lara and Jolene ignored theirs: they were way too stressed about last night.

"Everyone was, like, the child of a Rolling Stone or a Mama and Papa," said Jolene. "Rock 'n' roll kids make me feel so terrible about myself. I had a total Shame Attack."

"Me too," agreed Lara. "But then I have a Shame Attack after most parties." Lara is so insecure sometimes it's criminal. But I guess it's one of the reasons she fits in so well on the Upper East Side.

A Shame Attack is a bit like the Fargos, only it's intellectual, not beauty-related. Only girls in NYC and Paris get them. They are much feared because apparently they get inside your brain and keep you awake night after night. Jolene always takes a 10mg Ambien (the in sleeping tablet) when she gets an Attack, which is usually at 5 AM, just when she is about to finally get off to sleep after taking her first Ambien at 1 AM. Her latest SA was brought on because she'd taken a vintage gold Rolex off the boy to her right at last night's dinner and said she'd meet him for cocktails at the Mercer Hotel the next evening to return it. It was all very sexy and flirtatious. She'd totally forgotten she was engaged when she agreed to it all. Lara's came on because she hadn't read the *New York Times* since 9/11 and didn't know the most dangerous terrorist cell in the Middle East had been captured last week. She was freaking out all night because she was terrified that people would now think she was a self-obsessed Park Avenue Princess with no interest in Israel or anything below Seventy-second Street. (Which is pretty close to the truth but I would never be cruel enough to actually tell Lara how narrow-minded most of us think she is because she has a heart of gold, she really does.)

"I've never had a Shame Attack," I said. I'd come close, sure, but I don't think I'd ever had a full-fledged shame crisis.

"Never?" said Lara, turning whiter than her minuscule skirt.

"Look at her," said Jolene. "Of course she's never had one. She even looks like she's never had one."

"I'm going to get something really beautiful for Zach's mom at the sale," I said, changing the subject.

The Chanel sample sale drives most New York girls to frantically gobble up as many gilt quilts as they can for themselves and totally forget everyone else. (Then they go down with an attack of GQG: gilt quilt guilt.) I decided I would do the opposite and use the opportunity to perform an uncalled-for act of kindess: I would buy the best purse for my mother-in-law-to-be.

"Oh, what a cute idea," said Lara.

"What a terrible waste," said Jolene. "She won't understand it. She comes from Ohio."

I ignored Jolene's protestations and called Zach's office from the table: I wanted to check what color his mom might like.

"Hey. The office," came the reply.

It was Zach's assistant, Mary Alice. She talks in the monosyllabic bark favored by a clique of cool bicoastal assistants. (Even though she has had her picture in *Paper* magazine more than three times, Mary Alice is transparently miserable. She always dresses in shapeless, avant-garde Belgian clothes, which would make anyone unhappy. When I tried to help and explained that being a champagne-bubble-about-town was preferable to being a depressive-about-town she said, "Yeah. Right," and didn't do *anything* about herself.)

Resolutely chirpy, I replied, "Hi! It's me—"

"I'm taking messages only. He'll return," M. A. interrupted.

All the Manhattan assistants were doing the "message-return" thing after they found out it's standard at Spielberg's H.Q. on the West Coast.

"I need to ask Zach a very urgent shopping question—"

"Who's speaking?"

M. A.'s started pretending she has no idea who I am recently. Apparently that's protocol at Calvin Klein's New York office.

"Its *me*!"

"'Me'?"

"His *fiancée*."

"He'll return."

The line went dead. What was going on with Zach? This was getting weird. I looked up to see Jolene and Lara staring at me as though something really sad had happened, like I'd let my roots grow in or something desperately depressing like that.

"Are you okay?" said Jolene, cautiously examining her steak, which had just arrived.

"Fine!" I said.

I smiled my most radiant, in-love smile as if to say, *I'm happier than you can imagine.* If Nicole Kidman could look that glamorous while she was divorcing Tom Cruise, I could smile my way through a few unreturned phone calls. But it's really hard, you know. I realized that day that actresses like Nicole really deserve all those free clothes because looking blissfully happy when your blood is turning to tears in your veins is *extremely* skilled work. I say, Nicole didn't deserve an Oscar, she deserves the Nobel Prize.

"Why won't he talk to you?" added Lara.

I felt sick. Was M. A. blocking my calls or was Zach cooling off? I tried to put my doubts to one side. What was I thinking! Zach adored me. Why had he just given me that wonderful necklace otherwise? The simple explanation must be that M. A. wasn't passing on my messages.

"It's not *him,*" I said, maximizing my smile. "It's his assistant. She's very protective. Professional, you know."

Before I could go on I was interrupted by Julie yelling, "Hey girls! Did you miss me?" from the other side of the restaurant. She waved at each table as she walked toward us. Julie knows everyone in New York, absolutely everyone.

Julie's look that day could be described as walking-safety-deposit-box. She was unashamedly swinging several Van Cleef & Arpels bags. On her index finger was a gold cocktail ring shaped like a rose and studded with garnets; she had new gold hoops in her ears; on her arm was a platinum and emerald bracelet.

"Presents!" she said, collapsing on the banquette and dropping her loot. She handed the three of us a tiny bag each. Inside was a pavé diamond heart identical to the one around Julie's neck.

"Julie, you can't!" I gasped.

I honestly meant it, but at the same time prayed that Julie would ignore my protestation. I just adore diamonds, they make a girl feel really good about herself, especially when she's feeling a bit low.

"Oh, don't worry, honey. They were almost *free,*" said Julie. "I wanted to celebrate love, which is why I got us all a heart." She had a triumphant look on her face that signified one thing—a recent shopping success of the illegal kind.

"Julie, you've been stealing stuff again, haven't you?" said Lara.

"Almost!" She gulped. She glanced furtively about her and whispered, "I've just been to the Van Cleef über-*über*-private-favorite-clients-only studio sale that, like, virtually no one gets invited to. I got so much cheap stuff you won't believe it. They virtually gave me those hearts."

Lara looked like a block of salt. She had gone into mega-sulk mode. This tends to happen to Lara on a daily basis. She spoke in a low, very intense voice.

"But *I'm* their favorite private client! That's *it*, I'm *leaving*," she said, throwing down her napkin, grabbing her phone, and stomping angrily from the restaurant.

She must have been *très* traumatized because she left her monogrammed Kelly bag behind, a bag she'd waited over four and a half years for on the Hermès list. Poor Lara. Some girls just can't deal with the brutal hierarchy of sample sales. I mean, the whole thing is so political, sometimes I wish Condoleezza Rice would come in and sort it all out.

"Drat. That is a Shame Attack waiting to happen. I'm going after her," said Jolene gathering up her things. As she was leaving the table she said to me, "My driver will pick you up at 6:45 AM tomorrow. Don't be late, and remember to find out which bag Zach's mother wants."

"Well. Some of us get to go to Chanel sales and some of us get to go to diamond sales. That's just the way the cookie crumbles, sales-wise!" Julie sighed. She was beyond thrilled with herself. "*Poor* Lara. She needs to reevaluate her value system. I mean, someone kind *really* needs to tell her that if she's not careful she's going to become one of the most superficial twenty-four-year-olds on Park Avenue. Heartbreaking really."

Julie's honesty about her good friends is refreshing, but it's lucky I am not the gossipy type or most of her good friends wouldn't be her good friends for long. Suddenly Julie looked uncharacteristically solemn. She said she had something difficult to tell me.

"Charlie's gone back to LA. I'm gutted of course, but I insisted he send me flowers once a week and he agreed *immediately*—"

"How cute," I said. Julie obviously had Charlie wrapped around her little finger, even though they'd known each other only a few weeks. There was a pregnant pause, and Julie shot me a severe look. "What's the problem?" I asked.

"There isn't one, because that is how a man *should* behave." She started to whisper. "And yours is not behaving right. He's making you miserable." How Julie could not see that I was officially Deliriously Happy I know not. "Look at you, you're *totally* ana," she went on. "Which would normally be the best compliment I could pay another girl, but right now you're just *too* ana."

I couldn't believe what I was hearing. It is the general consensus in Manhattan that a girl can never be too rich or too ana. But there was something I hadn't told Julie which accounted for my extra weight loss. The last time I'd seen Zach, at the engagement party, he'd mentioned he was leaving town the next day to photograph a project in Philadelphia. Then Jolene saw him out the next night at Bungalow 8 on Twenty-seventh Street. When I heard that I swear I dropped seven pounds. Why had he said he was away when he wasn't? Then, another major factor in my ana-ness is that it's tradition that a girl as madly in love as I am can't eat a thing anyway. Still, Julie continued relentlessly, "You can't marry him. Just imagine what it would be like—you'd practically disappear with worry. You should be happy and relaxed during an engagement."

Actually, Julie's wrong about that. Apparently everyone's completely stressed out during an engagement. It's *supposed* to be incredibly stressful. I said, "Julie, he's just freaked out and exhausted right now. He just shot that Luca Luca campaign and he's really upset about that new photographer the agency took on who's been getting all that press—"

"Exactly! You want to marry someone who cares about how much press *someone else* is getting? What about someone who cares about *you* and puts *you* first?"

"He does care about me, Julie, and he's The One."

"He's not The One, there's no such thing as The One . . ."

Julie literally didn't stop talking even while she was eating her panna cotta, which had just been put on the table by a waiter. Her lips—which looked awesome dabbed with that new M.A.C. Lipglass that everyone's obsessed with right now—kept moving but I tuned out. I couldn't hear a thing.

I was overcome by a moment of deep introspection. How could I forget Zach's peonies, and the dinners and the gifts and everything? According to the laws of romance that I learned from historical movies like *Sleepless in Seattle*, there is only one One and there's nothing you can do about it. (It's like, Jackie and JFK were inevitable. Imagine if she'd said no. The whole course of American fashion history would have changed.) I'm all for Jean-

Paul Sartre and free will and so on, but when it comes to The One, it's not like you have any say in the matter, even if he's barely speaking to you.

Thank goodness I could see everything so clearly. That's the genius thing about introspection. You go in as lost as a Chinese noodle in a Sicilian lasagne and come out thinking straighter than Fifth Avenue.

Julie's voice faded back in.

". . . So, that's what I've heard about him. He's not a good person. Apparently he's got a reputation for torturing girlfriends in a sort of weird psychological way. Darling, maybe he *is* a psycho. People don't say things like that unless there's a reason."

"I totally agree," I said.

I had no clue what I was agreeing with but at least I was smart enough to agree with whatever it was Julie wanted me to agree with. Hopefully that was the end of this particular anti-Zach lecture.

"I gotta go," I said. "See you at the crack of dawn with Jolene."

We'd been at the Four Seasons long enough already. I didn't want to hear another word about why I shouldn't be getting married. I got up from the table and left the restaurant. I was going to prove Julie wrong.

I called Zach again the minute I was home. My fingers trembled slightly as I dialed his number.

"He'll return!" came the voice. M. A. had not even let me speak this time. I couldn't bear it any longer.

"Actually, its *très* sweet of you to offer a return, but I

would like a connection immediately, please," I said, as kindly as I could manage.

"I'm not some kind of AT&T operator."

"Please tell Zach it's his fiancée and I urgently need to discuss an urgent emergency."

"I'll take a message."

"But Mary Alice, you never give him any messages from me. He hasn't returned one message I've left with you in the last week."

"All his messages are on his board. He gets every single one."

I don't think M. A. was being 100 percent truthful about her talent for leaving messages. I felt sorry for her being so depressed the whole time, but that didn't mean she could get away with not giving Zach his messages.

"Please," I begged, "please get him."

The phone was covered and I could hear muffled voices. Then—bliss—Zach came on the line.

"What?" he said.

I was right about M. A. *Of course* Zach wanted to chat with me. The horrible thing was, now that I had him on the phone, I had no idea what to talk about with him.

"What?" came the voice again. He didn't sound overjoyed to hear from me.

"Nothing, darling!" I blurted.

"If you've got 'nothing' to say, can you not interrupt me when I'm trying to work?"

Oh, I remembered. I'll offer to get his mother the purse.

"I'm getting your mom a gift and I want to know, would she prefer a pink gilt quilt Chanel purse or a baby blue gilt quilt? Or maybe the primrose yellow?"

"I have no idea. Is that the 'emergency'?"

"I'd love to have dinner."

Silence. Zach must still be *très* upset inside about the new photographer at his agency because a photograph she had taken was on the front of the *Herald Tribune* today. And he was so busy and everything, I felt guilty for disturbing him at all. I know, I'll cheer him up, I thought. I said, "Can I take you out for a romantic dinner at Jo Jo? Tonight?"

"What is it with you and the most expensive restaurants in the city? How am I supposed to get any work done if I'm constantly baby-sittin' you?" he replied.

Sometimes I wonder if Zach understands me. Surely he knows that the most expensive restaurants in Manhattan are the ones with the best French fries? And it wasn't like I was asking him to pay.

"Don't you want to see me at all?" I asked timidly.

"I'll call you later."

He hung up.

Well, that was progress of a sort. He'd agreed to call later. This was just a very busy time for him. I mean, as Zach often said, it's very pressured being the hottest young photographer in New York, so it's hard to make time for dinner at Jo Jo. I *totally* understood. I wanted to show him I could be very mature about not going for dinner at Jo Jo and then maybe he'd take me to Jo Jo as a reward.

So that night, even though I had been invited to

1. the premiere of Cameron Crowe's new movie
2. the opening of the Rothko show at the Guggenheim
3. cocktails for Lexington Kinnicut's latest book about himself
4. Jolene's dinner for her skin analyst

I made an executive decision to have an early night so as to be as fresh as possible for Chanel the next morning. Also, I wanted to be home when Zach telephoned. I could hardly claim to need to go to Jo Jo if I was at four different parties when he called me on my cell. When he did, I would say I was destressing watching a DVD, because I had been working so hard on my career, which was semi-true. On the very q-t, the truth is I didn't own a DVD player. In fact, I have well-founded moral and social objections to DVD players: there is nothing more depressing than a single girl in New York, a DVD player, and a pile of watched DVDs—it's an admission of worryingly low popularity levels. If you get as many invitations as a girl in Manhattan should get, you barely know where your apartment is, let alone have time to watch movies in it.

I dressed up for the imaginary DVD in my new black net lingerie threaded with pink ribbons. If you are going to be pretending to watch a DVD all night, do it in Agent Provocateur just in case someone sees you. By half past midnight I hadn't heard a thing from Zach. I couldn't deny it any longer: I was attracting about as much attention from The One as a leftover blini at Le Cirque. For the first time, a very scary thought crept into my mind: maybe Zach didn't love me. Maybe he really was a "psycho," as Julie put it. I didn't even want to contemplate what was happening. I couldn't imagine anything more painful than a) breaking up with Zach, and b) admitting to Julie she was right about him. God, b) was almost more horrifying than a).

Suddenly, the buzzer went off. I was startled. I never have visitors after midnight except when I am having illicit affairs, and I couldn't recall starting one of those recently. I picked up the handset.

"Who's there?" I said.

"Me. What are you doing?"

It was Zach. I was delirious with happiness. Julie had zero idea how much Zach adored me. I acted very unanxious as I replied nonchalantly, "Nothing. Just watching a DVD." I let out a deep sigh of contentment. "Darling, come up," I said, buzzing the door.

Thank god I was dressed for Brazil. I could hardly wait for Zach to appear. Remembering that nonchalance was key, I went and lounged *très* attractively on my pale blue sofa. I lit a cigarette even though I don't smoke.

Zach walked in. He didn't kiss me hello. I think he was in one of his moods. He was impossible to converse with when he was like this. But god, he was attractive. I lost my appetite on the spot, as usual.

"Put some clothes on," he said. "I have to tell you something."

What did he have to tell me that was so serious? Obligingly, I threw this to-die-for chinchilla coat I had on an extended one-year loan from Valentino over my shoulders. Zach sat on the sofa. Once upon a time he would have thought the fur coat was really funny. Tonight he barely looked at me. He was freaking me out.

"Can I watch the DVD with you?" he asked.

God, Zach was confusing. There I was thinking something was wrong and all Zach wanted was to cuddle up and watch TV with me. Casually remembering I didn't have a DVD player, I said with over 100 percent confidence, "Of course! I got the new Scorsese."

Zach's face lit up. He adores those vile Scorsese movies. Ultra-casual, I added, "Why don't I make us a mojito first?"

I was thinking on my toes now. The Scorsese movie was a huge success, so the main thing was to make sure Zach thought I had both the Scorsese and a DVD player without him ever discovering that I owned neither. And that I totally *loathe* Martin Scorsese's gritty realism.

"I'd prefer just to watch the movie," said Zach.

"Sure!" I said brightly.

Be Nicole Kidman, I told myself. *Give Oscar-winning performance of Perfect Cute Girlfriend despite trauma of moment.* I slipped my very high peep-toe Manolos on. I slipped the chinchilla off. Surely Zach wouldn't still want to watch the DVD when he saw my heels-and-lingerie look from behind? I walked over to the armoire in which I "kept" the DVD machine. Then something beyond lucky happened. I felt Zach's hand on my back. Finally this lingerie was getting me somewhere. In one flick of his wrist it was history and we were on the sofa. How could I have been so suspicious about that trip he never took to Philadelphia? I take it all back, I really do, I thought to myself.

Everything was going to be good again after tonight. Zach was super-attentive in all the right places. Please don't tell anyone this or they will say I got what I deserved because I was being a horrible showoff, but I felt compelled to let Julie know that the romance was going absolutely brilliantly again and that we were whipping up some very serious tiramisu on that sofa. While Zach was investigating my new bikini wax I grabbed my phone and surreptitiously texted the following (Daphne had taught me how to do it while physically constrained):

everything brilliant zach making tiramisu love moi xxx

I got an immediate reply.

can i borrow rabbit trim prada for frick benefit?

Sometimes Julie makes the worst fashion choices. I knew the Fendi chiffon would be better with her hair but I was worried if I sent another message Zach might notice.

"Honey, let's go to bed," I said, taking Zach by the hand. "We can make out all night."

But a funny look came over his face. He stood up and started to put his clothes back on. Finally he spoke.

"I'm not marrying you. That's what I came here to tell you."

I tried to speak. Nothing came out. Eventually I whispered, "But we just, I mean . . . you know . . ."

"So?" he said, looking out the window.

I put my thong and chinchilla back on and sat under the *Drowned Truck* photo I'd hung a few weeks before. What had I done? How did we get from the scented body moisturizer and matching lingerie stage of our love affair to this? What could possibly have happened since I last saw Zach?

"But why?" I whispered.

"We had fun, okay. Let's just call it quits and move on," he said, not even looking at me.

"Is there another girl?"

"You're too selfish for me. You're not what I want anymore. I need a really independent girl. Someone who doesn't need constant attention."

A single tear crept down my cheek. My phone beeped.

"Sorry," I whispered. It was a text from Julie:

great! say hi to zach from me, jules

"Julie says hi," I croaked. My voice had virtually disappeared. I was starting to shiver, but it wasn't cold.

"How the *fuck* does she know I'm here? No one knows what I do," said Zach. He narrowed his eyes suspiciously.

I mumbled, "Mmm . . . I guess . . . I must have—"

I never finished the sentence. Zach grabbed the phone from my hands and scrolled through the messages. This was a scrape worse than the almost-discovery that I didn't have a DVD player.

"Tiramisu? You were textin' your fuckin' friend while I was fuckin' you? *Selfish* isn't even a bad enough word for you."

"I can get better, darling," I pleaded. "I know I'm a terrible, selfish girl but I can improve."

"You won't. It's all Me-Me-Me with you. Do you ever think of anyone else but you? Do you ever think about me?"

"All I do is think about you!" I said. "All I do is wonder how I can make you happy—"

"Is that why you fuckin' forgot to ask about my doctor's appointment today?"

"I didn't know you had one—"

"You should *automatically* know stuff like that about me if you're going to marry me."

"But you won't even speak to me," I implored him. "Your assistant won't put me through."

"That's because I tell her not to put your fuckin' calls through."

I was crying big-time now. Huge, hysterical tears as big as a Harry Winston diamond were shooting down my cheeks.

"How am I supposed to know what you want if I'm not allowed to ask you?" I wailed.

"Stop asking me stuff!" he screamed. "I told you, you should just *know*."

I sank off the sofa. My legs collapsed like two strands of that really thin spaghettini they do at Da Silvano. I half-knelt, half-lay on my zebra rug at Zach's feet. Married girls must be really smart if one of the requirements of wedlock is being able to think of everything their husbands need without ever having to communicate with them. Zach headed for the armoire.

"You don't have a fuckin' DVD player, do you?" He started banging the doors. As I had suspected there was no DVD player to be found in there. "You have 'social objections' to those, don't you? You don't like Martin Scorsese. You've never even seen *Apocalypse Now*."

"That was Francis Ford Coppola, darling," I said.

"Why do you always have to contradict me!" he yelled. "If you love someone, you don't disagree with them. But that's it, isn't it, you don't understand how to love anyone except yourself, and you don't even love yourself, do you? You don't even know who you are. You wouldn't notice an apocalypse unless it had a Gucci label on it."

"Actually it's Chloé I'm into," I whispered sadly. He didn't know anything about me, you see, even something as big as that.

Zach stared at me blankly, then he unlocked the door

and left. You could say I had learned the meaning of the words "Shame Attack." The tears were coming faster than an avalanche in Aspen now. As if that wasn't bad enough, the whole thing completely ruined *The Talented Mr. Ripley* for me forever.

6

Someone was whispering.

"If she didn't make the Chanel sale, it really must be bad. I mean, maybe she actually, like, loved him."

"I always thought his photos were beyond icky," hissed another voice. "There is no way I could marry someone who thinks a drowned truck is cute."

I heard a door opening.

"Sshhh! You two! You'll wake her up. I'm going to the pharmacy to get her some more Xanax. Watch her *quietly*." The door closed and someone disappeared.

Where was I? It was too much effort to move my legs or arms or open my eyes. My body felt like a wedge of brie that's been left out of the refrigerator too long. Every few minutes my head felt as though it was being stabbed by a needle just above my right eyebrow.

Silence. A few sighs. Then, "God, look at her. She looks totally ana, but not in a great supermodel way, more in a bad Karen Carpenter way. Ee-ow."

"Apparently she showed up at five AM complaining of a

Shame Attack extraordinaire, crying that her wedding was off. Julie said she was dressed in a stolen chi-chi and a thong and that was *it*."

There had obviously been a wedding disaster. The heavenly thing about anti-anxiety pills like Xanax is that you can be at the epicenter of your own personal romantic tragedy and you don't even notice.

"She would have looked awesome in a wedding dress. Ooooh, so sa-a-a-d. Vera Wang is going to *freak*. Apparently she went to India three times to supervise the beading of the veil personally. It was going to be the most exclusive veil Vera had ever created. It was going to take a whole year to embroider. What's she going to do with it now?"

"Why don't you help? Take the veil yourself for your wedding. That would be kind. Then you'd be the one with the Vera veil."

"Oh, y-e-ssss! I could take the veil as an uncalled-for act of kindness."

"Everyone at 660 Park would think you were the most generous friend she has. God, can you imagine the *humil-i-ation* of a disengagement? Imagine being the girl-who-almost-got–married. How will she ever be able to be seen drinking a Bellini at Cipriani again? Eew, god, the shame."

Hopefully these kindhearted people had brought me to a lovely lunatic asylum like the Broken Engagement Ward at Mount Sinai.

"You know I don't gossip, and I trust you not to say a thing to anyone, but I heard it ended because he caught her texting Jules while he was, you know . . ."

"What?"

Whisper whisper. A lot of *psssht, shhhpsst, psssht*.

"No-ooo!"

"Yes-s-s-s!"

"Oh my god. That is brilliant. Do you think she'd teach me how to do that?"

I cracked open my eyes. The room was almost dark and I could just make out two blonde manes frantically flicking back and forth. I said weakly, "Daphne can teach you."

Two heads shot up, and Jolene and Lara stared back at me.

"Oh thank *god*," said Jolene. "She's alive."

"Where am I?" I mumbled.

"You're in the guest bedroom at Julie's apartment. She just had it done up by Tracey Clarkson, you know, who does absolutely everyone in Hollywood. It's so chic in here you can hardly imagine."

"Why am I here?"

"Your fiancé callously dropped you after having sex with you and—"

"Eew!" yelled Lara. "You don't have to give her all the intimate sexual details."

Even Xanax doesn't erase details like that. Every ghastly moment was branded on my brain. I was sick with shock and horror. Now I know exactly what that poor girl in *The Exorcist* must have felt like.

"Darling, you need to eat," said Lara. "We'll order from room service. What do you want?"

"Just a silver fruit knife," I said.

"What?" said Jolene.

"A silver fruit knife," I repeated. "So I can slit my wrists with style."

"She's totally clinical," whispered Jolene to Lara.

Oh good, I thought, it would only be a matter of time

before I was shipped off to We Care Spa, this lovely therapy center in California. Publicists in New York are regularly clinical because it means they can take vacations there almost once a month and catch up on their A-list networking. Apparently you can get the latest Japanese hot stone massages there.

The tragic thing about Xanax is that eventually someone like Julie says you can't have any more of it. When it wore off a few hours later, fear sidled through the French windows and snuck under Julie's 473-thread-count sheets. Loneliness snaked around my body like the fumes from one of her Diptyque candles. I started to sweat, my face damp, my body boiling as I came to the icky realization that a broken heart is a broken heart no matter who designed the guest bedroom you are having it in. I must warn Julie that unfortunately Frette linens are absolutely no safeguard against personal romantic tragedy. I called for Julie and she came tiptoeing in.

"Please let me call Zach," I croaked. "I need to sort everything out."

Julie hadn't let me near a phone since I'd arrived the night before.

"Engagements and divorces are the only things that really make people happy," she said. "You're lucky to be out of it. Don't call him and make things worse."

"But I love him," I whispered weakly.

"You're not in love with him. You're in longing for him. How could you love someone you hardly saw? My analyst says you are infatuated with a romantic ideal. It's the idea of him not the reality that you want. The reality is that he's a total monster."

There is nothing I hate more than a professional opinion I haven't asked for. Julie's shrink had no idea about my One and Only.

"Why did he send me all those gifts, and tell me I was the wittiest girl in Manhattan, and ask me to marry him? It doesn't make sense," I pleaded.

"You know what? It does. For a guy like Zach with a bit of money and style, sweeping a girl off her feet is easy. It's much harder to really *be* with someone and make them part of your life. He prefers the chase," said Julie, as if she were Oprah or something.

"Please let me call—"

"Just rest," she said sweetly.

She left the room. She also left her cell phone on the bed. I dialed Zach. After the usual set of negotiations with the assistant, he finally came on the line.

"Yeah," he said, just like normal. Maybe nothing had happened.

"Should we meet, and you know . . . discuss—"

"I'm too busy," Zach interrupted.

"But this is serious. We should talk about it," I said.

"I'm leaving town. I'll call you." He hung up.

I felt desperate. Even though I knew Zach had behaved appallingly, I guess I still loved him. There is nothing as painful as being madly in love with someone who isn't madly in love with you anymore. How did we get from *it's so cute you can't cook* to this, I wondered as I lay in Julie's guest bedroom. I felt like I was in one of those majorly depressing Meryl Streep movies where everyone lives in the suburbs and wears bad clothes and can't understand what happened to their relationship.

"I'll never get him back now," I wailed to Julie when she put her head around the bedroom door later that day. "I feel so sad. I called him and he said he's leaving town."

"I don't understand why you keep going back for more," said Julie, exasperated. "I told you, he's a monster and now he's proven it."

I knew Julie was right, but that didn't make it any easier. There's an irrational behavioral pattern shared by many New York girls where the worse a man is to them, the more they want him back. If they do get him back, he's viler than ever. Then they end it because he's being vile, like he was all along, and they look sane and rational and together. The main point of the exercise is to become the reject-*or* instead of the reject-*ee*. I would have thought Julie would really understand, bearing in mind that she's probably the most irrational girl in town.

She tried everything to cheer me up. But mostly anything she or anyone else said made me feel worse. Like when she said to me, "He doesn't deserve someone as great and pretty as you anyway," I felt beyond depressed. After all, that's exactly the kind of thing I say to girls who aren't particularly great or pretty to try and make them feel better after boyfriends have dumped them.

I didn't leave Julie's guest bedroom for three days. Zach never called. I developed a severe case of breakuprexia, which is this illness all girls in NY and LA get after a breakup where you get beyond ana and can fit into a size two. I couldn't eat a thing—even my favorite vanilla cupcakes that Julie specially ordered in for me from Magnolia Bakery downtown. My flesh turned to bone. Lara kept trying to cheer me up about my appearance by saying she wished she had breakuprexia too then she wouldn't have to spend so much on nutritionists and personal trainers. The truth was, I looked like a chopstick and felt as raw as a piece of Nobu's yellowtail. Only, it would have been better being the yellowtail because at least everyone wants yellowtail, and no one wanted me. You know you've checked into Heartbreak Hotel for real when you feel less desirable than uncooked fish.

There were other signs that something was very, very wrong with me. Like the only music I could bear to listen to was Mariah Carey, which, when I look back on it, was almost more worrying than the breakuprexia. When Julie offered to get in Xenia, the Polish manicurist who goes on all the *W* magazine shoots and buffs absolutely anyone who is anyone's nails, I whimpered, "No thanks." I must have been beyond clinical to turn down Xenia, I mean, I am such a New York grooming addict that my nails actually *hurt* if they don't have NARS Candy Darling pink varnish on them. But you know what? Aching nails were nothing compared to the pain I was in now.

On the fourth day Julie announced she was taking me out. The Vandonbilt twins were throwing a lunch in aid of their charity, a Guatemalan girls' school. The twins made Julie feel *très* awkward about being Julie because even though they were far richer than Julie, they acted totally broke-slash-cool all the time and were always helping other people. "And, you know, they tilt their heads to one side as though they are really listening to you and speak real quiet as though they are perfect. But then, you know, in a moment of weakness they go to Barneys and spend a gajillion dollars on makeup and think no one's got any idea," said Julie.

"I don't want to go. I'm too ashamed to ever leave the house ever again," I said.

"Listen, I don't wanna go either, sweetie, but those Vandy girls are my cousins and I need to show them I can be just as benevolent as them. Why they live in that *medium* apartment and wear those *medium* clothes when they could have the best that Dolce & Gabbana has to offer I will never understand." Then she added softly, "You can't stay here forever. You've gotta go out at some point."

I struggled out of bed and somehow got dressed. I was freaked out when I looked in the mirror: my hair was stringy, my face blotchy. My pants hung depressingly from my frame and my T-shirt sagged forlornly from my chest. I looked like one of those really sad Marc Jacobs groupies who hang around the Marc stores on Bleecker Street on Saturdays. The only difference was they spent a fortune trying to look this undernourished. Julie, who was in an upbeat pink sundress, loved my despondent appearance.

"You look totally heroin chic," she said. "The Vandys are gonna kill themselves when they see you." Well, at least something positive may come from the visit, I thought.

Julie wanted to stop at Pastis, down in the meatpacking district, for a bowl of decaf latte before we hit the Vandy lunch. "I gotta get in the downtown mood," she said. I was terrified: Pastis is like the trendiest place in New York. What if there were people there who could detect that I was recently disengaged?

"Don't worry," said Julie, seeing my troubled expression. "We won't bump into anyone we know down there. No one gets up in the West Village before twelve."

As we were chauffeured downtown I started to feel better. It felt good to be out of bed at last, and it was fun being in Julie's new car, an SUV luxuriously upholstered in caramel leather. I wasn't crying hysterically anymore. I could actually chat as we headed down Fifth Avenue.

"You wanna come to the beach this weekend? You can have the guest house all to yourself. Daddy would love to see you," said Julie.

"Sure!" I said brightly.

"Hey, good girl!" said Julie. "You're going to be good again so soon you don't even know it."

But here's the thing about a broken heart: just when you feel a teensy bit less hysterical about it, it bites you in the heel and you're more hysterical than you ever were the first time you got hysterical. As we sped across Fifty-seventh Street I glimpsed a huge billboard with a giant picture of a ring set with three diamonds. Underneath the photograph were the words THREE WAYS TO TELL HER YOU LOVE HER. My first crying attack of the day started immediately. Why were the people at De Beers trying to make me feel so bad about myself? Didn't they know that advertising engagement rings was extremely traumatic for the disengaged population?

"Oh my god!" said Julie. "What's wrong?"

"It's that ad for an engagement ring, it's reminding me."

"But sweetie, you never had an engagement ring, so it's not really relevant."

"I kno-ooo-w!" I sniveled. "Imagine if I had h-h-had an engag-g-g-gement ring *h-hiccup* h-how much more upset I'd be. Oh god, I can't bear it."

"Here, darling, have a Versace tissue, they always make me feel so much better."

I wiped my nose and tried to concentrate on something bland like the inside of the car. I pulled *New York* magazine from the pouch in front of me. MANHATTAN's 25 MOST ROMANTIC PROPOSALS read the headline in pastel pink text. Whoever the editor of *New York* magazine was, they were totally sick to do this. It reminded me of work: I'd totally forgotten to reschedule the Palm Beach story. I couldn't deal. I snapped my eyes shut and kept them like that until we arrived at Pastis.

As Julie had predicted, the brasserie was empty. We sat at a corner banquette sipping coffee. I felt much better again: it was a great place and our waiter was totally hot. Julie read *Us* magazine and I managed to swallow a mouthful of eggs benedict.

"Julie, do you think it's really true what's happened to me?" I said.

"Well, it's in *Us* magazine and once something's been in *Us* magazine it's official," said Julie, holding up the Hot Stuff Extra! section.

I gasped. As you know, when it comes to gossip I am a believer. Now that I was Manhattan magazine gossip, everything must be real. This was truly hideous.

"O-o-h, no, I can't even keep it a secret now. I'm so embarrassed," I cried.

"Look at it this way, at least you won't have to go through the hell of actually telling anybody the wedding's off, since they'll all read about it. It's better this way, honestly," replied Julie. "Free negative publicity has advantages."

"Hey!" A chirpy voice interrupted us. It belonged to a girl who was way too pretty for me to deal with right now, Crystal Field. She was tan and carrying a mini basket out of which peeped an adorable Teacup Pomeranian wearing a red bow in its hair. Teacup puppies are very in (because you can take them as hand luggage on the plane to Paris) and so are mini baskets from Chinatown to carry them in. Crystal is very in. In fact, Crystal is perfect. It was *très* tragic to have Crystal appear at a moment like this in my life. She was depressingly glowing. A few seconds later Billy, her boyfriend, joined us. Billy is very gorgeous and very in, too. They held hands. They were openly "in love." This did not concern me: Crystal and Billy were simply too in to have a real relationship. It wouldn't last.

"You're both so tan," said Julie.

"The honeymoon," smiled Billy. "We just got back."

Why did thrilled couples feel some unfair need to go around brutalizing uncoupled people like me? It was beyond selfish. Then Crystal asked me, "When's your wedding?"

I stared at her for a few moments. This was a moment more humiliating than I had ever faced in my life. I was actually going to have to *tell* someone, *in public,* that I was fiancé-less. It took some time before I answered, so long in fact that Crystal and Billy started looking nervous and the dog started yapping. Finally I just said, "It's off."

Silence. No one knew what to say when faced with such a tragedy at midday in Pastis, a place where the clientele knows only pleasure.

"Eew," said Crystal. Her mouth stuck in the shape of a large O.

"Yeah, eew," said Billy. Even supposedly straight men in New York have started saying *eew* to keep in with their girlfriends. They made excuses and left abruptly.

No one wanted to be near a romantic failure like *moi* in case I was infectious. Love was everywhere in New York but I couldn't get any of it. It felt a lot like that time Gucci brought out that Jackie bag. It was sold out in about nine minutes and everyone had one except me. I put myself down on the wait list, hoping something would change, but the fact was I was never going to get a Jackie because there just weren't enough to go around, like there isn't enough love.

By the time we arrived *chez* Vandy I felt about as self-confident as Chelsea Clinton before she found out about straightening irons. Julie assured me no one at the Vandys' would have cute husbands in tow. The twins lived in a converted sweatshop way down on Mulberry Street. Everyone was lounging on giant floor pillows from Moss and drinking antioxidant tea. Veronica and Violet Vandonbilt were both wearing custom jackets printed with the words IT'S OUR WORLD YOU'RE JUST LIVING IN IT on the back. When they saw us they tilted their heads massively and said, "Oooh. We're sooo sooorry for you. We got our acupuncturist in especially when we heard. Group hug!"

Suddenly everyone started asking Julie why the Vandys were so sorry for me and before I knew it the whole party was giving me group hugs. Julie led me off to a secluded pillow.

"Do not go near the twins' acupuncturist," she said. "God, why do they have to be so *nice*? It totally creeps me out that they don't even know you and they are offering you needles. And have you seen how much they flick their hair? It's so tacky."

The Vandys came and sat with us. Julie was all smiles, asking them what they were up to.

"Actually, I'm opening a thirty-thousand-square-foot spa on the Bowery," said Veronica.

"And I'm buying a jewelry store on Elizabeth Street," said Violet.

"How wonderful!" smiled Julie. "How generous of Daddy Vandy."

"LVMH is backing us," they said in unison.

"I love your bracelet," said Julie, rapidly changing the subject and grabbing Veronica's wrist. "What is that?"

Veronica was wearing a gold ID bracelet engraved with the number 622.

"Oh, John has one, too," cooed Veronica, tilting her head. "That's the number of our honeymoon suite at Cipriani Venice. Mmmm."

Even highly sensitive nice people like the Vandys had to remind me that I hadn't had a honeymoon and probably never would. I wiped a stray tear from my cheek. "Oh, noooo! Group hug," burst out the twins. This was too much to bear. Suddenly my whole body started to hurt, even my nails, which felt like they were bleeding or something. Thank god for Julie. She made a quick excuse and rushed me out to the car and we sped back to the safety of her apartment. This was getting serious, I realized. I needed a replacement fiancé or life in Manhattan would be so intolerable I would have to move somewhere foreign like Brooklyn.

The next day I went back to my own apartment. There was one message on my voice mail. It was from Mom: "We've all heard. Are you sure you're cancelling? It's very embarrassing for me in the village having to cancel the castle *again* so maybe *you* could do it this time. Okay. Be in touch."

The place seemed very empty. The phone didn't ring. No invitations *at all* arrived by messenger. As I'd suspected, absolutely no free clothes came randomly from fashion designers now that I was disengaged. I drifted around the apartment in my nightdress (actually rather a gorgeous vintage one) worrying how I was ever going to meet my deadline. The office wanted their Palm Beach story, but the only thing I could effectively achieve was sitting in my study, despairing. It seemed so quiet that I actually started to relate to the sad girls who owned DVD players.

I decided to go buy one and watch movies for the rest of my life since I was never going to be invited anywhere ever again. I got dressed and left the apartment. On the way to The Wiz I stopped off at Magnolia Bakery on Bleecker Street for an iced vanilla cupcake. I ate it in the taxi on the way to The Wiz. Those cakes are so sweet, I swear you can self-medicate with them. It lifted my mood, if only for a few minutes.

A trip to The Wiz on Union Square is enough to make your nails ache like mad even at the best of times. My god, I thought, as I wandered past a million cell phones towards the TVs, the champagne bubble about town has lost her fizz. It was a depressing moment. I picked out a machine and got on line. Then my cell rang. It was Julie, asking where I was. I told her. She freaked.

"The fucking *Wiz*? Buying a *DVD player*? You're having a nervous breakdown."

"I am not having a nervous breakdown," I said, breaking into hysterical sobs. "I'm one hundred percent absolutely totally great."

About fifteen minutes later Julie arrived and led me into the car. We headed up to Bergdorf's—Julie couldn't forfeit her highlight with Ariette even for my nervous breakdown. When we arrived we were ushered through to the color room. I sat and watched as Ariette started on Julie's hair. Ariette also started on the disengagement. She wanted all the juicy details—a request that Julie loyally denied. She just said, "Ariette, *baby* blonde, please, think CBK, not Courtney Love, and do not mention my friend's failed relationship."

"Sweetie, you need to get in therapy *right now*. You are having a nervous breakdown. Trust me, I'm having one 24–7, I know what I'm talking about," said Julie, turning to me.

"Julie, there's no way I am going into therapy," I said. I mean, look what it had done to Julie. She wasn't exactly the poster girl for analysis.

"Fine," said Julie. I couldn't believe I was getting out of it so easily. "I've got a much better idea. You know what I do every time I'm having a nervous breakdown and I'm over therapy?"

I shook my head.

"Rehab at the Ritz," she said.

Julie thinks a stay at the Ritz Hotel, Paris, can cure all mental illnesses, even the super-duper troublesome ones like schizophrenia. But Paris? With a broken heart? It would kill me.

"I just want to stay in your guest bedroom for the next six years," I said.

"Since you are mentally ill," replied Julie, "and have no idea what is good for you, I am committing you and taking you to Paris. If you're going to go nuts you might as well do it somewhere chic. You'll be able to dine out for months on how crazy you went in Paris." Julie's eyes were sparkling with the potential social advantages of a best friend with a nervous system in shreds. "Oh, don't cry! You've escaped a terrible marriage, with a psycho photographer who takes really weird pictures. God," she sighed heavily, "sometimes I wish it was me having this nervous breakdown."

Julie had a point. I mean, even in the depths of romantic woe I could see the appeal of suffering an ultrasophisticated collapse in Paris with lots of shops close by. I'd much rather have one there than somewhere deadly like the psychiatric department of the Beth Israel Medical Center, where there are no good boutiques as far as I know. The only thing I was beyond paranoid about was that niggling deadline. I took a very irresponsible executive decision only to announce my French trip after I'd returned from it. That way no one could stop me before I left on the grounds that I had a pressing story to write.

Ooh, I thought to myself, as I stepped onto the Air France plane the next evening, this *crise de nerfs* (that's French for mental crisis) is going *absolutely brilliantly.* I was almost cheerful that night. Even when I saw a hot young couple in the aisle next to Julie and me, trying to upset me by publicly sharing a bottle of echinacea as though they were the pre-divorce Tom and Nicole or something—you know, one droplet for him, one for her sort of thing—I just smiled and thought, next time I'm really in love I'm going to do that too. I was definitely getting better.

When we got to the hotel early the next morning everyone on reception was just glowing with pleasure to see us.

"Congratulations, *mes chéries,*" said the concierge, Monsieur Duré. He always takes care of everything Julie wants there and knows her needs "beyond intimately."

"*Merci, monsieur,*" I said in my intermittently fluent French, which was coming in truly useful already.

French people are so nice to people about nervous breakdowns I can't imagine why they have such an icky reputation. M. Duré was the cutest, kindest person I had ever met in my entire existence.

"So, Duré, where are you putting us? Somewhere heavenly I hope," said Julie. "Oh, and could we have some *café au lait* sent up to the room immediately, darling? And a *petit* bit of *foie gras* would be divine too."

Duré led us to the first floor and a double doorway. It was painted duck-egg blue and SUITE 106 was written on it in gold leaf. This *crise* was making me really, really happy already.

"*Voilà!* Our *plus romantique* suite. We are so 'appy to 'ear of the engagement," said Duré, grandly throwing open the doors.

The sad thing is I never saw the view because I passed out on the threshold. This was very lucky because it gave the maids time to change all the pale pink "engagement" roses to violets before I got to see them.

"Duré, it's a *dis*engagement," Julie was whispering angrily when I came to.

"Oh! What is a disengagement?" Dure asked.

"It's when the marriage is stopped," I sighed.

"Ah, *vous-êtes une* spinster?" he said.

"*Oui,*" I replied. I got through an entire box of Julie's Versace tissues in the next ten minutes, despite the loveliness of our suite. It had a huge drawing room with a balcony and a view over the Place Vendôme. Two bedrooms led directly off it, both with en-suite bathrooms stuffed with soaps stamped with the Ritz logo and shampoos and shower gel in glitzy Ritz bottles. Usually this would have cheered me up. Today the glamour of the bath accessories had zero impact on my mood.

The problem with negative mind states is that they are about as predictable as ex-boyfriends—you never know when they're going to come back unannounced. One minute you can be feeling as happy as a rap star in a blacked-out SUV, and the next second something takes your mind to a place almost as hideous as the lobby of Trump Tower. (I say almost because even the ugliest emotional place you can go isn't as poorly decorated as that golden interior.) I must have been beyond deranged to think things would improve in Paris. I spent my days listlessly trailing after Julie at Hermès and JAR, where she bought a ring set with a cushion-cut cognac diamond for $332,000 because she'd heard Roman Polanski had given his beautiful young French wife the same one. She never wore it because it was insured only while in a safe.

The Ritz depressed me more than some of Laura Bush's worst outfits. Duré barely acknowledged me. The maids cast pitying glances my way, even when I tipped them with fifty euro notes I had borrowed from Julie's wallet. There were no Prospective Husbands here either—I was convinced one of those would resolve my feelings of inadequacy immediately. I had come to the detrimental conclusion that despite everything brilliant Gloria Steinem and Camille Paglia and Erica Jong had said on the subject, it would be *très* embarrassing to be in New York minus a fiancé. My mind spiraled tragically: why would anyone want to marry me anyway? I wasn't interesting, I wasn't really pretty (kind people just pretended I was), and the only boyfriends I had had were with me because they felt sorry for me. Never again would I get the round table at Da Silvano; I could forget about the chef's special white truffle pasta at Cipriani that he made for favored guests; my platinum Bergdorf's complimentary card would be taken away the minute the board of directors found out what had happened; when they saw how beyond my breakuprexia had become, the designers would stop sending me clothes to borrow; the VIP room at Bungalow 8 would be off limits; and never again would I see a movie before everyone else because there would be no more invitations to premieres. If I was lucky, the most I could look forward to was a friends-and-family screening for Showtime's Movie of the Week.

It wasn't as though I could hang out with Julie. On our third morning she had spotted the only PH in the place—Todd Brinton II, the twenty-seven-year-old Brinton's frozen TV dinners heir. He was immaculately dressed in the European uniform of the jet-set kids—pressed white shirt, gold cuff links, jeans, car shoes. Julie thought the sexy thing about him was that he looked like an Italian race car driver but was an American, so she could understand him. I had barely seen her since they met.

"What about Charlie?" I said to her one night. It was late and we were drinking cocktails in a corner banquette in the Hemingway bar.

"He's so cute!" she replied. "He calls all the time. Adores me. I think he might visit. He's very worried about you . . . And don't look at me like that, there is nothing wrong with having two boyfriends. My shrink thinks it's very healthy for me, because then I don't get obsessed with either of them."

I became more clinical by the day. Every gilded corner of this palace for paying guests made me worse. There were references to death everywhere. The women breakfasting in *L'Espadon*, the mirrored and swagged dining room, had had so much Botox they looked like they'd been embalmed. The bath in my room was so vast I feared I would drown in it. Then there were the bathrobes: every time I looked at one of those beautiful fluffy peach robes embroidered in gold with the words RITZ—PARIS, all I could think was how chic it would be to be found dead in one. It was tragic really—I mean, there was a time when a totally exclusive hotel robe could make me delirious with happiness. I remember the first time I wore one of the pale gray robes at the Four Seasons Maui, I felt as good as I did one of the *very few* times I took cocaine.

It was obvious: I was meant to die in a Ritz bathrobe. It was the only thought that had made me happy in days: I would kill myself in *très* glamorous circumstances. I finally understood the whole Sid and Nancy, Romeo and Juliet scenario—it was better to die than live with the pain of a broken heart. I would wear the fluffy Ritz robe with Manolos—I lived in Manolos and frankly I wanted to die in them, too. The next day I asked Julie how Muffy's sister's daughter had killed herself.

"Heroin," she said. I had no idea where they sold heroin in Paris. "Why do you want to know? You're not feeling suicidal, are you?"

"No! I'm much better today," I said. This wasn't a total

lie because, now I'd decided on death, I felt great about life again.

"I don't know why these kids just don't OD on Advil," remarked Julie. "It's so much easier than getting crack or whatever."

Advil? You can die from Advil? I had a whole bottle of it upstairs. I wondered how many Advil it would take.

"Well, anything over two would be an overdose, I guess," said Julie.

It was horrible to think that three of those little headache pills could leave you dead. I would take eight just to be sure. God, why didn't more people kill themselves if it was this unstressful?

"You want to come to Hermès this afternoon?" continued Julie.

"You went only yesterday," I pointed out to her. "Don't you think you should cut down a little? It's getting to be a habit."

If I wasn't going to be around anymore, the least I could do was leave Julie with some helpful moral guidance.

"At least I'm not addicted to Harry Winston like Jolene," said Julie. "Then I'd really be in trouble. Now, you coming or not?"

"I think I'll go to the Louvre," I said innocently. "Don't worry about me."

Julie left and I went back into my bedroom. Death would not be immediate. I had many things to sort out first, such as

1. My outfit
2. My suicide note
3. My will

but hopefully I could prepare everything and be dead by the time Julie got back. I knew she'd go straight from Hermès to meet Todd and party all night with him. She rarely got in before six AM.

I called room service and ordered two mimosas and a plate of *foie gras*. There would be things I'd miss about life, like room service at the Ritz, which is so quick I'd barely said the word *mimosa* before it appeared. And the little buzzer they have right by the tub labeled FEMME DE CHAMBRE that you push if you need something urgently, like a glob of bubble bath or a *café crème*.

Now I finally understood why I adored that Sylvia Plath poem where she says that dying is an art, like everything else. I scribbled my good-bye note on that beautiful Ritz notepaper they do here. It would be very Virginia Woolf—tragic but smart. She wrote the best suicide letter ever—no self-pity, very brave—and it worked brilliantly. I mean, everyone thinks she's a genius, don't they? I started writing. I would be brief:

To everyone I know, especially and including Julie, Lara, Jolene, Mom, Dad; my maid Cluesa, whom I entrust not to hoard my personal effects in the manner of Princess Diana's butler; my accountant, from whom I ask forgiveness for never paying the $1,500 I owe him for preparing last year's tax return; and Paul at Ralph Lauren, from whom I fully admit sneaking an extra cashmere cable baby sweater last season—

I was only saying hello to a few of the people I knew, and already the note was as long as the guest list at Suite 16. I continued:

By the time you read this I will be gone. I am très happy here in heaven. Living with a broken heart was too painful for me, and I could no longer be such a burden to you all. I hope you understand why I have done this—I mean, I just couldn't bear the thought of a lifetime alone. Or the humiliation of never being able to get a good table at Da Silvano again.

I put the Da Silvano bit in for Julie. She would feel *really* sorry for me about that because she would kill herself too if she couldn't get that corner table.

I love you and miss you all. Say hi to everyone in New York for me.

Love,
Moi XXX

Next I wrote my will. You'd be amazed how easy it is when you really think about it. It read:

The Last Will and Testament of a Bergdorf ~~Blonde~~ Brunette

To my mom—My next highlight appointment with Ariette. Even if this conflicts with something really important like my funeral you should come to NYC for it because it's impossible to get in with Ariette if you are a regular civilian.
—My discount cards: Chloé (30% off); Sergio Rossi (25% off—a little mean but still worth it if you buy two pairs of shoes); Scoop (15%—totally mean discount but CBK had a personal shopper there and

maybe if you contact her she'll shop for you). I mean, Mom, you could look beautiful if only you'd pay someone to choose your clothes.

To my father—The lease on my NY apartment so you will have somewhere to escape from Mom.

To Jolene and Lara—The Pastis private number—212-555-7402. Ask for table 6, which is next to where Lauren Hutton sits. Use my name or they won't take the booking.

To my editor—The Palm Beach heiress story notes. You can find them under "v.rich.doc" on my laptop. (PS, Thanks for the extension on my deadline. Sorry I didn't deliver.)

To Julie, my best friend and the well-dressed sister I never had—White Givenchy couture tuxedo suit with Chantilly lace trim that I stole backstage from the spring show.

—My Ambien prescription—there's at least four refills for 30 tablets left, and Dr. Blum will never know.

—My favorite separates, including: McQueen laced leather jacket (1); Chloé jeans (16); Manolos, pairs of (32); handbags, YSL (3), Prada (2); Rick Owens ruffle dress (1)—if it's too avant-garde for you, I understand; $120 Connolly cashmere socks you stole for me from London store (12); James de Givenchy cocktail ring (1). (I know it's actually yours but you'd totally forgotten about it.)

The thought of leaving all those gorgeous clothes behind almost made me want to stay. I signed the document and asked the chambermaid to witness it. I mean, I didn't want anyone disputing the will later. Next, I typed the whole thing up on e-mail and clicked on SEND LATER. The e-mails wouldn't be sent for 12 hours—7:30 AM tomorrow morning. The TIME DELAY option on the new Titanium G4 Mac is totally genius and I fully recommend it to any suiciders. You don't want anyone finding you and waking you up after you've gone to all the trouble of dying. Can you imagine the Shame Attack that would follow?

Next I planned my outfit: obviously, the Ritz robe was compulsory. I decided my rhinestone-trimmed silver Manolos would go brilliantly with it. I laid it all out on the bed and found a mega bottle of Advil in my makeup bag. I drew the curtains and took off all my clothes. I put on the Manolos. I have to say, they looked awesome with nothing else on at all. I washed down eight Advil with the mimosa and lay down.

Nothing happened. I was definitely still alive because I could see the rhinestones sparkling on my toes, which, I realized with some horror, were manicured red instead of flesh pink, which would have looked way better with those shoes. Maybe eight Advil was a little conservative? I took another, then another, then another until there were none left. About thirty. Oops, I thought, I mustn't forget to put on that Ritz bathrobe before I die. I'll just have a *petit* sleep first though. Then I'll put it on . . . in a minute.

Ow. Ooow. My nails were really, *really* hurting. My head was agony and I felt nauseous. There was something scratchy against my skin. I was shivering. I opened my eyes then snapped them quickly shut. Oh! God! Beyond dreadful! Apparently I was still in my room at the Ritz. Maybe I was in heaven. Maybe heaven turned out to be a suite at the Ritz. I glimpsed the silhouette of a man.

"*Excusez-moi, monsieur*, am I dead?" I whispered groggily.

"Nope," came the reply.

This was *très* annoying. Why wasn't I dead, what went wrong?

"I found you."

"Who the hell are you?" I was furious.

"It's me, you crazy girl."

I opened my eyes. Charlie Dunlain was standing there looking down at me in a stern fashion. How dare he call me crazy? I was very sane and if by chance I wasn't, this was a very insensitive moment to be labeling me a lunatic. He had my will in his hand. So intrusive. I tried to grab it from him but I was too dizzy.

"Give me that. That is a very private document," I said. I managed to sit up a little, which made me feel less sick.

"Well, I'm gutted you didn't leave me anything."

"How the hell did you get in here?"

"The door was wide open," he said, looking a little less serious. I thought I could detect the beginnings of a smile.

He was sick, totally sick. That's LA movie-director types for you, no feelings at all, everything was just a joke. I looked at the clock: 7 AM. Not only was it way before my 10:30 AM waking-up time, but I wasn't supposed to have woken up at all.

"Charlie, what on earth are you doing in my room at seven in the morning?"

"I just got off the plane and I thought I'd come by and save you."

Charlie obviously had no clue about the women's movement. Didn't he know that since the 1970s it was illegal to go around randomly saving women?

"I don't want to be saved. I want to die."

"No you don't."

"I *do*. I hate you!" I croaked. "How dare you go around saving me like that! It's unforgivable."

"How dare I? How dare *you*." He was cross now. I was a little bit terrified of him suddenly. "The only thing that is unforgivable is what you've done," said Charlie.

It was *très* unkind of him to be so cross after all I'd been through. I mean, *hello*, what about some major sympathy?

"What's the point in saving someone if you're not going to be nice to them afterward?" I wailed.

"Stop being so darn spoiled and grow up," said Charlie. He really had no idea how to be nice.

I looked around me. The Ritz robe lay next to me on the bed. A gray coat covered me. It didn't belong to me. An icky realization crept up on me: it must be Charlie's. This was deeply embarrassing.

"Charlie, was I, you know, like, nude when you found me?"

"No," he said.

I was beyond relieved. Then he said, "You were wearing shoes."

That's it, I thought. I am never, ever not killing myself again. The whole thing was beyond humiliating. Now I was going to be the girl who couldn't get married *and* couldn't kill herself. Forget Da Silvano, I wouldn't even be admitted to John's Pizza on Bleecker Street now. I suddenly remembered the e-mail. I could stop it: I had thirty minutes before it went out.

"Charlie, pass me the computer, fast," I said.

The icon in the PENDING box was flashing. I opened it and clicked on DON'T SEND, relieved. I noticed the in-box was flickering: I had mail. Out of curiosity I quickly checked it. There was a note from my mother:

> *I do hope you haven't done anything silly, darling. I presume the e-mail was a joke. I do not admire New York style highlights, or shopping with discount cards. But if you're giving things away I've always rather admired your John Galliano knitted mink sweater. Just a thought. Love, Mummy.*

Somehow the will had been sent, alas. I had never been very brilliant with the extra features on my Mac. There were several more e-mails in the in-box, but I decided to read them later—I couldn't take the humiliation right now.

"Oh, Charlie, this is a disaster. Could you order me a Bellini?" I said.

"No."

I blinked as if to say, *Why not?*

"The last thing you need is alcohol. That would make you feel worse."

"No one could feel worse than me right now, not even me. What did you think of the note?" I asked.

"*What did I think of the note?* Who do you think you are, Sylvia Plath?"

Charlie totally understood me at that moment. At least if I'd died everyone would have realized I'd read lots of important literature, like *Mrs. Dalloway* and *Valley of the Dolls*.

"Well, it's funny you should say that because I was totally going for the whole Virginia Woolf thing actually," I replied.

He grabbed me hard by my shoulders and shook me. I was shocked. "You've got to grow up and stop being so incredibly childish. This could have been serious," he said.

"Stop it!" I whimpered. "Stop being so nasty to me about it all! I'm just not feeling too good about things now. Life is terrible."

He let me go.

"Things might be terrible. But what about all the people who love you? Your parents, Julie, all your friends? Did you ever stop to think how terrible it might be for them if you killed yourself?"

"Of course," I said, which wasn't exactly totally true. I hadn't thought about anyone except *moi* since my disengagement. "They'd be better off without me like this though, I'm just a burden now."

"You've got to pull yourself together. Stop being so self-indulgent."

"I can't 'pull myself together,' I'm too unhappy," I said.

"We're meant to be unhappy sometimes. That's life. Hearts get broken. Bad things happen. You get through them, you don't go off doing selfish things like OD'ing. If you were happy all the time, you'd be some talk show host. Like Katie Couric."

I started to cry. Why do people have to be so mean about Katie? She can't help it if she's being paid like $60 million to smile until 2010.

"Stop being so harsh," I wailed. "I need some kindness."

"Kindness? Put this on and get some sleep." Charlie handed me the Ritz robe.

"I can't wear that," I said. "It's part of my suicide outfit. I know, why don't you take me to Café Flore for breakfast? I love St. Germain. That would cheer me up."

"You're going nowhere. You're going to stay here and sleep it off."

"Well, maybe later you could take me for a really glamorous dinner at Lapérouse. I mean, they do this *flambé tarte tatin* there that is beyond."

"I don't care," replied Charlie, "if the fucking Eiffel Tower is being fucking flambéed, you aren't moving."

For someone who was supposed to be a good friend, Charlie was being very hostile. Hadn't anyone told him you don't swear at suicide victims?

"You're sick and you need rest. You're staying right here all day and all night. You'll drink hot milk and eat rice and that is that," he said.

Rice? He hated me, he really did. Just then there was a knock at the door. It was Julie, with Todd in tow.

"Hey boo!" she squealed, hugging Charlie. "You're here! This is Todd-ee. We are gonna have so much fun." She didn't seem fazed by introducing her boyfriends to each other, but her face fell when she saw me. "My god, sweetie, what happened, why are you dressed like a street person?"

"Can we go next door?" said Charlie. "And maybe 'Todd-ee' could come back later. I need to talk to you, Julie."

Todd sloped off looking embarrassed, and Charlie led Julie into the other room. He closed the door. Typical. Just when I was about to get some much-needed compassion from Julie, Charlie whisked her away. God, he was so interfering! I couldn't wait for him to go back to LA, where he belonged, along with all those other impossibly controlling, anal-retentive movie directors. Suddenly, I felt like I was going to vomit. I staggered into the bathroom. I'll spare you the details.

Things didn't improve all day. Julie loved all the things I'd left her in my will and asked if she could have the Ambien tablets even though I wasn't dead. Once Mom realized that I'd managed not to kill myself, she said she was not at all happy that I was so honest in my will about her limited talent for fashion. The only person who was thrilled with his bequest was Dad.

The next night while Julie was down in the spa getting a blow-out, Charlie asked me to meet him in the bar. At last he had realized that a postsuicidal girl didn't need lectures, she needed champagne. I'd felt pretty dreadful yesterday—sick and weak and sad—but now I felt a little better. I was desperate for anything to distract me from thinking about what I'd done. I mean, I was embarrassed beyond belief, you can imagine. But when I got down to the bar Charlie didn't even notice my new Chloé outfit that Julie had bought me to try and convince me not to attempt to kill myself again. He was frowning and serious.

"Better?" he said.

"Totally desperately lonely and brokenhearted actually," I said. "Could you get me a champagne cocktail?"

Charlie called over the waiter. "A vodka for me and a Perrier for mademoiselle, please."

God, men are just as selfish as girls always say. Then he said, "You need a clear head if you're going to sort out your life."

"A clear head is not going to get me another fiancé," I said.

"You don't need a fiancé."

Charlie didn't understand that my life in New York would be ruined unless I found another fiancé. All anyone cared about in New York was who was married to whom, or was going to be. Didn't he know it was like the nineteenth century there? Didn't he know what had happened to poor Lily Bart?

Charlie continued, "You need to sort yourself out before you fall in love with someone else."

"I'll never fall in love again," I sulked.

"Don't be so cynical. Of course you will."

Then out of the blue, Charlie said, "Is Julie seeing someone else, here in Paris?"

Yes, and you met him, I thought. I didn't like to lie to Charlie, but when one is in a situation where one's loyalty is divided, I always say, lie anyway. I smiled reassuringly, and said, "No."

"Be honest," he said.

Can I be super-duper honest and admit something *très* terrible? I wasn't paying that much attention to this very tense conversation anymore because something happened while I was talking to Charlie that I never expected: I fell in love.

The entire time I was talking to Charlie a very handsome boy was making what I can only describe as very Brazilian eye contact from right behind Charlie's left ear.

"She's *nuts* about you. She never stops talking about you," I said ultratruthfully.

God, Mr. Brazil over there looked hot when he turned to the right. He had dark blond hair and a sun-kissed forehead. I imagined he'd just come back from a weekend in the south of France or something glamorous like that.

"She's seeing Todd, isn't she?"

A waiter interrupted us. "Mademoiselle, for you," he said. He put a glass of champagne in front of me. "From the Prince. Eduardo of Savoy." The waiter gestured toward Mr. Handsome. I mouthed *merci*. He nodded back.

"Todd's *gay*," I said, superconfidently.

I wondered if the Prince's parents would mind when he told them he was marrying me.

"Todd is about as gay as Eminem," said Charlie. He was silent for a while, looking into his drink. "I think it's over with Julie."

I tried very hard to focus my thoughts on Charlie's dilemma, but I couldn't help being distracted when I recalled that this particular H.R.H. had a famously wonderful summer house in Sardinia and estates scattered all over Italy in fact. Total PH material.

"I'm going back to LA tomorrow night," said Charlie.

He looked up at me for reassurance. It was odd, as if the tables had turned and it was Charlie who needed support and advice from me. I gathered my thoughts so I could make a great speech about Julie's virtues, but then wondered whether these two really were suited. I mean, Charlie was so bossy and Julie was such a delinquent. I made a lame attempt to make my case.

"But you and Julie are like . . . totally . . . great . . ." I trailed off, because I'd noticed that H.R.H. was reading Proust. How hot of him. No, how *smart* of him. The waiter approached and gave me a note. It read *Dinner, 8:30 PM,* VOLTAIRE. Charlie took it straight from me and shot me a furious look. He turned to the waiter who was hovering expectantly.

"Could you tell the young man that *mademoiselle* is not well enough to have dinner out tonight?" he said.

How dare he? Just when I was feeling a little better. He only wanted me to be unhappy because he was unhappy.

"Monsieur, tell him I'll meet him there," I said, gathering up my things.

Charlie glared at me and said nothing. He really hated me now. I really hated him back, so we were quits.

7

It was *très* lucky that whole little Advil plot of mine didn't work out. Eduardo quoted Proust throughout dinner. Can you imagine anything more intellectually stimulating than a man whispering, *"Il n'y a rien comme le désir pour empêcher les choses qu'on dit d'avoir aucune ressemblance avec ce qu'on a dans la pensée,"* to you over a glass of Château Lafite that's older than you are? Even though my semi-fluent French didn't exactly stretch to a translation, I knew it would be beyond romantic if I could have understood it.

"Giuseppe," said Eduardo to his driver after we'd left the restaurant and were in the car, "please take us home."

As I told Julie afterward—because she was super stroppy when she couldn't find me at the Ritz the next morning—I swear I had zero idea that when Eduardo said "home," he was referring to the family palazzo on the shores of Lake Como. He kissed me like a demon all the way from Paris to Como, a drive of about 800 kilometers. It should take about eight hours. But when you have a driver like Giuseppe you make it in five hours flat. I secretly hope he never drives me again. No one needs to get anywhere at 185 kilometers per hour.

I think Eduardo was just about the perfect man. He wore more Malo cashmere than an entire mountain of goats. His mom was an ex-actress from Hollywood and his father would have been the King of Savoy if they still had kings there. Usually the Italian royal family isn't allowed into Italy, but the government worshiped Eduardo's mom so much he'd been given special dispensation to go in and out as he pleased. He'd studied French lit at Bennington and lived in New York "working for the family," whatever that meant. I didn't inquire, I mean, I'd seen *The Godfather* and everything and you just don't ask Italians how they specifically get their money.

The palazzo was better inside than the Frick. I was living for the four-poster bed I woke up in the next morning. It was draped in Italian lace exactly like the kind Dolce & Gabbana use on their corsets. The shutters were open and I could see the lake and mountains outside, all Technicolor blues. No wonder there are no Italians in the Hamptons.

I was pretty amazed with the way life was turning out. I mean, I was alive, I'd avoided a potentially disturbing Julie-Charlie breakup scene *through no fault of my own*, and I was eating breakfast in bed in a place that made the Ritz look like the Marriott Marquis. Everywhere you looked in the palazzo, there was a butler in a black jacket and white gloves bringing you a freshly baked almond cake or something delicious like that. I couldn't believe how much better I felt already. Who knew you could recover completely from a suicide attempt in thirty-six hours? It was easier than falling off a cliff.

I must send a postcard to the girls in New York, I thought; I mean, they needed to know about this. We walked down to the local village to buy a few things. As we left the house, two ferociously tanned Italian men appeared. They were dressed identically in navy bomber jackets, dark pants, and sunglasses. They were both wearing ear pieces. They looked so fit I swear they'd spent their whole lives at Crunch gym on East Thirteenth Street. *Bodyguards,* I thought. How glam to have your own personal protection. Of course, I acted super-duper nonchalant; I mean, I didn't want Eduardo knowing I was totally freaked out by the security so I just said *"Ciao"* to both of them as if to say, *Everyone I know has armed guards.*

They walked us all the way into the village and back again, whispering into those little ear pieces. We didn't seem to be in any immediate danger of an assassination attempt or anything like that in the village—the only person we saw was a lone farmer herding a donkey along the main street. But it did occur to me that had someone wanted to identify and kill the Prince it would have been very easy to target him because there was no one else walking around the village that day with two very conspicuous undercover bodyguards trailing after him and a girl wearing heels and a black satin evening dress.

You know what's really awesome about being an H.R.H. with more staff than the first lady? You can decide what you want for lunch while you are out walking, call the house where there's a chef better than Jean-Georges Vongerichten on call 24–7, and have *melanzane* and *panna cotta* waiting the minute you get home. You can imagine what I wrote on my postcard:

Dearest Lara and Jolene,
Honestly I don't know why Princesses complain about being Princesses so much. It's 150% luxury. I advise you both get yourselves an H.R.H. A.S.A.P.
Love and kisses, Moi

I know Jolene was scheduled to get married and everything, but she should know what she might be missing out on in advance.

We were sitting in the drawing room after lunch drinking espresso when one of the staff rushed in with the telephone and handed it to Eduardo. He said something very fast in Italian and then put the phone down and jumped up. He was on high alert.

"Okay, we're leaving!" he said. "We go back to New York tonight."

"Why?" I said.

We were having such a heavenly time. It seemed crazy to go back to New York though it had crossed my mind in the last few days that I really needed to contact the Palm Beach heiress.

"*Carina*, I have some . . . family business to take care of. I'm sorry. But we'll come back here in the summer, I promise." I loved that Eduardo called me *carina*—it means "darling" in Italian.

He looked depressed.

"But I've left my passport and everything in Paris," I said.

"You don't need a passport with me."

God, how glam. Even the president needs a passport.

There were six e-mails from Julie when I got back to New York very late that night. I dreaded reading them—Julie was never going to forgive me for leaving her alone in Paris, or, rather, alone and rejected by a man in Paris. It would be her turn to have a nervous breakdown now. The first one read,

Honey,
Everything going GREAT with Charlie. He adores me. He's off back to LA for work. I'm staying on in Paris for a few days shopping. So glad you disappeared off with His Royal Whatever. Heard he's totally hot. Sent Todd back to NYC—I adore him too but he was kind of getting in the way.
Kisses,
Julie

Thank God. Julie still had Charlie. Even though he'd been undeniably vile about the whole Advil incident and I'd made an executive decision never to speak to him again, he made Julie happy. That was all that mattered.

Julie's other e-mails listed her various shopping purchases in Dickensian detail. She was mainly scooping up Marc Jacobs outfits at Colette. This seemed sort of weird since she could just buy them for a lot less on Mercer Street back in New York. But as she said, "Look, if you are going to have to wear Marc Jacobs because it's just too good, at least stand out from the crowd and be able to say you bought it in Paris." I e-mailed her back and asked her to bring back my passport and clothes. I knew this wouldn't trouble her at all, because, like all Park Avenue Princesses, Julie always has someone else pack her bags and then ship them because they are always three times as heavy as the baggage allowance.

You know how I was totally gutted after the disengagement because my apartment suddenly became an invitation-free zone? Well, the minute everyone in Manhattan knew I'd been a guest of the Prince at the palazzo, my mantelpiece became so crowded with stiff white cards I needed a crane to clear it. I was secretly concerned that these were transparently tactical invites sent *in case* I became a Princess. But I decided to imagine that I was receiving them because I was genuinely popular. Otherwise I would have been headfirst back into that Advil bottle. Denial can be very beneficial for one's social life.

There's nothing like dating an "of" in New York. Apart from the fact that Eduardo was just dreamy on the looks and personality front, everyone in New York wants to marry an "of." Felipe of Spain, Pavlos of Greece, Max of Sweden, Kyril of Bulgaria—those boys have gorgeous American girlfriends and wives coming out of their ears. Like most exiled royalty, they all love being in New York, where they feel appreciated. (Apparently Europeans aren't nearly as friendly to them as us.) No one here minds at all that the Princes don't have kingdoms anymore. Most people in New York think Savoy is a very swanky hotel in London, but they still adored Eduardo. It doesn't matter where you're "of," the point is to be "of" Somewhere. A New York girl would kill to marry a domain-less Prince and get to call herself a Princess. The only people who mind about the whole kingdom thing are the Princes themselves, who take it all *très* seriously.

Eduardo lived in an immaculate bachelor pad on Lexington and Eightieth. It was an excellent place for late-night trysting. Whenever I couldn't fluently translate all that French quotation stuff Eduardo was into, I amused myself by scanning the walls and bookshelves, which were crammed with paintings and sepia photographs of his ancestors in crowns and majorly sparkly tiaras. Who knew they were so into Harry Winston back then? If only they put that in the history books, New York high school girls would consider the unification of Italy a very important part of their education.

The minute Julie hit New York we met for a decaf latte at Café Gitane on Mott Street. Gitane is wall-to-wall with supermodels dressed like street urchins in very expensive Marni clothes. Everyone thinks it's supercool. I have to admit I've picked up a few fashion directions from the girls there myself on occasion. Julie actually fit in surprisingly well because she was wearing her new "French" Marc Jacobs combat pants which looked genius on her. She'd chosen a table in a dark corner, which was odd because Julie usually wants to sit in the most prominent spot wherever she goes.

"Hi, darling," she said when I arrived. "I know, I know, you're looking at me weirdly because this is a freaky table for me but I'm being, like, *low-key.*"

I was confused. Julie is actually politically opposed to being low-key.

"Why? It's so not you," I said.

"*Ssshhhh!*" she whispered, putting her sunglasses on. "We don't want anyone hearing us."

"Why?"

"You're on suicide watch."

"I'm fine. I'm totally off the Advil and *so* into Eduardo. Look at me, everyone says I'm radiant."

"We all know the secret of radiant in New York after a breakup—Portofino, okay. So don't even think about trying that one on us."

"Us?"

"Me and Lara and Jolene. We're watching you 24–7. You're moving into mine, no arguments."

"*No way,*" I said. "Look, Tracey made that room stunning, but I don't want to live there."

"You have two options. Either you live in The Pierre with me, or you go into therapy."

Julie was as transparent as a glass of San Pellegrino sometimes. Living with her was okay for five minutes when I was sick, but I didn't want her stealing all my clothes. That was her real motive, I was sure of it. She never, ever gives anything back, even big things like Versace pantsuits. She's a black hole for fashion and you don't want any of your nice stuff near it.

I was convinced therapy would make me ill. Girls in New York who are in therapy are the worst to be around. They talk about their childhoods nonstop. Julie thinks therapy has all the answers and is totally into getting really upset over her childhood to try and figure out why she has so many tantrums. She just can't admit that the tantrums are adult spoiled-brat tantrums. She thinks it really traumatized her that her mom forced her into Lilly Pulitzer dresses between the ages of four and ten in Palm Beach when all the other kids had been allowed to wear CK jeans. Julie's shrink traced her adult addiction to shopping back to this public humiliation.

"Julie, I'm not doing either of them. I'm fine, I'm better," I insisted. "I've fallen madly in love with someone else."

"You've only known him a few days! You're infatuated. Even if this royal kid is the real thing, you need to figure out why it is you stayed with Zach when he was treating you worse than the shit on the soles of his sneakers."

"But Julie, I've forgotten all that now. It's like I was never even engaged to Zach. I don't even feel like it happened to me. I feel like it happened to someone else, in a movie. That wasn't really *me*."

"So who was it then? You can't pretend this stuff didn't happen. If you don't figure it out now, you're going to end up under someone else's sneakers."

Why did Julie think it was such a smart idea to relive something vile that I'd very successfully blocked out of my mind? She's met with way too many head doctors. My view is that the best way to deal with icky things is to forget about them.

"You nearly died a week ago and you think you're 'fine'?" said Julie. "You could have grade two bipolar manic depression or something terrible like that. This is *very serious*. At least get a brain scan or something."

Like most New York girls, Julie gets an MRI every time she gets a headache. She is so familiar with the grading system of depression she could diagnose it. She continued, "Does Eduardo know what happened?"

"Of course!" I said. "I told him everything."

I would hate for Julie to know that I told her an outright lie, but *of course* I hadn't told Eduardo a thing about what had happened in Paris. He thought I was there for the boutiques, like all American girls. The truth is, I absolutely hated myself for the whole Advil thing. Charlie hated me for it. Julie wasn't exactly thrilled about it. I didn't want anyone else hating me. It would have been so not smart to tell Eduardo the truth about me at this early stage or he might hate me, too.

"Well, that makes me feel better about him," said Julie. "But at least think about seeing Dr. Fensler. Even if you feel fine it could be useful."

"Can we talk about something else?" I said.

Entre nous, the truth is that when Eduardo was out of town—which he was a lot because of business—I sometimes felt a little Advil-y again. I'd thrown away all the pills in the apartment, but when I was alone at night those Ritz-robe-type feelings would come back and freak me out. Whenever I remembered Zach even for a second I felt like going straight out to Bigelow's Pharmacy on Sixth Avenue and buying the biggest damn tub of tablets I could find. I could never seem to call Eduardo at the really bad moments because his cell hardly ever worked in these godforsaken places like Iowa that he had to travel to. A lot of the time he was away on weekends, too. On top of all this, when I'd called the Palm Beach heiress to rearrange, she'd replied, "I already did the interview. The magazine sent someone else."

One Sunday—and Sundays are murderous, aren't they?—I almost felt like running out to The Wiz again and buying a DVD player. Eduardo was unreachable on one of his trips. I was a reject, the stale bagel that no one wanted. I kept staring at Zach's *Drowned Truck* photo. I'd never noticed before, but it looked slightly out of focus. Maybe it wasn't such a great photo after all. I decided to take it down, but it left such a gaping hole I had to put it up again, which made me even more miserable. By the time I called Julie, it was four in the morning, but she was awake: she was fasting on blueberries now and the hunger pangs were keeping her up.

"Julie," I said, "I'm so sad."

"Why sweetie, I thought you and Eduardo were in total bliss," she said.

"I adore Eduardo but Zach's the one I want. I'm thinking of calling him. I'm sure he misses me."

"Ooohhh. Hold on," she said. "I'll call Dr. Fensler first thing and make an appointment for you. You'll never get in otherwise."

Dr. Fensler has the glammest waiting room of any shrink in the city. It's definitely nothing like the lunatic asylums I've heard most rich people like Julie go to in New York. Everything about it is gorge, including the Christian Liaigre table that is beautifully arranged with fashion and gossip magazines, even the ones that are really hard to get like *Numéro*. I scanned the room. It was better than a front row at a Michael Kors runway show. All the other girls there were beyond stunning and almost all of them looked like actresses or socialites. I am sure I saw Reese W., but I couldn't quite make out if it was her because her sunglasses seemed to cover almost her entire face. The really important detail about the waiting room was that all the girls looked *très* happy: everyone was just gorgeous and surrounded by shopping bags and decked out in those new Tod's strappy sandals that you can't find anywhere and were perfect for the warm June day outside. They were all discussing very nontherapy subjects like their next vacation in Capri and how great St. Barths was last Christmas. These girls looked like they didn't have any problems at all. In fact, they looked like they didn't even *know* what a problem was. There wasn't a frown or a cross face among them. I was definitely the most miserable and underdressed person there. Dr. Fensler was obviously a genius. I could hardly wait to meet him. I was sure he didn't take health insurance.

About ten minutes after I'd arrived, a pretty young nurse in a white velour sweat suit showed me into a treatment room. It was very new therapy: no old leather couch, no analysis books on the shelves, just a bright light and a high lounger exactly like the ones by the pool at the Mondrian Hotel in LA. I sat and waited. I was a little nervous. Anyone who's had therapy knows it's excruciating having to reveal everything about yourself to a total stranger and then be informed that you better try to change. The thought of it was very unappealing. But if I left looking as hot as those girls in the waiting room I'd do it gladly.

The door opened. Dr. Fensler—coiffed and tan—peeked in.

"He-e-e-y! Hi!!! Am I thrilled to see you!" he said. He sounded way overexcited. He obviously hadn't noticed that I hadn't dressed up for him as though I were off to a cocktail party. "You look *fan*-tastic! My god, that *skin*. Have you been living in a *refrigerator*?"

Before I could reply he chirruped, "Just gotta inject two lips. Back in *ten seconds*. No one does a lip fix quicker or prettier than Dr. Fensler."

Lizardlike, he darted out. Julie was deranged. She

hadn't sent me to her analyst. She'd sent me to her dermatologist. I called her immediately on my cell.

"Julie," I said sternly, "Dr. Fensler is a cosmetic dermatologist!"

"I know. He's a genius. Everyone who's anyone wouldn't be seen at a party without stopping by Fensler first."

"But Julie, I'm not going to a party. I'm already at my own party and it's not fun and I'm trying to leave and I'm not sure Dr. Fensler is the man to get me out of it. I thought you said I needed therapy."

"Darling, dermatology *is* the new therapy," said Julie. (Julie thinks that anything that is new is good just because it is new.) "Have you seen how tragic people who go to shrinks are? Shrinks make people *un*happy. But here's the thing about Dr. F—you go in for an innocent little Botox shot and you come out feeling happier than if you'd done ten years of therapy. You look pretty, you feel great. Easy. Some girls in New York have got a bit compulsive about it, they go every day. Now, I *do not* want that happening to you but I think a little dermatological therapy would be a very positive experience for you. It's kind of like cheating but cheating in a good way."

Now I understood why all those girls outside looked so happy. They were classic Botox junkies. No frowns, no expression, just smiles.

"Julie, I don't think this is right for me. I want to talk to someone about what's been happening. I don't want that frozen Botox look everyone thinks is so in."

"No one is saying you have to get Botox. I'm saying, get a peel, maybe get an enzyme jab. You can tell Dr. F. everything. Five percent of the time he's injecting, the rest of the time he just listens, which is what you need. Look, he understands the whole Manhattan relationship thing better than any couples counselor I've ever met and I swear I've met every single one on the Upper West Side. Would I ever send you anywhere but the best?"

"No."

I was *très* tempted. I mean, I'd never heard of therapy that made you look like a Michael Kors girl before. If I was going to be miserable at least I could be attractive with it. I try not to be as tremendously vain as Julie, but sometimes you've got to be when your sanity is at stake.

"Okay. So try it. It's on me. And by the way, did you see K. K. in the waiting room? I'm convinced she's been doing that new Botox mask thing from Paris but she swears her motionless face is just from rubbing in Persian rose oil for twenty minutes a night. She's a lousy liar. No one looks that good with herbal remedies."

Dr. Fensler popped his head around the door and trotted in. "Julie," I said, "I gotta go, he's here."

"So, tell me everything," he said. "Broken up with your boyfriend?"

I nodded.

"I am going to make you beautiful, and happy, like all my girls. You'll never think about him again. Don't worry! You can come every day if you need it. A lot of girls do when they're going through a trauma like this."

He came closer and started examining my skin.

"Ee-wchhh!" he yelped. "I see a pimple. Have you been flying recently, to Europe?"

"Yes," I answered. Maybe this man was a genius after all.

"Jet lag acne. Everyone's got it. It's new, totally new. You're depressed, you're stressed, you're circling the globe like a maniac, you can't handle the time zones, your hormones are up the wazoo—*bang*! Jet lag acne. You know all the supermodels come *straight* off the Air France flight from Paris to me. In, out, peel, jab, and they're fantastic again. They look better and they *feel happier*. Now tell me about this boyfriend you lost."

I told him the whole story, exaggerating a few parts to make it more entertaining. Naturally I left out the most humiliating bits, like the thing about never going to Brazil. I didn't want Dr. F. knowing really private stuff.

"There's more," he said. "You're hiding something."

Reluctantly I told him about my Parisian suicide attempt, which I'd edited out. I also admitted the excruciating truth about never getting any Rio after the trip to LA.

"Well, he was either blind or gay," joked Dr. Fensler, trying to cheer me up. "That kind of rejection is very upsetting."

"I feel really bad about myself," I said. "The feelings won't go away."

"Nothing that a quick Alpha-Beta peel won't remedy," said Dr. Fensler, snapping on plastic gloves.

He prepared some bottles of potent clear liquid and asked me to lie down. He dabbed the first solution on my face. It stung.

"Ouch!" I squealed.

"Ah. Very good! Your skin is going to look immaculate when you leave here. Every cell will be perfection. You will never let anyone hurt you like that again. You must be wondering why you stayed so long with such an unpleasant person."

I nodded. I couldn't speak because the fumes from the chemicals were so strong.

"You know what that's all about? Staying with a jerk?"

I shook my head. I was still very confused about my attraction to someone who, I realized after the fact, had been completely horrible to me.

"Classic dysfunctional relationship. They chip away at you until you feel like you're nothing without them. No one can understand why you stay. But you do. From your end, it's a typical case of low self-esteem. My dear, you build up that self-esteem and no one will be able to touch you. When you get it back, men will be drawn to you *uncontrollably*. Self-confidence is highly sexually attractive. You have to love yourself before anyone decent will really love you. I can make you beautiful on the outside but you gotta make yourself beautiful on the inside, too. Lecture over. Okay, I'm putting the second solution on now."

This burned even more than the first one. I couldn't imagine how this could possibly be good for your skin or your soul. I managed to utter, "Well, I think my self-esteem is improving. I've met this new guy who looks out for me like I'm the most precious thing in the world."

"Where is he?" asked Dr. F.

"Oh, travelling. For work. He travels a lot," I replied.

"Well, just make sure he isn't married and living in Connecticut with three kids!"

I giggled. Dr. Fensler was really amusing me.

"Now I am going to leave this last layer to sit for five minutes and then you will be glowing, my dear. You are a fabulous girl. Don't settle for anyone who doesn't treat you like the princess you are. No more bullies, no invalidators, no energy drainers."

I had no idea what an invalidator was, but I would avoid it. Maybe the right dermatologist is the secret to personal happiness in New York, like Julie says.

Dr. Fensler fussed around his countertop for a while and then asked, "How was the sex with the guy you were engaged to?"

People ask the most personal questions. It's so intrusive the way they just ask you about Brazil as though they were talking about a casual vacation to Palm Springs or something.

"Well, I mean, hmmm. When we had it, it was . . . the best," I said, embarrassed.

"Uh-oh! *Beware!!!*" said Fensler. "Never, ever marry the best sex of your life. It only happens with someone who is very dangerous for you. It's passionate, exciting, but it generally indicates that you are pushing each other's dysfunctional buttons. Be very wary of men you are crazily sexually attracted to—they're the dangerous ones for you. That's what all analysis says in one form or another."

I didn't choose that particular moment to admit that sex with Eduardo was a million times better than sex with Zach. What was I supposed to do? End it with him precisely because I was so attracted to him? Date someone I found repulsive? This was where the whole therapy thing cancelled itself out. You couldn't actually do anything about the things you were supposed to do things about. Dr. Fensler held a mirror up to my face.

"Now, take a look at yourself. Phenomenal."

Dr. F. had done something amazing. My skin was glowing. I looked more like someone who'd just come back from a month in the islands than a girl recovering from a French suicide attempt. I suddenly felt overflowing with self-esteem. The feeling was on a par with how good I felt the first time I bought a silk Pucci headscarf and actually wore it on a yacht in the manner of Christina Onassis.

"I feel wonderful, thank you so much," I said as I got up to leave.

"Keep that feeling. The second you don't have it, come straight back here for some more wonderful, got it?"

The thing about going to the dermatologist, unlike seeing a therapist, is that it makes you feel really happy about yourself right away. As I passed through the waiting room, I promise you I literally *waved* at all those gorgeous girls in there. Eduardo adored me, Zach was all in the past, and I looked like a million bucks.

Honestly, if I'd known about Alpha-Beta peels before, I'd never have ended up with someone lousy like Zach in the first place.

It was auspicious that Dr. F. had plumped my epidermis, because Eduardo was due back in town that night, and I was anticipating some more best-Proust-of-my-life with him, regardless of the doctor's advice. Aerin van Orenburg—the young reclusive daughter of Gustav van O., who always says he has more art than the Gettys—had decided to come out of her seclusion and throw a wild costume party. The rumor was that since college all Aerin had done was stay home and knit gold lurex shoe bags for her massive collection of Christian Louboutins. Everyone wanted to go to Aerin's party. But Aerin, being the contrary kind of girl she is, had invited only half of everyone who wanted to be there.

Aerin loved her own contrariness. Her theme was super-obscure and confusing for everyone: it was "Robert and Ali."

The idea was that the boys should dress as the 1970s movie mogul Robert Evans and the girls as his one-time wife Ali MacGraw. The thing about throwing a costume party in New York is that if you're going to do it, you've got to be super original about it. I've heard that some really cruel NY girls actually burn costume party invites if they feel the theme is "tired." Apparently you cannot throw a party with any of the following themes ever again here: Mick and Bianca; Boogie Nights; Bill and Monica. Also leather 'n' leopard is off-limits because everyone just cheats and zips straight into Roberto Cavalli.

Lara, Jolene, and Julie loathed the theme. Unless they wore wigs they couldn't imitate Ali's hair.

"So wear a wig," I told Julie, who had called for a costume summit.

"There is *no way* I am putting icky brown hair over this gorgeous blonde. Ariette would *die*. How can Aerin do this to me after I totally looked after her at Spence?"

It's rare that a brunette like me has a social advantage over a New York blonde. But for once I did. I could hardly wait for the party tonight.

"Why don't you get Ariette to do a nonpermanent brunette for the night?" I asked Julie.

"Eew! No! I mean, my god, my hair might start *growing* brown if I did that," replied Julie. The fact is that Julie's hair does grow slightly brown, but I made an executive decision not to remind her. "I'm going as the blonde Ali MacGraw. She would have looked much cuter like that. Why does Aerin have to be such a pain? She's just trying to upset everyone and get written up as the most original Park Avenue Princess in the *Suzy* column."

"You don't have to go," I said.

"Are you kidding me? *No one's* been invited. I *have* to go. It's the highlight of my week. Even though it's only Monday, so my week hasn't really started yet."

Julie hung up. She called back a few seconds later to say, "Sweetie, don't tell Aerin I said that thing about her thing being the highlight of my week because I would hate for her to know *her* party was the highlight of *my* week."

Eduardo had arranged to meet me at the party, which I freely admit was the highlight of my week. Julie decided to bring Todd as her date: he was obviously back on her extensive boyfriend-of-the-minute list, and Charlie was back in LA. (Thank god. The idea of him frowning at me across a crowded room full of Robert and Ali lookalikes was not appealing.) Aerin has an allergy to sparing any expense. She'd transformed her entire place into a replica of Robert Evans's famous house in Beverly Hills. *Love Story* was playing on a giant screen in the library. Matsuhisa had been flown in from LA to do the food. Apparently the real Robert and Ali were there because Ali was Aerin's godmother or something. Thing was, it was impossible to spot them among all the other Roberts and Alis.

Something strange happened in the middle of the party. I was lounging by myself on a velvet sofa when Todd sat down beside me. He was barely recognizable in his Robert Evans velvet flares and huge tortoiseshell sunglasses. He seemed agitated. Suddenly he looked at me very intensely and said, "I must have your number."

Creepola, I thought to myself. Todd was Julie's. I was off-limits.

"Why?" I said.

"I need to call you. I want to . . . There's something I need to say to you, " he said.

Todd was really grossing me out. He was looking at me with stealthy eyes.

"Todd, I don't want you calling me, okay?"

He walked off. He looked embarrassed.

The party was so fabulous that it seemed like I'd been there for only five minutes and suddenly it was 1 AM. Time is so insidious at the best parties. At the worst parties it isn't, which is so annoying. Julie left with Todd. I went outside and hailed a cab.

Inside the taxi another insidious feeling crept up on me. *Where was Eduardo?* He never showed up. I checked my cell. No messages. I called my home voice mail. He hadn't called there either. I called his cell and there was no answer. I called his apartment. Nothing.

I was *not* desperate, really. It was just this was not how I wanted to be treated. He'd stood me up and left me to be harassed by Todd. Thank god for Dr. Fensler. I was so overflowing with brand-new self-esteem that night that I decided I would tell Eduardo it was all over in order to show him that I was a certain kind of girl with a certain kind of high self-esteem who must be treated like the best emerald in one of his great-grandmother's tiaras. After he had begged me to take him back I would *reluctantly* agree if he promised to modify his behavior. After all, this was Eduardo's first misdemeanor and wasn't it legal procedure to let criminals off for a first offense?

By the time I got home my self-esteem was still *almost* intact, which I thought was an excellent result considering the beating it had taken tonight. I headed straight for the phone and saw the MESSAGES button flashing. I dialed voice mail. Eduardo better have a great excuse. But it wasn't him. There were three messages from Todd (how did he get my number?) asking me to call him back. This was sick, I mean, it's a form of incest to go after your girlfriend's best friend. And Todd knew I was dating Eduardo. They'd been at school together and were old acquaintances.

I was woken at 6:30 AM the next morning by the phone ringing. I picked it up even though I consider it unethical to make contact with the outside world before 10:30 in the morning.

"Its Todd—"

"Todd, it's so early!"

"I have to talk to you."

I was loving this whole positive s-e thing Dr. F. had given me but did I really want Todd being attracted to me?

"Todd. You are cute. You are Julie's. I'm not seeing you. You're crazy," I said.

"But—"

"I'm going back to sleep."

I hung up.

It was obviously the era of insanely early morning calls because about ten minutes after that the phone rang again. *Oh, eew,* I thought, *I cannot deal with this Todd drama any longer.*

"Yes?" I said sternly.

"Is that you, my *carina* honey petal?"

It was Eduardo. He was whispering. No man had ever called me his *carina* honey petal before, but I was not swayed from my course: even though I would eventually be lenient, I must show no clemency now. In my most high-self-esteem voice I said, "Eduardo. I'm disappointed. You let me down last night."

I really was. I mean I'd made a huge effort to look like Ali MacGraw at the peak of her stardom and he'd totally missed my fashion moment.

"I don't think we should see each other again," I said.

"*Non!* My darling, I am stranded at the airport in Florida. You know that hurricane that hit the coast down here? The airport's right in the middle of it. They wouldn't let my pilot take off. I had to stay in a ghastly Sheraton hotel. I'm exhausted and all the phone lines were down until now. I am so sorry I couldn't reach you last night because you know, *je t'adore*."

I was hit by a mega-guilt attack. To think I'd been so untrusting when Eduardo was sleeping under some horrible synthetic hotel sheet. Still, I didn't say a thing.

"Let me take you to dinner tonight. To Serafina. Best pasta in New York. How can you say no?"

I couldn't. If you'd ever eaten the champagne and clam pasta at Serafina your self-esteem would have collapsed immediately, too.

A convenient stone's throw from Barneys, Serafina on East Sixty-first Street is New York's H.Q. for H.R.H.s. Apparently Albert of Monaco goes straight there from his plane just for the pizza porcini, and the "of Greeces" and "of Belgiums" rarely eat anywhere else. There are ofs everywhere you look in that place. They're very civil to one another but Eduardo says the Greeces are violently jealous of the Belgiums because the Belgiums still have a country, even if no one would ever dream of going there if it were the last place on earth. It makes no sense to me. I mean, I'd rather have no country at all and live somewhere exciting like Manhattan than have one like Belgium and actually have to be in it when it has nothing but beer to drink and no chance of an Alpha-Beta peel.

I decided on that gorgeous pastel peppermint satin number by Louis Vuitton for dinner. Looking back on it, I guess I must have been subliminally trying to communicate to Eduardo that I was the perfect candidate for Princess of Savoy. That dress was exactly the kind of thing Grace Kelly would have worn if she'd been a brunette. It was an excellent outfit for being cross with Eduardo in, because he wouldn't be able to focus on anything I was saying and would hopefully agree to all my terms immediately, which constituted the following:

1. Improve record on absenteeism. Work travel acceptable Monday through Friday only.
2. Replace hopeless Motorola cell phone with digital cell that works everywhere, even on father's Learjet.
3. Another visit to the palazzo *très* soon.

The second I walked into the restaurant I saw Eduardo at the entrance looking all tanned with his hair slicked back. He said, "My *carina,* you are *bellissima* tonight." All my terms slid from my mind and right out the door of the restaurant. I couldn't remember a single thing I was annoyed about anymore. (Luckily I had written down my terms on the inside of my hand: I had warned myself that forgetfulness might descend when I glimpsed Eduardo again.)

We had a great table with a view of the whole place. That night was gorgeous Swedish Princesses night: there was a table full of them in the center of the restaurant. No one could take their eyes off them. I think this was because they were natural blondes and no one could believe their hair was real. Then there were "of Greeces" everywhere you looked with their pretty blonde American wives, and I could see Julie in a far corner with Todd—eew!—and a whole table of "of Austrias." There was an East Village–type kid in one corner dressed in all that Gothic stuff you get on East Ninth Street. He seemed out of place until he came over and greeted Eduardo, who introduced him as Iago of Denmark. *Hamlet,* I thought, *how cute.*

Iago joined us for dinner. (This was not exactly on my list of terms but I had omitted to add a clause stating "no romantic dinners *à trois* with obscure Danish Princes.") They mainly talked about the issues that concern minor European royals such as—

1. When are they going to get their countries back?
2. Who crashed the most cars while at Rosey?
3. Is the south of France going to be completely overrun by Russians?
4. How are they going to get invited on the King of Spain's yacht again this summer?
5. Is Nikki Beach in Saint Tropez still chic? Or is it more glamorous to show off your tan/girl/self at La Voile Rouge?

"Of" conversations are actually super-dull, but if you want to be a Princess you have to act like they're the most fascinating thing in the world. You also have to pretend you think it would be awesome if the royals got their countries back, even if you are a very democratic girl like me who thinks monarchies are way out of date. I secretly believe most of these young Princes couldn't rule their own apartment buildings, let alone a nation. (This excludes Prince William, who is so hot he can rule the universe if he wants.)

After Iago left, Eduardo looked me in the eyes and said very romantically, "Tiramisu?"

"Eduardo, I am very upset. I am not dating you anymore and I am certainly not going to bed with you," I replied.

I didn't want Eduardo thinking he could have me back *that night*, even though I would definitely let him have me back that night. It was actually very hard to focus because that damn Todd kept making peculiar faces at me from the other side of the restaurant and motioning toward the bathroom. Men in New York are totally sick sometimes. I tried to ignore him.

"Actually," said Eduardo, "I meant, would you like to eat some dessert?" How embarrassing! "I know you're upset and I'm not expecting anything from you. You have every right to be angry with me," he went on.

This was sweet but I was disappointed. I'd been counting on some very stimulating Proust tonight—after much coaxing from Eduardo, of course. I said I'd eat the dessert: since it was the only tiramisu on offer, I might as well have some. After that the nicest thing happened. The waiter brought the tiramisu and it was in the shape of a heart.

"Forgive me?" said Eduardo.

"No," I said, meaning yes.

"Come to Sardinia on Spain's boat with me in two weeks?"

"No," I said, meaning, *Shall I run to Eres on Madison right now and get that new white bikini that's in the ad?*

Anyway, when I got to the bottom of the tiramisu—

which was beyond delicious—there was a pink crystal heart just sitting there waiting for me. Eduardo could disappear on work trips and never call me *all the time* if he wanted.

"Forgive me, *Principessa*?" he said.

"Forgiven," I said. I love a happy ending that involves a gift.

"Let's go," said Eduardo.

"Okay, just let me run to the restroom," I replied.

I wanted to gloss my lips and blush my cheeks before we got home. You could say I was beyond overwhelmed. Eduardo was perfect. He'd apologized gracefully and admitted he was wrong and I was right about everything without my even having to state my terms. I couldn't even imagine why I'd been with someone like Zach when there were Eduardos out there to be had. I slipped into one of the stalls. The door to the restroom opened and someone rushed in, breathlessly. I'd heard those Swedish girls were always doing cocaine back here. I sat stock still.

"Hey," said a voice. "You gotta hear me out." It was Todd.

"Todd, leave me alone, I'm not interested," I said.

"Julie sent me. She's insisting I tell you the truth."

That was weird.

"What?" I said.

"You gotta stop seeing him," he replied.

"No way, Eduardo's adorable. We're going for the weekend on the King of Spain's yacht."

"Break it off, I'm telling you. You're gonna get hurt."

I came out to the washing area and opened my makeup bag. I have to admit it was kind of great having two men fighting over me but I acted like it was *horrible*.

"Todd, I know you like me but I'm with Eduardo and you're dating my best friend," I said.

"I don't wanna date you," said Todd.

What? How depressing. He just wanted to sleep with me. That was almost worse.

"I just want you to be happy, that's all. I know Eduardo really well from school and stuff and he won't make you happy. I told Julie tonight and she told me to corner you and not let you leave the ladies' till you knew."

"Todd, stop trying to ruin everything! He's waiting outside for me, I've got to run," I said pulling open the door.

Todd slammed it shut. He stood across it.

"Let me out," I said.

"He's married and living in Connecticut with three kids under five."

"Don't be silly. That's the most ridiculous thing I ever heard."

"It's true."

"It's not."

"Haven't you wondered why he's away 'on business' every weekend?" said Todd.

"It's work," I said firmly.

"Italians do not work on the weekend!"

"Eduardo does," I replied.

"And does his phone never work at 'work'?"

I absolutely refused to believe it. I really needed a trip to Rio that night, you know. That's a total secret by the way.

"I know him, he's a classic cheater. I'm sorry," said Todd.

"Shut up!" I said. I tried to push him away from the door.

"'*Il n'y a rien comme le désir pour empêcher les choses qu'on dit d'avoir acune ressemblance avec ce qu'on a dans la pensée.*' Did he say that to you?"

How did Todd know this stuff? This was weird.

"Know what it means?" said Todd.

"It's Proust."

"So what does it mean?"

I didn't answer. I'd never asked Eduardo what it actually meant. It just sounded great.

"Let me translate," said Todd. "'*There is nothing like desire for preventing the things one says from bearing any resemblance to what one has in one's mind.*' He's been using that line forever."

I was stunned. Todd read Proust? And there I was thinking he was just a regular illiterate rich kid. I take it all back, I really do. I couldn't even look at him. I grabbed my purse and speedily exited the restaurant through the back kitchen.

Fool, I thought as I escaped. If only I really had learned perfect fluent French, this would never have happened.

Front Row Girls—the 101

1. Spiritual Home: New York fashion shows. Always in front row at Oscar, Michael, Carolina, and Bill (that's de la Renta, Kors, Herrera, and Blass).

2. Age: twenties, or very early thirties at absolute oldest. One well-known FRG has been twenty-three for over eight-and-a-half years now.

3. Breeding: grandfather started major merchant bank/cosmetics brand/aerospace empire. Slightly WASPy ancestry a plus. Dressing WASPy a minus.

4. Dress size: sample—i.e. 0, or 2 at largest. If you get onto the front row and you're not thin, you need a lot of personality to make up for it.

5. Vacation: grandmother's house in Palm Beach; best friend's private island; staying home in apartment (such a treat when you never do).

6. Classic fashion tip: honey-colored alligator stilettos. They disappear to the naked eye and elongate legs.

7. Shopping philosophy: always buy retail. FRGs never borrow.

8. Best friends: other Front Row Girls. FRGs don't converse with Second Row Girls—it's very bad for their necks to twist back like that.

8

Usually the moment I vow not to contact an ex-boyfriend, like all brokenhearted girls, I telephone them *immediately*. Eduardo sent me endless handwritten notes and Fauchon chocolates but I didn't contact him, even though I was so strung out about the whole affair I can't recall ever being that strung out. I mean, Zach was bad enough, what with no ring and no Brazil, but Eduardo had been so deceitful. Who'd think you'd be unlucky enough to get two men like that in a lifetime? Still, I wasn't overly traumatized. You see, Dr. F. really had done something miraculous with my self-esteem, which was a lot less dented than you'd expect. I agreed with Julie when she declared, "There's only one Prince worth knowing and that's The Artist Formerly Known As."

I decided to put my failed affairs behind me. It was very clear that the PH was a very prospective thing indeed. My new resolution, or rather my old resolution, which I decided to revive, was to focus on my work. Everyone was talking about this Front Row Girl named Jazz Conassey—

the Conassey lumber heiress from Wisconsin—recently arrived in New York. She was decked out beyond belief at all times in very, very petite skirts, tiny vintage couture coats, and sunglasses like a millennial Twiggy. She must have studied fashion in Paris because you do not get to be that good at fashion sitting in a forest in Wisconsin. Anyway, that lovely editor who had so kindly let me off my career when I had all those unmentionable Advil problems wanted a story about her. I agreed immediately. Not only did I want a check to run out and splurge with, I also wanted to examine Jazz's closet, which was rumored to be stocked with a piece of Pucci from every collection.

Jazz lives in a grand apartment block—47 East Seventieth. It's the ideal address for a fashion addict because the lobby is literally opposite the side entrance to the Prada store on Madison. I'd heard that Jazz was a talented multitasker: she was known to shop Prada while she was simultaneously on the line to her personal shopper at Barneys. I called her right away.

"Hey, it's Jazzy!" It was her voice mail. "If you need to reach me, from the twentieth to the twenty-third I'm at the Four Seasons Milan at 011 39 2 77 0 88. From the twenty-third to the twenty-eighth I'll be at my mother's in Madrid at 011 37 24 38 38 77. After that you can reach me at the Delano, Miami. Or try my cell phone, which is 917 555 3457. Or my European cell is 44 7768 935 476. Love you miss you mean it later."

How Jazz had time to collect Pucci with such a fierce vacationing schedule I know not. I elected not to leave a message—after all, it wouldn't be picked up for a week. I tried the Madrid number. Mrs. Conassey picked up. I asked if I could speak with her daughter.

"*I* would like to talk to my daughter. If you find her, could you please tell her to call her mother?" she said and hung up.

I tried the European cell. Voice mail came on. "Hey, this is Jazzy. If I don't pick up please call me on my US cell 917 555 3457."

I called the 917 number. That voice mail directed me back to the New York apartment. Front Row Girls are as notoriously unavailable as supermodels. I dialed the New York number again. Someone picked up. I could hardly believe my luck. I snapped to attention.

"Jazz?" I said.

"This is housekeeper," said a distinctly Filipino voice.

"Is Jazz in?" I asked.

"Yea."

"Can I speak to her?"

"She a-sleepin'."

It was lunchtime. I was shocked. Until now I was under the impression that I was the only person I knew in New York who isn't up before 10:30 AM. I said, "When she gets up can you ask her to call me back please? Can you tell her we want to write a fabulous story on her for the magazine?"

"Yea. You number?"

I gave it to her. At least Jazz was here, which made things easier.

It didn't surprise me that Jazz didn't call me back that day. Front Row Girls never call anyone back. They don't need to. Everyone calls them, endlessly. They're the society equivalent of the most popular girl in high school. I telephoned the apartment the next day—after lunch. The maid picked up again. I asked to speak to Jazz.

"Not here," said the housekeeper.

"Where is she?" I asked.

"She go Mustique yesterday."

My heart sank. Mustique is one of those godforsaken Caribbean islands where you cannot get a cell phone signal anywhere.

"When's she returning?" I asked. My deadline was in a few days.

"Don' know! Never know when Miss Jazzy here or no," replied the housekeeper.

"Do you have a number for her?"

"Sure!" said the housekeeper, repeating Jazz's impotent cell number.

New York society girls are beyond elusive. They have access to so many impossible-to-reach-without-your-own-jet vacation hideaways that even the CIA would have difficulty tracking them down. I doubted if a GPS system could find Jazz now.

"You must come, I'm throwing a meeting for Save Venice," Muffy had said. "Unless someone does something, that town is going to do a disappearing act. We don't want Venice to be the David Blaine of historical cities."

That was how I found myself at her house a few days later. Muffy pretends she's saving Venice for charitable reasons but between you and me, it's because Muffy is literally addicted to the scene at the Hotel Cipriani there. She'd die if she couldn't go there for a month every summer. She's the only person I know who "throws" meetings. If she donated all the money she spends on catering her meetings to the

Save Venice trust, she'd raise three times as much money as she does, without having to throw a single benefit.

The idea at this particular meeting was that everyone there should sign "reminder" notes to the Save Venice Ball. Apparently handwritten signatures make people more likely to buy tickets and show up than printed ones.

"Start signing," said Muffy when I arrived midafternoon, pressing a wedge of invitations into my hands. "Go sit in the library and I'll come join you. Champagne? Or would you like a lychee and mango macaroon? I had the dough flown in from Paris specially. They melt on your tongue."

I popped one in my mouth. It was sinful, it really was. The cost of that macaroon would probably have paid for at least six new bricks in St. Mark's. I went into Muffy's library, which is painted Bordeaux red, like everyone else's libraries on the Upper East Side, and sat with a group of girls. They had stacks of invitations in front of them. No one signed a thing or licked an envelope. There was too much to discuss.

"Oh," sighed Cynthia Kirk. "All this sitting on boards and philanthropic work!"

Cynthia is a wealthy young committee princess. Her goal in life is to become queen of the Manhattan benefit scene.

"I know! It's *constant*. Absolutely," said Gwendolyn Baines, her direct competition for this particular role.

"You're only as good as the last money you brought in. Charity is brutal. Worse than hedge funds," said Cynthia.

"And when you've got someone doing construction on your fireplace *as well!* It doesn't bear thinking about," complained Gwendolyn.

"Fund-raising! I barely have time to shop for clothes anymore."

"Likewise. But I've realized *under pressure,* I can live my life on bags, shoes, and jewelry. It's all about the accessories. The rest is just whatever."

"My trick, because I am under *terrible stress* with the museum, is Michael Kors shifts for summer. You just zip'n'go! You zip, and *zoom!* you're out of the house in three minutes."

The atmosphere was more tense than a scene from a Chekhov play. Any minute now one of the girls was going to faint or die just for the attention.

"Oh, there you are!" said Muffy, poufing down beside me on the sofa. She was even more breathlessly exhausted than the fund-raisers sitting around me. She patted her immaculate forehead with a laundered linen handkerchief. "If I'd known saving Venice was this tiring I might have chosen another city that isn't *drowning,* like Rome, which is just collapsing," she sighed. "Now dear, this Eduardo character. What a brute! In my day if you were married, you told your girlfriend. That was the marvelous thing about Studio 54, the openness. Everyone knew where they stood. Are you all right?"

"Muffy, I'm fine. I'm just going to get a full bio next time," I said. If there's one thing I'd learned from the Eduardo episode it was this: no more men without full background checks.

"I know someone who has the résumés of some of the most eligible men in the city," said Muffy.

"You do?" said Cynthia.

"Yes, but this is not about you, Cynthia, you're married. This is about you," said Muffy, looking straight at me.

"Actually, Muffy, that's really sweet of you," I said. "But

I don't want an 'eligible man.' I'm taking a break from all that. I've decided to focus on my career."

"Oh dear, no! You do not want to be working so hard or you'll need Botox by the time you're thirty," Muffy replied, her face falling dramatically. "Look at the lines on Hillary Clinton's face. Too much career going on there."

Muffy is aesthetically opposed to serious career girls. She thinks working destroys your skin cells. Sometimes Muffy is so old-fashioned I think they should install her as an exhibit at the Met.

"You must meet my friend Donald Shenfeld. Divorce lawyer to anyone who's anyone who needs a divorce."

"Muffy, Eduardo isn't getting a divorce any time soon," I said.

"It's not for him, it's for you," Muffy replied.

Maybe Muffy had early-onset Alzheimer's. I hardly needed a divorce since I'd never even managed a wedding. She went on, "Donald's fabulous. He's arranged a lot of fabulous divorces and a lot of fabulous relationships in this city. He divorced me at the same time as he was divorcing poor Henry. He realized we were the perfect couple, he introduced us, and look at me now! I've got the most wonderful homes! Donald Shenfeld knows who's coming, who's going, and here's the really criminal part, who's *about* to be coming."

"I would love to meet with him," said Gwendolyn.

"Gwen, you're taken," snapped Muffy.

"I know, but why not be aware of who's on the market? Just in case."

I wondered if Gwendolyn's and Cynthia's husbands were as busy searching for second wives as their wives were searching for second husbands.

"See," said Muffy, turning to me earnestly, "you have got to be ahead in this town. An eligible divorcé comes onto the market and boom! Gone quicker than you can say 'Did you sign a pre-nup?' It's a huge advantage to have someone like Donald looking out for you, in advance."

"Don't you think a man who's about to get a divorce isn't exactly a prime candidate for a relationship?" I said.

"That's where you girls get it so wrong. You're looking in all the wrong places. The divine thing about a divorcé is that you know they're the marrying kind. You can't say that for a single man, can you?"

Muffy has very logical thought processes that make no sense at all sometimes.

"Donald has someone fabulous for you."

"Muffy! *Stop,*" I cried.

I didn't want to know. Of course she totally ignored me, saying, "Patrick Saxton. Forty-one. Still has hair. As good as divorced. Film business, you know, he runs some huge movie studio. Bicoastal. Private jets absolutely *everywhere,* which warms my heart because you know I hate to think of you flying commercial even if you are a working girl and that's what all the others do. He's dying to meet you."

Blind dates are for sad NY girls with no nice clothes. There was no way I was going on one.

"I've heard he's phenomenally rich," said Cynthia, eyes widening.

"I don't want a rich guy," I said.

I meant it. Everyone I know with a rich boyfriend or husband is always complaining about money. They never complain about the shopping opportunities though.

"He's not *that* rich," said Muffy. "He's not make-you-miserable, my-own-yacht rich. He's four houses rich, which I think is just rich enough."

Some New York girls would date Patrick purely for the extra closet space. But "as good as divorced" sounded a lot like "married." This one was totally off my list before he'd even got on it.

❧

Voice mail is the modern American equivalent of Chinese water torture. Jazz's was running 24/7, on every land line and cell phone. The next day I left several messages again, hoping she might call back. I didn't want this story to go the same way as the Palm Beach heiress. There was nothing to do but sit and wait by the phone. Instead of brooding on my fiancé-free, date-free life, I decided to be positive and plan my Save Venice outfit—the party was in two days' time.

Just as I was calling Carolina Herrera's office to see if they'd lend me a gown, the other line rang. I snapped off my Carolina fashion call and picked it up. A sweet, girlish voice with a Marilyn Monroe edge came on the line.

"Hi, this is Jazz Conassey. I'd love love love to do the story."

"Jazz!" I said. "I've been trying to contact you. Where are you?"

"Ooo-hh," she yawned langorously. "On a boat somewhere, I don't know where, but it's so fun, you should come down here."

Girls like Jazz always invite everyone everywhere, even

people they've never met, and even when they have no idea where they are.

"When are you back in New York?" I asked.

"I don't know! Don't ask me questions like that! Maybe tomorrow? I was thinking of going to this Save Venice party. Daddy's virtually saved Venice single-handed, so I'm under a lot of pressure to be there."

"I have to go, too. Why don't we meet there and we can do the story the next morning?"

"But those things are dull. *So dull.* And I'm on the boat and everything. It's so nice down here. And you know, I don't really want to be in a magazine much anyway."

Talking society girls into doing what you want is like playing chess. You have to be at least three moves ahead. All you need to know is, ask for what you don't want and you'll get what you want. Ask for what you want and you'll get what you don't want. I said calmly, "You *shouldn't* do the story then. *Definitely not*. Have a great time on the boat and—"

"No, wait, *maybe* I could manage it. I could meet you at the party?"

"Are you sure?" I said. "I don't want to interrupt your vacation."

"Hey, I'm *always* on vacation. I need a break from vacations actually. They get *so dull.*"

I said, "How will I find you at the party?"

With a giggle she replied, "I'll be the girl in the shortest skirt with the best tan."

How one dresses as a doge of Venice in a miniskirt I know not but if I had legs like Jazz's I would rewrite fashion history, too.

“God, it’s very S.P.D.V. tonight,” said Julie with a sigh, scanning the Save Venice crowd, which was gathered in the grand ballroom of the St. Regis Hotel.

We were hanging at the bar drinking strawberry cocktails. Julie was dressed in a long, narrow column of gold lamé—vintage Halston, which is so in right now it’s insane. She refused to dress for a theme after the Ali MacGraw scenario had sent her into a fashion depression. I didn’t exactly look Venetian either, but I was living for the draped navy evening gown Carolina had sent over for me. It would be a tragedy to have to return it.

“S.P.D.V?” I said. Sometimes Julie’s lingo is way too abbreviated for me.

“Same People Different Venue,” she explained, looking supremely bored.

Julie was right. The Save Venice party was a jungle of the same socialites, dresses, and jewels you see at every benefit in New York. I roved the party looking for a beauty in a mini but all I saw were girls in apartment-sized ball gowns. That much net in one dress can be majorly traumatic sometimes. The congestion in the restroom when two girls wanted to pass by each other was worse than the New Jersey Turnpike at rush hour.

Lara and Jolene were there in matching pink and blue Bill Blass dresses. They’d recently started shopping in duplicate in case they wanted to dress the same. Neither of them had seen Jazz. In fact, no one had seen Jazz at the party. I was getting stressed out. Was I ever going to get another story done? I took my seat and tried not to worry.

Julie, Lara, and Jolene were all at my table. They were overexcited because they'd been given the task of judging the best-dressed girl at the party.

"I nominate you," said Lara to Jolene.

"No," said Lara, "*you're* the prettiest."

"No way. You're the prettiest," said Jolene.

"You are!" said Lara.

"Okay, girls. Let's just be honest," interrupted Julie. "*I'm* the prettiest, but we can't award the Dolce & Gabbana gift certificate to ourselves, so let's get on and choose the winner."

I couldn't see the fun in the best-dressed competition. All I could think about was how I was ever going to write my story if my subject was constantly unavailable. This career thing can really upset your social life if you aren't careful.

I chatted a little with the man to my left, a Wall Street hedge-fund guy. I didn't even notice the seat to my right was empty until I heard a voice saying, "I'm sorry I'm late. So rude of me."

"No problem," I said, looking around. I found myself face-to-face with a man wearing an immaculate tuxedo with a freshly laundered handkerchief in the front pocket. His fair hair was combed back and he was smiling. This person was 100 percent charm school.

"I've been chatting with our sponsors and we got very involved. But the main thing is to raise as much as we can for this charity."

I hadn't caught the guy's name. As he went to sit down, I sneaked a peak at his place card. It read PATRICK SAXTON.

Sometimes I could literally murder Muffy. Even if Patrick was some kind of total saint who gave all his money and time to Venice, that didn't mean I'd changed my mind about not being interested in an almost-divorced movie mogul who probably had future-ex-wife issues I couldn't even imagine. Across the table the negotiations for the best-dressed guest were getting more intense than the nominations for the Pulitzer Prize.

"Louise O'Hare deserves to win. Who else actually personally commissioned Olivier Theyskens to design a Venetian dress?" said Jolene.

"No way," said Lara. "Kelly Welch got Lars Nilson over from Paris to make her frock, which counts as more effort."

"Apparently Louise has a backup dress from Ungaro," said Jolene.

"It's *Ooon-garo.* Not *Un-garo,*" said Lara. "And anyway, having a backup dress is a sign of terrible insecurity. We need to consider the girls' personalities, too."

Julie butted in. "Hey, this isn't a Miss Universe competition! My god! I think someone else should decide. You two are too obsessed to pick a fair winner. Why doesn't he choose?" said Julie, looking at Patrick.

"Absolutely not," he smiled, raising his palms. "I'm not qualified."

"Dude, you don't need qualifications to say who's the cutest," said Julie. "Just decide who deserves to win."

Patrick gazed around him, wide-eyed. It was like he'd never seen a pretty girl before. For a movie tycoon he seemed kind of cute, personality-wise, which is very rare, actually. He quickly pointed at a girl sitting alone in a corner.

"I think she took the most trouble," said Patrick.

Jolene and Lara gasped. "Madeleine Kroft!" they said in unison.

Lara and Jolene were alarmed. Madeleine Kroft was exactly who they *wouldn't* have chosen. She was a sweet, preppy, twenty-three-year-old who hadn't lost her puppy fat. She was dressed like she had hired her outfit from a Halloween store on Bleecker Street. She was painfully shy, and rarely spoke without turning a violent shade of tomato.

"No way!" hissed Jolene. She cleared her throat. Collected herself. "That is *so nice*. I never would have thought of giving the prize to her."

"Oh my god," echoed Lara. "This is like the nicest thing that's ever happened to Madeleine Kroft. I feel *so bad* for not suggesting her. She's like the nicest girl ever."

Patrick got up and went over to Madeleine. We all watched as she started jumping up and down with excitement. Julie snuck around and sat in his empty seat. Then she whispered to me, "He's cute. He's rich. He's the nicest person we've ever met in New York. You should date him."

"Even if he were available, which he isn't, I'm sure he wouldn't be interested in me, which is lucky because I wouldn't be interested in him," I said.

He returned with Madeleine to the table. "Oh my god!" she gasped to Lara and Jolene. "Oh my god, this is the best day of my life. You two girls are the best. You're both really special people. Thank you so much for choosing me. You can come down to the compound on Hobe Sound whenever you want."

Jolene handed her the Dolce & Gabbana shopping certificate. Madeleine looked at it and suddenly seemed sad.

"What is it?" said Jolene.

"I can't fit into any of the clothes at that store," wailed Madeleine desperately. "Why do you think I have to dress like this?"

"Well there're tons of accessories there you can buy instead," said Jolene.

"That's even worse. I hate it here. I feel like a meringue in a room full of chives."

"You're a very beautiful girl, Madeleine. Don't be upset, this is a good thing!" said Patrick.

"Really?" she said.

"I promise. You're a lot prettier than all those chives," said Patrick.

Madeleine beamed at him and took off into the crowd. The whole way through dinner, Julie, Lara, and Jolene gazed at Patrick like he was Mother Teresa or something. After coffee was served he turned to me and said, "Can I offer you a ride home?"

"Yes!!!" shrieked Julie excitedly. "She'd love a ride."

We took a cab. Patrick said he never used drivers for parties because he hated the thought of them waiting outside all night for him. Maybe Patrick really was as down to earth as he seemed. I mean, I've never heard of anyone in New York who can have a driver but doesn't.

"Listen, I leave for Cannes tomorrow night for a couple of days for the film festival. Would you like to be my guest? I'll be doing a lot of business, but it could be fun," he said.

I would love to be your guest, I thought. *But you are married and I have my career to think of. And I don't want to give the impression that you have any chance of any extramarital predivorce Brazilian activity with me tonight, which I would if I said yes.*

"I'm sorry, I can't," I said, smiling sweetly.

Do you know what a huge self-esteem boost it is to turn down a trip to Cannes? I highly recommend it when you are feeling a little low about yourself; it's as effective as an Alpha-Beta peel. The cab came to a halt outside my apartment.

"Sure?" he asked.

"Sure," I said, thinking, *Am I?* "Good night," I added, getting out of the cab.

❧

As I walked into my apartment my cell rang. It was Jazz. I'd totally forgotten about her no-show.

"Hey! It's me," she said. "I got so, like, totally beyond delayed tonight and then it seemed so rude to show up three hours late to the party so I just stayed here at the 60 Thompson. We can do the interview now."

"Jazz, it's one AM," I said.

"So?"

"Why don't we do it tomorrow?"

"Because I'm leaving for Cannes in, like, six and a half hours."

Of course she was. Duh. FRGs are always leaving for somewhere fabulous imminently. I had no choice but to pull on a pair of jeans and hop into a cab.

Jazz never explained why she had taken a suite at 60 Thompson that night, but from the state of it she had been having a party that was way more fun than Save Venice. She plopped herself into bed, like a beautiful, tan rag doll while a maid cleaned up around her.

"Thank you so much," she said to the maid. "You're so nice here, I love you! You're the best. Can you bring me a tea?"

"Of course, miss," said the maid adoringly. "What about some cookies, too?"

"Oooh, I love you!" said Jazz.

She patted the duvet and beckoned me over. "I'm gonna

tell you everything about us, the Front Row Girls," she began. "The thing is, I just adore being a Front Row Girl. It's so nice to *always* be in the front row . . ."

There is nothing like an Alexander McQueen bag arriving unannounced by messenger to distract you from all your good intentions regarding your career. The next morning one arrived containing an exquisite party dress and a handwritten note, which stated,

> *Sure? You could wear this for the amfAR benefit in Cannes. Depart 6 PM tonight, Teterboro.*
> *Yours, Patrick*

Teterboro! All New York girls know that that ugly word means something very pretty. Teterboro means "I have a plane." Teterboro is a delightful airport that deals only in noncommercial flights. If you're ever out in New Jersey on a Friday night and you're wondering why the highway is gridlocked with chauffeur-driven sedans, it's all the moguls running to catch their G-Vs down to Palm Beach. I consider it beyond unfair of Patrick to let it slip that he had a jet at his disposal at this juncture. It made it much harder to turn down his offer. Most New York girls have a thing about private jets that is so overwhelmingly powerful that they literally cannot say no to a trip. I would *occasionally* include myself in that particular group. However, today my inner child just wouldn't stop reminding me that Patrick was still married, whatever Muffy said. I would forfeit the trip, even if it was a sin to turn down such a gorgeous dress.

I put the bag in the hallway to be returned. I tried to block the whole idea of a fabulous trip to Cannes from my mind. I sent Patrick a text telling him I couldn't come.

The instant I'd sent the message, of course, I regretted it. How miserable it suddenly seemed not to be going to the Côte d'Azur after all. Maybe reading about some glam party would cheer me up. I flipped to the *Suzy* column in the latest *W* magazine. It fell open on a page of photographs. There, staring at me from the biggest picture on the page was Zach, with Adriana on his arm. Adriana A! The Luca Luca mannequin! How could he? He'd always said she was a nightmare. And look, Adriana was wearing the absolute latest Lanvin swingy dress, one that I coveted. Much as I didn't want to look any closer, I felt compelled to examine the frock: as I did so, I noticed the caption beneath the photograph. It read, "Photographer Zach Nicholson with his fiancée, model Adriana A." Zach was engaged again, already, to Adriana A? I couldn't believe it. It was too dreadful to contemplate. I snapped the magazine shut.

How was I going to write the FRG story now? Paralyzed by a combination of sadness and jealousy, I couldn't focus at all. Maybe that trip to Cannes *was* a good idea after all. It would certainly take my mind off how hip Adriana looked in that dress. If I stayed here I would start obsessing about Zach again, and Adriana A. or not, he wasn't worth it. Maybe being in Cannes would improve my concentration. In fact, I told myself, there is nowhere better for attending to important work than on a PJ. I texted Patrick again:

Ignore previous message. Love to come.

A few minutes later I got one back:

Ignored. Pick you up at 5 PM, Patrick

I would write the FRG story on the plane and e-mail it back the next morning. No one had to know I was away. It was the only option for my very unstable career at that point. It's such a comfort to be able to make a sensible decision in an emergency.

Patrick buzzed my door on the dot of five. I grabbed my little suitcase and flew down the stairs. A dark Mercedes was waiting on the street, its engine purring. I hopped in the back seat.

"Sure?" said Patrick.

"Sure," I said.

We sped off. The interior was ice cool and very soft. For a man who never hired drivers this was not exactly in keeping with Patrick's personality. Still, I say, complain not when you are in the back seat of a Mercedes on the way to a very glamorous trip to the Riviera.

The Hotel du Cap in Antibes should be renamed the Hotel du Deals. Everyone who's anyone in movies stays there during the festival even though it's a thirty-minute drive from the Croisette, where all the movies are, and it's ninety minutes if the traffic's murder, and the traffic is *homicidal* during the festival. Geography-wise, it's a lot like choosing to stay at the Mark if all you want to do is shop in Mulberry Street.

The whole du Cap thing is like a bizarre cult or something. I mean, if I were Cameron Diaz and I was blonde and rich enough to stay anywhere I wanted, I'm not sure I'd choose a hotel that requires you to pay your bill *in advance, in cash,* has nothing on room service but club sandwiches and shamefully tiny scoops of sorbet, and where the TVs in the rooms are so old they should be on the History Channel.

That's what I thought when we arrived in the pitch black at 6 AM this morning. It was something like 12 AM New York time—G-Vs get to Europe quicker than regular planes, which I guess is one of the advantages of a plane you can only just stand up in. We couldn't get a morsel to eat or a bed until Patrick had handed over a wedge of cash the size of a shoe. Honestly, they should call it Motel du Cap.

Patrick is beyond gentlemanly. I had warned him in no uncertain terms on the way over that I was not available to him for trips to Brazil, in view of his marital status. Without actually saying it, I think I managed to communicate my real message: were he ever to be *a lot* closer to a real divorce, I *may* be convinced to travel to South America with him. The great benefit of an ultra-chaste attitude is that your host is forced to book you into your own suite. Totally on the d-l, because I would hate Patrick to find out I said this, your own suite is a lot more relaxing than sharing with a man you hardly know who is trying to talk his way into your own personal Ipanema Beach all night long.

I woke at 11 AM feeling jet-lagged beyond belief. I dizzily threw open the shutters. Oh! I gasped. *That's* why everyone's here, I thought. Miles of impeccable green lawn stretched down to the Mediterranean, which sparkled like one of those antique cushion-cut blue diamonds they sell at Fred Leighton on Madison. Who cared if there was no food here! You could fill up on view. The ex-fiancé getting a new fiancée suddenly didn't seem to matter quite so much anymore.

There was a knock at my door and a busboy entered. He was carrying a silver tray loaded up with baguette and orange pressé. A notecard was perched on top:

Meetings all day. Have fun at the pool. I will pick you up at 7 PM for the amfAR party. So glad you are here, Patrick.

Remember that Eres bikini I was obsessing over for the thwarted cruise on the King of Spain's boat? Well, I wasn't at all hysterical anymore about not getting to wear it there when it was even more perfect for here. The du Cap (everyone just says "the du Cap" here) is one giant fashion opportunity. It was the ideal place for a white two-piece with silver buckles at the hips.

I strolled through the bar and out to the pool which is on a cliff edge overlooking the ocean. I was just pulling up a chair when a voice yelled, "Hey, over here!"

It was Jazz Conassey. Of course it was. I walked over to where she was sprawled like a tanned pretzel on a white mat.

"Hi," I said.

"Dev-a-station factor!" she said, staring at my bikini.

"What?" I said.

"I'm devastated," said Jazzy.

"Why?"

"Your bikini."

"Is there something wrong with it?"

"No! Noooo! I'm devastated in a good way, it's a hot bikini. I'm paying you a compliment."

"Well, thank you so much, Jazz. I'm *devastated* by your outfit, too," I said.

She was in a batik-print swimsuit and had more diamonds wrapped around her neck than an entire red carpet of Hollywood starlets. I think she was acting out the FRG version of hippy chic.

"Jean-Jacques!" called Jazz to the poolman. "Bring my friend a mat?" Jazz turned to me and added, "You really don't want to be in a *chair* at this particular pool. It's all about the *white mats* here."

"I was thinking of getting a cabana," I said.

"Don't," replied Jazz. "Those cabanas are so, like, *secluded*. You can't be seen there. You want to be seen."

I followed Jazz's order and lay down beside her on a white mat. The etiquette at the du Cap could inspire a whole new volume from Emily Post.

"I'm starving," I said. "I'm going to order a club sandwich. Do you want anything?

"No, I'm on the du Cap diet," replied Jazz.

The du Cap diet, it turns out, consists of peach Bellinis, peanuts, and Ritz cookies. As Jazz rightly said, the peanuts were way more delicious than the club sandwiches, which, frankly, are better at a Holiday Inn.

"So, have you written the story about me yet?" said Jazz.

"Yes," I lied. The magazine wanted it right away. But I couldn't bear the idea of going indoors and working when there was some world-class tanning to be done out here. "What are you doing here?" I asked Jazz.

"Doing? I'm not *doing* anything. I'm just hanging with this friend who's got, like, six movies out."

"Seen anything great?"

"Not yet, but there's a screening this afternoon of this really hot little indie movie out of LA that everyone's talking about. I heard the director's totally hot. You want to come with me?"

"Sure," I said. "What's it called?"

"*The Diary.* Everyone's saying it's as funny as Woody Allen was when he was still funny."

We left the hotel at four. Jazz had somehow managed to secure the only driver in the whole of Antibes with an open-top jeep. We whizzed down the driveway of the hotel and onto the coast road.

"So what are you wearing to the ball tonight?" yelled Jazz, her hair swirling around her in the wind.

"McQueen. Patrick gave it to me."

"Devastation factor! You're here with Patrick Saxton *and* he got you a dress? Wow. Amazing."

"I'm not 'with' with Patrick. I'm just with him. I don't even know him."

"Look here's the info about the movie," said Jazz.

I scanned the sheet of paper she handed over. It read,

The Diary
A comedy
Written and directed by Charlie Dunlain

Charlie? Charlie didn't make successful, funny movies. He made depressing low-budget intellectual films no one ever saw. It was bad enough being discovered dead by a hopeless movie director, let alone the darling of the Cannes film festival.

"Jazz, I can't come. I gotta turn in that story." I tapped the driver on the shoulder and said, "Can you drop me here, please?"

He pulled up. I hopped out of the car.

"But you said you'd done the story!" said Jazz.

"See you tonight," I said, walking back toward the hotel.

Just when I'd been feeling more cheerful about everything, the thought of Charlie's stern, disapproving face in the Ritz bar came right back to me. He'd bring on a really negative Advil-type mood swing. Even worse, the story about Eduardo and me had done the gossip rounds, so he would be more unimpressed by me than ever. Anyway, I wanted to be on time with my story. It's important to be super-duper reliable when you have a career, particularly when you've been somewhat unreliable for several weeks.

Later, as I was putting the finishing touches to my story on the laptop in my room, the telephone rang.

"*Bonsoir,*" I said. I was determined to improve my hopeless fluent French.

"Hey! It's Lara. Are you having the best time? Is George Clooney there?"

"It's so nice here. You should come sometime," I told her.

"Can you believe Charlie got that award?" said Lara. "We read about it in Cindy Adams."

"He did?" I said. "Oh."

Why do the best things always happen to the worst people, and the worst things, like premature balding, always happen to the nicest people? God, I hoped that didn't mean Charlie would be at the amfAR party.

"Are you okay?" said Lara.

"I'm great," I replied.

"Are you freaked about Zach and that airhead model?"

"A bit, I guess."

"Try not to think about it. Those two are so over they don't know how over they are. Call when you're back."

"I will."

"*Au revoir,*" said Lara and hung up.

I e-mailed my story off at 6 PM. It was only midday in

New York, so I was at least an hour ahead of my deadline. I ordered two peach Bellinis from room service to celebrate. Before a party, two Bellinis make you feel not at all nervous, you know, which is a brilliant pre-party ploy if you have a nonaddictive personality. In fact, after drinking both Bellinis I started feeling so wonderfully not-nervous that I began thinking that maybe I would *love* to bump into Charlie Dunlain at amfAR, in the gorgeous McQueen, as the date of a well-regarded movie producer. Then he'd see that I wasn't a suicidal loser who attracted ghastly men.

The only issue I have with those Bellinis, in retrospect, is that when I put on that lovely floaty chiffon dress that Patrick had gotten me, I guess I wasn't totally being 100 percent careful what with all those bubbles floating around my system. I got the frock over my head. I tried to pull it down. Oops. It was stuck, forming a cage from the top of my head to my belly button. I couldn't move. I couldn't see. My arms wouldn't go down or up. I must have forgotten to undo the zip. I slowly tried to wriggle the dress off. As I was released I heard a violent ripping sound.

6:25 PM. I undid the zip and started to put the dress back on. That was when I saw it: a devastating—and I mean that in the original sense of the word—wound gaped from the back of the dress. It was beyond unwearable. It wasn't even fixable.

Patrick would be here in thirty-five minutes. Desperate, I ran over to Jazz's room and hammered at the door. FRGs always have exquisite backup dresses available.

"I'm having a party dress 911," I gasped when Jazz let me in.

"Hey, no problemo, sweetie. You can wear my backup," she said.

What a saint! Jazz was ready to party in a red vintage 1970s Valentino column scattered with silk roses. She looked awesome. I felt less freaked. If Jazz's backup dress was anything like this I doubted whether that mini-meltdown I'd anticipated would ever hit me. She glided to her closet and pulled out a silk gown.

"It's Oscar. New season. Very now. Here," she said.

I took the dress from her. It was steel gray taffeta. There was a lot of dress. I was secretly excited. I slipped it on. I ran to the mirror.

I looked like an iceberg. No, seriously, I did. Why did the only bad dress that Oscar had *ever* designed in his *entire* career end up on me on what potentially could have been the most glamorous night of my life? Now I know what Halle Berry must have felt like the night she won the Oscar. I mean, imagine, up she went to get that cute little gold thing in front of the whole world and she's dressed like an ice skater. No wonder she was having an anxiety attack. I couldn't say anything, I mean, it was so sweet of Jazz to lend me the dress, but she knew I was disappointed. She said, "Soooo, it's a little WASPy. But French people don't realize how uncool it is to be WASPy. They'll never know, I promise."

I didn't have time to freak out. I raced back to my room and slipped on my black mules—which would have looked chic with the chiffon but looked like two anchors with the iceberg—and scooped up my black clutch. The phone went.

"I'm in the car downstairs," said Patrick.

"Coming," I said, as though there was nothing to be alarmed about at all.

He wouldn't even notice what I was wearing, I told myself. Men never do. I sidled down the stairs—the dress seemed to be wider than the staircase—and tried to glide into Patrick's car. In fact, I barely managed to force myself and the block of dress through the door. Sometimes fashion makes you feel like a wedge of pâté.

"Hi," I said.

"Hi," said Patrick. His face fell as he regarded my outfit. "I thought you were going to wear the Alexander McQueen dress. That's Oscar de la Renta."

Weird. I am super-suspicious of men who know as much about fashion as me. I told Patrick what had happened.

"I'm sorry, this is Jazz Conassey's backup dress!" I giggled.

Patrick didn't exactly giggle back. In fact, Mr. G-V was not the slightest bit charmed by my tale. He barely spoke to me all night. That's the problemo with gay men and straight guys who are too into fashion: they're all over you when you're in some really interesting *avant-garde* McQueen number, but show up in a WASPy iceberg and *they* turn into icebergs. Patrick was polite but cool all night. He was captivated by Jazz's rose-strewn Valentino, but I drank so many peach Bellinis that my self-esteem barely noticed. The only thing I could congratulate myself on that night was not seeing Charlie Dunlain. There was no sign of him all evening.

Another note arrived with breakfast the next morning.

We leave at 1 P.M. A car will take you to the airport and I'll meet you there. Happy sunbathing!
Patrick

He didn't sound too pissed. Maybe Patrick didn't mind about the iceberg after all. Maybe he wasn't as superficial as I'd thought last night. Sometimes I can be way too judgmental.

The phone rang. Oooo-www!!! My head was hurting. My nails were agony. Even my *hair* was hurting, which is unique to a Bellini hangover. It was Jazz.

"Hi, I'm flying back to the city with you," she said.

"Great. I think we leave at one."

"I'll see you at the airport," she said.

See. Patrick wasn't terrible. How kind of him to offer Jazz a ride home.

Still, if Jazz was travelling with us I needed to redeem myself with a top-class, private-jet outfit. Head aching, I gingerly pulled on a crisp white sundress. I put on flat gold sandals and gold hoop earrings and tied my hair in a ponytail with my favorite Pucci headscarf. Then I lay in bed with a bag of ice on my nails until the car arrived to pick me up at midday. Patrick really was a saint, sending cars and notes 24-7. Maybe he'd send a new dress to replace the one I'd ruined when I got back to New York, though of course I wasn't 100 percent expecting it.

On the way to the airport we drove through Juan-Les-Pins. It's a cute little place with more shoe and bikini shops than you can imagine. I couldn't resist a thirty-second shopping spree. The driver stopped the car, saying, "Five minutes, *mademoiselle.* It's forty-five minutes to the airport from here."

About twenty-five bikinis, fourteen sarongs, and six pairs of wedge-heeled espadrilles later—you know how it is in the Hamptons in summer, it's required procedure to change pool outfits between every meal—I hopped back in the car. The shopping easily made up for last night's humiliation. I mean, the girls in New York were going to kill themselves when they saw the espadrilles I'd gotten them. I say, if you are lucky enough to go on gorgeous trips abroad, take your girlfriends something fashionable back. It was only the middle of May and I had a few weeks until Fourth of July weekend, but for a New York girl it's never too early to start bulk-buying beachwear.

The driver dropped me at Terminal One. I headed for Gate Zero, where all the private planes depart from. No sign of Patrick or Jazz. They probably hadn't arrived yet. I approached a man dressed in uniform.

"*Excusez-moi, monsieur, je cherche Monsieur Patrick Saxton.*"

"*Il est parti, mademoiselle,*" replied the man.

I looked at my watch. 1:30 PM. I was only half an hour behind schedule. Surely Patrick hadn't gone without me?

"What?" I said.

" 'E leave one hour ago with girl with tan."

How could he? How could *she*? Especially after I had written that really nice article about her. I suddenly felt weak and shaky: those du Cap Bellinis catch up with you at the most inconvenient moments.

"How am I supposed to get to New York?" I said. No doubt this lovely pilot would shove me on someone else's G-V later. I mean, I was totally dressed for it.

"*Je ne sais pas,*" the man exclaimed, tossing his hands in the air.

He turned abruptly and walked off. My outfit had done nothing to influence him. As he was almost out of the lounge he pointed through the glass windows ahead. I followed his arm with my gaze. Across the street I could see the entrance to Terminal 2. My heart sank. Look, I don't have anything against airports *per se,* but I could see more people crowded into that lobby than there were at the whole of the Macy's Thanksgiving Day Parade last year. The trouble with going on a private plane is that afterward you never, ever want to fly commercial again. My advice to anyone who is about to fly private is to *only* do it if it is going to become the norm. Honestly, at that moment I wished I'd never seen the suede ceiling or eaten the delicious sandwiches in Patrick's gorgeous little G-V.

What was I thinking! If I wasn't careful I was going to turn into Patricia Duff or someone really spoiled like that. I could fly commercial, like just about everyone else in the world. Summoning up all my self-esteem I dragged my much-increased baggage across the street. The heat was burning. By the time I got to the Air France desk I felt like a tuna melt.

The stewardess behind the counter was gray-haired and impeccably groomed. She looked at me as she might regard a used Band-Aid.

"*Oui?*" she said. "Can I 'elp you? *Madame*."

Why do French ladies always go out of their way to upset young girls like *moi* by calling them "Madame"? It's cruel, especially when you've got a Bellini hammering at your brain.

"*Mademoiselle,*" I said. "I've missed my flight to New York. When's the next one?"

"Three PM. Okay?"

"Sure," I said.

"That will be 4,376 euros."

"What?" I gulped.

"We 'ave only business class available."

"What about taking a later flight?

"We are *completely full*."

I was close to tears. I didn't have 4,376 euros to blow on a one-way ticket to New York. Still, I bit my lip and handed over my Visa card. I would write off the whole trip as a very pricey disaster from which I had learned a costly moral lesson: never dress as a WASPy iceberg if you can dress as an ice princess in Alexander McQueen instead. But, god, it would have been so much cuter to have spent those euros on something fun like that pink striped wing chair I want from ABC Carpet & Home on Broadway.

"*Merci,*" said the stewardess, swiping the card. "You will be boarding in 'alf an 'our."

"Which gate, please?" I asked.

While she was checking, I gazed down the line of counters. A couple of desks down I spotted a familiar figure. I craned my neck to get a better look: it was Charlie Dunlain, checking in at the LA desk. Oh, god, I really didn't want him to see me. I *loathe* chance encounters, particularly with people who recently saw you when you'd just overdosed on Advil. Even worse, I suddenly noticed that Charlie was way cuter than I remembered. He looked tan and amazingly at ease with himself. He's like the only person I've ever heard of who actually looks better in airport lighting. That's success for you, I guess. Seeing him at that moment made me positively diabetic, I swear it. The shock made my blood sugar drop like crazy. Suddenly I felt giddy: maybe I was going to faint with embarrassment. I snapped my head back and stared in the other direction.

Still, this wasn't as bad as it could have been last night, I reminded myself. I mean, here I was, *not* in the WASPy iceberg dress, in a top-class outfit possibly slightly reminiscent of Lee Radziwill in Capri in the seventies, acting completely unsuicidal, totally normal, just taking a plane to New York like any normal, unsuicidal girl. Maybe I should say hello. Then I could leave and never speak to him again.

"Hi!" I called out, suddenly embarrassed. There. Done. So what if he hated me, I didn't care in the slightest. Charlie turned and looked at me. God, I felt faint again. Those Bellinis are so sneaky sometimes.

"Oh, hi, er . . ." he said awkwardly, and added, "I think someone wants you," gesturing toward the counter.

I turned back to find the stewardess glaring at me.

"Madame," she huffed, handing me back my credit card. "*Alors,* I regret you cannot travel. Your card has been denied."

"Can you try it again?" I asked anxiously.

"*Non*. Could you move aside please?"

Suddenly I felt really, really sorry for used-up supermodels. This must be exactly what it's like for them: one minute it's PJs everywhere, the next minute you can't even get arrested in coach. As I started to gather up my things, Charlie called out, "Hey, let me walk you to your gate. It's right next to the departure lounge for LA."

Eew, god. It's one thing being abandoned by a private jet. I would actually even say it's a positive learning experience. I mean, no one has to know, right? It's quite another being discovered smack-dab in the middle of the G-V abandonment process by someone you know. There was no way I could let Charlie find out I was ticketless and cashless. He'd be so disapproving. He sauntered over and picked up my bags.

"Wow, are they letting you take all this as hand baggage?" he asked.

"Of course," I said, as if I always take a suitcase and four shopping bags as carry-ons.

"Are you . . . okay?" said Charlie, looking concerned.

"Fine!" I replied. Surely Charlie's rave reviews in Cannes had obliterated all memory of the Advil incident.

"Really? I've been worried about you, after . . . Paris," he said awkwardly.

"I'm fine. Everything's great."

I don't tell lies, but when I do I am *très* convincing. We headed toward Departures. Inside, I was freaking. I mean, how a ticket was going to transpire between here and the boarding gate I knew not. I didn't want to be humiliated again in front of this man. If only Charlie wasn't such a gentleman, carrying my bags like someone out of *The Palm Beach Story,* I wouldn't have been in any risk of being found out. In the meantime, I tried to chitchat with him as if everything were as great as I was pretending it was.

"I'm glad you and Julie, you know, cleared up everything," I said.

"Yeah, we figured it out. What a girl. The incredible Julie!" he said with a fond smile.

She'd really done a number on him. He was totally into her. He didn't have a clue what she was really up to. None of her boyfriends ever did. You know what? With my sudden bout of hypoglycemia, combined with my Bellini headache, I felt a little sad for Charlie all of a sudden. I mean, he was probably an okay person, whether I disliked him or not. It's like that Thierry Mugler perfume, Angel; I loathe it, but it doesn't mean it's a bad perfume. I mean, millions of people think it smells totally awesome. I guess Charlie was my Angel, if there's such a thing as an analogy between men you hate and scents you hate.

We arrived at security. I couldn't get through without a boarding pass.

"Actually I'll say good-bye here," I said breezily. "I need to use the restroom."

"Have a safe flight," he replied, handing me my bags.

"Will do. Thank you."

Charlie turned toward the long security line. I'd done brilliantly. He had absolutely no idea about anything. I waited until he had walked away and then picked up my things and headed toward a café. There's nothing like a five-dollar orange pressé to really lift your spirits when you've been abandoned by a movie mogul and almost rescued by a patronizing and annoyingly cute movie director. I sat at the counter, dipped my head into my *International Herald Tribune*, sipped my juice, and wondered what on earth I was going to do. I think a little tear crept down my cheek. Now that I was alone, outfit or no outfit, I was miserable. I felt like a fool.

"Planning on missing your flight?"

He was back. What was wrong with the guy? Just because Charlie was dating Julie that gave him no right to interfere in my personal travel plans, or my personal suicide plans, for that matter. He stood there smiling at me as if my life were some kind of comedy or something.

"Yes," I snapped grumpily. I'd lied enough for one day. I didn't care what Charlie thought of me anymore.

"Why?" he asked.

"It's private," I answered.

"Are you all right?"

"Well, if you really want to know, I've been abandoned by some guy who brought me here on his G-V. There's no space in economy. The Air France people won't accept my credit card and my fiancé's already got another damn fiancée."

To my horror, a big fat tear rolled down my cheek.

Charlie passed me his handkerchief, and I grabbed it, furious he was witnessing another scene.

"Is this that Eduardo guy?" said Charlie.

"Eduardo's married!" I said, my voice cracking. "And so is Mr. G-V!"

Even though he was now armed with the pathetic truth about my lousy situation, Charlie still looked mildly amused.

"Well maybe this is good?" he said.

"It's not good, it's a tragedy," I said.

"It's good to learn not to take vacations with men you hardly know."

What was he talking about? I had known Patrick for at least twenty-four hours before I agreed to the Cannes trip. He had that look on his face again, as if I should know better. Maybe I should.

"Come on," he said. "You need to get on that plane."

Charlie rushed me back to the ticket desk, whipped out a credit card, and bought me a ticket then and there. He handed me my boarding pass and we went through security together. All the while I looked at the floor and walked in a state of embarrassed silence. At the gate, the last passengers were boarding the New York flight.

"Go on," he said, pushing me toward the door to the plane.

"Thanks. I'll pay you back," I said, mortified.

"Forget it. Chalk it up to experience. Just do me a favor, don't go accepting rides on private jets with married men, okay?"

I made my way onto the aircraft, livid. Charlie really didn't understand. It's physically impossible for a New York girl to turn down a ride on a private plane, ever.

Julie Bergdorf's Reading List

1. American Ballet Theatre fall benefit committee list. Julie says there's so many family intrigues going on there it's better than Tolstoy.

2. Ian McEwan's *Atonement,* specifically page 135. That's the hot sex scene.

3. *Vows* section of *Sunday Times*. It's important to know who's off the market.

4. Talking of markets, the FTSE 100 is why Julie loves the *Wall Street Journal.*

5. Barneys New York spring catalog.

6. Last ten pages of *The Corrections* by Jonathan Franzen. Julie's figured out that no one ever guesses she hasn't read the whole thing if she mentions Chip's relationship with the neurologist.

7. Running list for Michael Kors's fall show.

8. *The Drama of the Gifted Child,* by Alice Miller. It's really helped Julie not be so hard on herself for being so dramatic. She says it was almost compulsory reading at Spence.

9. Julie's address book. You wouldn't believe who's in there, and neither can she.

10. Paris couture schedule. It's useful to know it by heart.

9

Whenever a celebrated chef opens a new restaurant in New York, which is just about every five minutes as far as I can tell, the whole city gets pretty psyched. It's like all these girls who normally won't touch human food suddenly think eating is cool again. Most tastings are populated with razor-slim society girls who are determined to be seen at the tasting and taste nothing. Then they tell the chef how much they adore his new edibles and go back home and starve themselves for the rest of the night.

A few days after I'd gotten back from Cannes, Julie and I attended just such an event on the Lower East Side. China Bar is a retro-inspired Asian restaurant serving 1970s Chinese food in an ultra-modern space. Everyone told the chef that his deep fried duck ribs were "exquisite." They would. They hadn't tried them. Muffy went too far though. She told the celebrated chef "your wontons are better than at Mr. Chow's," which was just a total falsehood. I don't approve of lies, unless it's for a good cause like helping people. I mean Julie tells the best lies, like when she's raising money for her school's charity, she tells donors that, you know, Michael Douglas and Catherine Zeta-Jones are opening a new wing, when in actual fact *she's* opening the new wing. But telling an impressionable young cook he's a genius when his food should be at the bottom of the Hudson River is just plain cruel.

When we arrived the restaurant was so crowded with girls not eating and men not noticing them you could barely move. Julie whipped two saketinis (the new in drink—it's a cross between sake and a martini) off a tray and we grabbed a free booth.

"Hey sweetie, I'm sorry you saw that thing about Adriana and Zach," said Julie.

"Thanks," I said.

"Anyway, it proves he's completely fickle. Thank god you didn't marry him. So, tell me about Patrick," said Julie, changing the subject.

"I loved the du Cap, but . . ." I stopped mid-sentence. I hoped Charlie hadn't told Julie what had happened at the airport. I didn't want anyone knowing Patrick Saxton was such a hopeless date that he'd actually abandoned me on another continent. Luckily I didn't have to explain. Jolene interrupted us.

"He-e-e-y!!! How are you?"

Jolene had a Shanghai Cosmopolitan (the other new in drink in New York—it's a Chinese version of a Cosmopolitan) wobbling in one hand and was dragging Lara along with the other. Jolene was wearing tailored white pants that flared at the ankle and Lara was in a black minidress covered in zippers. Maybe she thought punk was back or something. Maybe it is. Lara looked bored but Jolene's face was pink with excitement.

"Michael Kors!" announced Jolene dramatically as she reached the table. "He!" Dramatic pause. "Is!" Another pause "GOD!!! Look! Have you seen his spring slouchy pants?" She spun around to show off her new silhouette. "It's the skinny-wide leg. Makes your legs look narrow without doing the Jappy skin-tight thing." (Jolene is 50 percent JAP but in 100 percent denial about it.)

"Michael Kors understands the inside of a woman's thigh," she went on, "like no other man I know—"

"Enough already, Jolene!" said Julie, exasperated. "You need to focus on something else. Like, what about reading something now and again?"

"I read all the time," said Jolene. "I would estimate I read *Vogue* magazine *at least* once a day. Anyone want another Shanghai Cosmo? Back in a minute," she said and flitted off. She was like a demented dragonfly tonight. Lara slid onto the seat next to me.

Julie looked irked.

"I swear I'll be committed if one more person mentions those new slouchy pants that they think they discovered before anyone else. There's nothing to say about those damn pants except go try them on," she complained.

She had a point. The chitchat at New York parties was so low-brow sometimes I could barely keep up. Julie's face suddenly brightened.

"Wait!" she cried. "I'm going to start a reading group, you know, a book club. It's the only way to improve Jolene's cotton wool brain. It would improve all of us."

"I just like going kickboxing at Equinox to improve myself," said Lara, grimacing.

"Exactly the problem," sighed Julie.

Jolene slipped back into the booth with another drink.

"Jolene, do you wanna join my book club?" shouted Julie over the din of the party.

"Is that like Oprah's Book Club?" Jolene replied enthusiastically.

"Not exactly. It's more like I'm going to hire a really cute brain-box NYU professor to teach us all about important literature. I wonder what we should read?"

"What about Virginia Woolf? She looked really good in that movie *The Hours*," said Jolene.

"No one is allowed to mention clothes if they come to my book club, Jolene. And that includes you, Lara," said Julie, shooting her a look. "They're only allowed to discuss books. Okay?"

"I totally get it," said Lara. "But is it okay to watch the movie of the book if you haven't got time to read the book of the book?"

"Has anyone ever told you you're *totally Dead Poets Society*?" said Julie.

She was perched bewitchingly on a stack of books in the office of Henry B. Hartnett, a young English lit teaching assistant at NYU. A few days after the China Bar party, Julie had called around the English department at NYU in search of a tutor. She was determined to start a book group, particularly after Muffy told her on the q-t that Gwendolyn Baines and Cynthia Kirk were planning to start one. Julie had to be first.

A little nervous, Julie had asked me to go with her to meet the NYU "professor" as she'd called him. Julie had come dressed as Sylvia Plath, in a box-pleat gingham skirt and a plait, after seeing Gwyneth Paltrow in the movie. She was even wearing flat shoes. I was shocked. I mean, until now Julie had always pretended she didn't know what flat shoes were. She had asked me to dress "academic" so that NYU would take us seriously. That morning I'd dutifully thrown on a navy blue vintage shirtwaist. The only thing was, I just couldn't resist adding black fishnets and red Christian Louboutin heels before I'd left the apartment that morning. Life is just too boring without the little fashion extras, isn't it?

Henry appeared to have little experience with young women, and even less with Park Avenue Princesses. He seemed bashful, keeping his distance behind a wide desk stacked with examination papers.

"Dead who?" said Henry, baffled.

"You're cute. I mean, in that brainy outfit you're wearing and being so shy, Professor," said Julie. Henry was cute, no argument. His "brainy" outfit consisted of worn-in cords, a linen jacket, and English brogues. His shirt was slightly fraying at the collar.

"Actually, I'm not a professor; I'm not tenured yet. I'm just an instructor. You're applying for school?"

"*Professor!* Do I look like a *student*? I don't wanna go to school, I wanna, like, improve myself, and my girlfriends, who need a lot of improvement, believe me. It's like all they can talk about is Michael Kors and what a genius he is and I can't stand it."

"Who?" said Henry.

"I'm *loving* that you don't know who Michael Kors is!" cried Julie. "Can you teach us about literature, and books? I live at The Pierre, it's real nice, I'll send a car for you, I'll take care of any expenses, I'll pay you whatever you ask. If you could just lend your mind for a few hours, we'd all really appreciate the improvement. Don't say no! Don't!"

Before Henry could reply, Julie continued, "And I could cater whatever you want. What do you think? Shall I get Elaine's to bring the eats? Would that be literary enough food for you?"

"I think some cheese and crackers is all you generally need."

"So you'll do it, Professor? Oh, I'm so, so happy."

"I'm not a professor, Miss Bergdorf."

"But you will be one day, right? I mean, I could get Daddy to get you promoted *right now* if you want, it's not like he isn't totally paying for this place already. Okay, so, I'll send someone to pick you up at six on Tuesday, which is a really good night for a book club because nothing ever happens on Tuesdays."

"There's just one more thing, Miss Bergdorf."

"Yes?"

"We need to decide what book you want to read. Because you all need to read it before Tuesday, so we can discuss it."

"Eew," said Julie. You could say there was a minor flag in her enthusiasm when faced with the reality of actually reading a whole book. "But that's what I need you for, to tell us what to read."

"A lot of people enjoy a book called *In the Heart of the Sea,* by Nathaniel Philbrick. I couldn't put it down," said Henry.

"Oh, a love story! Is it like that movie *Titanic*?"

"A little, but with sperm whales," said Henry. "If you like the *Titanic* story, you'll find this most appealing."

Patrick Saxton had been calling like a maniac since I got back from Cannes. He claimed that he'd left me at Nice airport for security reasons—apparently because of terrorism or something, your plane has to take off exactly when you said it would. I've always thought half the point of having a private jet is so you can take off whenever you like, or never take off at all if you suddenly didn't fancy it. According to Patrick this wasn't so.

"I begged the pilot to wait longer," said Patrick over the phone a few days later. "But French air traffic control wasn't allowing any waiting on the runway that day. I'm so sorry, I hope it wasn't too inconvenient for you. I was really worried about you."

Oops. Maybe Patrick was Mother Teresa after all.

"I'm sorry I was late. It was really dumb. But you could have left me a message," I said. Or a ticket.

"I tried! They wouldn't let me. I did book you onto the three o'clock to New York, though, I thought you'd just figure that out."

"You did?"

"Of course. I would never have left you there with no way home. What kind of a person do you think I am?"

"I'm sorry. I was totally freaked out and not thinking straight."

"I'd really like to see you again," he said.

"Well . . ." I trailed off. Did I want to see Patrick again? I guess I did. He was charming and fun and, once he was divorced, could be a prospect. "Maybe," I said. I didn't want to sound too keen.

"Great, I'll call you to arrange something. By the way, could you give me Jazz's mobile number?"

"*What?*" I said, unable to contain my disbelief.

"She left her passport on the plane. I've asked my assistant to messenger it back to her, but we don't know where she is."

Maybe Patrick was genuine. I couldn't tell anymore. I didn't reply for a few seconds. Anyway, the other line was beeping like crazy. I had to get Patrick off the phone.

"I've gotta go," I said, gave him Jazz's number, and switched lines. "Hello?"

"Hey, it's Jazz. We were so worried about you, what happened?"

"I got delayed, shopping for bikinis," I replied.

"You're just like me! I've missed so many flights because of shopping, you can't even imagine. God, Patrick was so mean not to wait. Still, he's the worst date in New York, so what can you expect?" said Jazz.

"He is?" I said. "Everyone says he's a saint."

"Listen, I've known Patrick forever. I've been dating him on and off since I was fifteen. It's fun, as long as you know he's taken. He's gorgeous, but he's married."

"Muffy said he is getting a divorce."

"He's been saying that to his girlfriends since the day he got engaged! His wife will never let him go, and he'll never leave her. She's the one with the money. It's her plane, not his. Everyone knows that."

"Oh," I said.

"They have an arrangement. No one gets Patrick Saxton. He likes it like that. Don't you adore married men? They don't hang around like lovesick puppy dogs."

"I guess that's one advantage," I replied.

"Anyway, do you have Patrick's new cell number? He asked me to the Venice film festival with him this fall—I'm definitely going. Don't you love that plane, with those pink gumdrops in the restroom? Of all my friends who go private, Patrick's plane is the best."

I gave Jazz the number and put down the receiver. If only I could be as superficial as Jazz, life would be a lot less trouble.

I never knew the "incredible pressure," as Julie described it, of inviting twelve of New York's wealthiest girls into your home until Julie dragged me into the paranoid world of dinner party décor. Honestly, she got so distraught organizing her book club meeting you would have thought she was planning the inaugural ball at the White House.

The minute she had invited everyone and sent them a copy of the book to read, Julie was besieged by a mountain of anxieties exclusive to the junior princess gang. She worried that her friends were only attending her book club in order to check out what Tracey Clarkson had done with her apartment. They would "dissect" her taste the minute they were out the door and probably criticize her "for not having something zebra. *Everyone* has a little zebra something in the house now," she said. She fretted that her friend Shelley—who always has a Royal Doulton bowl filled with perfectly ripe pomegranates perched on her coffee table to match the hand-painted Zuber wallpaper—would be unimpressed by her own bowl collection. Then there were the plates and espresso cups: she wanted to bring in that French fancy china that everyone else has, even though she didn't know the name of it and was too ashamed to ask. She'd heard that the in demi-tasse spoons were Buccellati's silver ones and wondered if she could get hold of any in time. She worried that the material on the bottom skirt of the sofa must be pulled tight down to the floor so that it didn't look like someone had just sat there, and wanted the cushions to be well plumped, but not overly plumped. Would her housekeeper's pressing skills be adequate when it came to starching her linen cocktail napkins? The sharpness of the corners of cocktail napkins are the standard by which New York hostesses are judged, she claimed, her face full of fear. She was even freaking out because some of the girls she had invited were not in the photo frames on her walls. If anyone were to notice this, it could precipitate severe social recriminations, like being excluded from certain high-profile baby showers.

She was a nervous wreck, and she hadn't even realized she didn't have anything to wear yet. Her friends only aggravated things.

"Wade Roper is so rich-person-passé," claimed Jolene authoritatively of one society florist. "How about using Martine Wrightman? Oh, but we'll never get her because we just never will."

"Don't get the invitations from Mrs. John L. Strong at Barneys, get them from Kate's Paperie and write them by hand. You want this to seem casual," said Mimi. "If you get them calligraphied it looks like you've got way too much time on your hands."

Julie called me weepily a few days before the party. "I can't cope," she said. "I wish I'd never even thought of this stupid book club. It's a big fat joke."

Although I secretly totally agreed, it was too late for Julie to get out of it now.

"I'll help you," I said, even though I didn't really have the extra time. I still had work to do on the Jazz story.

"I've heard that there's this new dinner party decorator everyone's been using in TriBeCa. He'll do something fun and crazy and no one will believe it. Shall I call him?"

"Okay. Can you get here in an hour?"

Before I managed to get a hold of Barclay Braithwaite, a young dinner décor designer just up from Alabama (all party organizers are always just up from Alabama, and they're always not straight), Mom called.

"Darling. I haven't heard from you at all. How are you?" she said.

"Oh, fine," I said, thinking, I'm about as far from fine as the moon is from Earth.

"You don't sound fine to me. You sound American. When are you coming home? We miss you."

"I'm not, Mom. I like it here."

"It's not Mom, it's *Mummy*. Now, I hope you are coming to your father's fiftieth. You know he's expecting you. Three weeks' time. I think it might be rather grand," whispered Mom. "Everyone in the county wants to be invited, so try not to spread it around too much. We don't want to upset the locals. You know how they get! It's too awful really, especially when you are after a new cleaning woman like I am. The Swyres may come if I can reach them. You don't know where I can get hold of them, do you? I would so love you and Little Earl to meet up again."

I couldn't believe Mom was still obsessing over the same issues she had been when I was six. She just doesn't realize that there are no knights in shining armor available, and I'm not after one anyway.

"I'd love to come to the party," I said. "I can't wait."

I meant it. I was suddenly hit by a pang of homesickness. Maybe it would do me good to drive down those English country lanes and see the hedgerows full of cow parsley again. I could even stay a few days at The Old Rectory and get some rest—although that might be difficult with Mom around.

❧

Julie was standing in the drawing room being fitted for a new pair of Rogan jeans by a tailor from Barneys when I arrived at her apartment. Barclay, dressed in his uniform of white jeans and pink Charvet shirt, was with me. I'd picked him up from his office in TriBeCa and we'd taken a taxi up to Julie's together.

"I know it's not about clothes, this whole reading thing, but I want to look casual, like I didn't think about clothes at all, which is why I'm getting the jeans done now, so I don't have to think about them," she said.

Sometimes I think Julie is more confused about life than Lara or Jolene, which makes her a very confused girl indeed. She turned to Barclay, beaming that gorgeous smile she saves for when she desperately needs something, saying, "Thank you, Barclay, for doing a party 911. I just want this event to be different. I want what no one else has ever had. How about it?"

"Can I have some iced water with rosemary please?" said Barclay. "They serve it at L'Ermitage at breakfast. Helps me think."

A few minutes later Barclay was perched on the edge of the sofa sipping his herb water as though it were the elixir of party planning. Decorating Julie Bergdorf's dinner, it soon became apparent, was going to make or break his career. He wanted it to be amusing, chic, and beautiful all in one go.

"I'm thinking, no more 'floral-floral.' Floral-floral has been done to death. For you Julie, I'm thinking ocean chic. For the hors d'oeuvres, lobster rolls, but shrunk. Tiny ones! Minuscule! The smallest, most darling lobster rolls in New York City. Then oysters, served on a real mother-of-pearl dish," said Barclay, scribbling on his notepad. "Now, if you just give me some time alone, I'll have a plan ready for you in a few minutes."

Barclay darted from the room. When he was out of earshot Julie whispered, "Have you heard the terrible news?"

"What's happened?" I said.

"It's Daphne. She called me from the Bel-Air yesterday. She's had to leave the house. Bradley's been having an affair with the decorator, and even though Daphne *loves* what the decorator did with the place in Beverly Hills, she feels ill whenever she stands on the Aubusson rug in the living room. Can you imagine, not being able to be around your own house? I feel so icky for her. I asked her if she wanted me to go out there and be with her, but she just said her yoga teacher was with her and that was enough. I'm worried about her; do you think I should go anyway?"

How grisly. Daphne had been such a perfect wife to Bradley, throwing him the best parties in Hollywood whenever he wanted and everything. When a girlfriend in crisis says she's okay, you must ignore her wishes and go straight to her side, regardless of how many yoga gurus she has at her disposal.

"Maybe we should both go," I said. "We could leave the morning after your book club."

Before Julie could answer, Barclay bounced back in. He said, "If you wanna get really wild, you keep the library serious, reading by the light of a sea lantern, and then you break out for dinner with this *fantasy* table," he said. "You walk into the dining room and splash! Coral! Driftwood! The table's covered with a cloth of *natural canvas!* I've never done anything but linen and lilies on the Upper East Side before. This could really shake things up. What about a centerpiece of Japanese fighting fish?"

"Great," said Julie. "But don't be too creative, Barclay, or everyone will guess it wasn't my idea."

"No one will ever know," he said, disappearing again.

Julie turned back to me. She said, "Anyway, Bradley says he wants Daphne back, but she's saying she wants to activate the pre-nup."

"No way," I said.

"I still think she should try and work it out. Bradley really adores her, he's just messed up, the bastard."

By the time Barclay got to the menu, he was so agitated he looked like a fighting fish himself. "For the diet crowd, when they get together, they don't want diet food—unless it's lunch," he said authoritatively.

Alarmed, Julie raised one beautifully waxed eyebrow. Diet food is the only food she understands.

"People want to feel safe and warm right now, protected. Have you seen what's going on in the world? It's ugly out there. I say, give those girls a good solid fish pie," said Barclay.

Julie gasped. Few of her girlfriends have ever been in physical contact with anything as substantial as a fish pie.

She only agreed to it because she thought it would really shock everyone.

After I'd dropped Barclay back at his office, I went home and called Daphne. She was going to be totally freaked out if Bradley really had done what Julie said.

"Get out!" said Daphne when she heard my voice. "It's so good to hear from you. How are you?"

"I'm good," I said. "But how are you?"

"I'm great!" said Daphne.

For a woman on the verge of marital collapse, Daphne sounded worryingly carefree. Maybe being at the Bel-Air was giving her a false sense of reality. It always does when I'm there, what with all those beautiful ponds and lily pads and swans rushing around everywhere.

"I heard what happened, with Bradley," I said. "Are you sure you're okay?"

"I freaked when I discovered he'd been doing the decorator—*in the inlaid bed I commissioned her to create, can you believe*—but since I've moved out, and come here, Bradley's all over me. He's been sending flowers, jewelry, fur coats—which is kinda sad actually because he should know that right now I'm a non-fur-wearing vegan—but you know, I think it shows a certain wish in him to repair the relationship. I want to be back with him. But I'm not gonna let him know that right away, naturally. Let him perspire a little first. I say, what's meant to be will be, and there's nothing you can do about it."

What had gotten into Daphne? Forget husbands, she virtually has a nervous breakdown if the pool boy leaves.

"Would you like us to come out there? We're really worried about you," I said.

"I'm fine. Wouldn't you be if you had the honeymoon suite at the Hotel Bel-Air?" she said. "You really don't need to come."

"Is anyone taking care of you? Looking after you?" I asked.

"Get out! Of course. Twenty-four-seven. I never knew I had so many friends. You know who's been the best though, like beyond sweet and kind when they really didn't need to?"

"Annie?" I said.

Annie is Daphne's best friend in Hollywood, even though Daphne says no one's really your friend in Hollywood.

"Noooo! No, *Annie*—the angel!—is taking care of *Bradley,* because Annie's husband Dominic is an agent at ICM and all Dominic wants is to be an agent at CAA and Annie knows Bradley can fix anything for anyone here if he wants to badly enough," she huffed.

I heard a sniffle and the rustle of Kleenex.

"So who's the saint then?" I said.

"There I was two days ago, sitting here with those swans driving me nuts with all their swimming around and Charlie comes by. He takes me to the Coffee Bean on Sunset for a nonfat soy Ice Blended Vanilla, which is like my favorite thing here—you have to try it—and tells me Bradley's a fool, that I'm a very special woman, and that Bradley never would have gotten where he has without me and then says what's meant to be will be. I don't think I know anyone in the movie business that goes around spontaneously comforting studio head's wives when they've got more to lose by supporting the wife than the studio head. He is *so nice,* it just made me feel so positive. I just feel, I can't explain it, really . . . happy," said Daphne, slightly giggly.

Daphne's never happy. She'd been brainwashed. She needed to leave town.

"Why don't you come to New York?" I said.

"Don't you think that's amazing for someone to be that kind?" said Daphne. "I mean, it was just so sweet."

"Julie's throwing a book club in a couple of days, she'd love you to come."

"Book club my ass!" cried Daphne with a laugh. "Those things are more like *Fight Club*. I'm staying here to figure things out with Bradley. I promise I'll call if anything happens. But isn't Charlie *sweet*?"

"I guess," I said reluctantly.

"Are *you* okay?" said Daphne.

"I'm great," I said.

"So I hear you've been in Cannes, with La Saxton. Is he as good in bed as everyone says?"

"Daphne! I haven't even kissed him. It was just a date."

"Get out! You know what they call him in LA?"

"What?"

"Patrick *Sex*ton. Isn't that genius!"

"I don't think he's my type."

"Get out! He's totally your type on a flirty, nonserious basis. Just watch out for the wife. She's a total psycho, especially if she thinks he likes someone for real. Listen, I'll be in touch, see ya!" said Daphne, and hung up.

Still to come for the *Essex* crew were the agonies of a mouth that has ceased to generate saliva. The tongue hard-

> ens into what McGee describes as "a senseless weight, swinging on the still-soft root and striking foreignly against the teeth." Speech becomes impossible, although sufferers are known to moan and bellow. Next is the "blood sweats" phase, involving "a progressive mummification of the initially living body." The tongue swells to such proportions that it squeezes past the jaws. The eyelids crack and the eyeballs begin to weep tears of blood. The throat is so swollen that breathing becomes difficult, creating an incongruous yet terrifying sensation of drowning. Finally as the sun inexorably draws the remaining moisture from the body, there is "living death."

In the Heart of the Sea wasn't exactly the Kate Winslet–Leonardo DiCaprio scenario I had been expecting. I didn't pick it up until late the night before Julie's book club. I read about half of it, and could barely sleep afterward. It's grisly as hell, all about the sinking of a Nantucket whaleship and how its crew survived by doing things like sucking the marrow from their dead shipmates' bones. It freaked me out even more than that Ethan Hawke movie with the plane crash where everyone cooks one another for breakfast. Gwendolyn Baines and Cynthia Kirk wouldn't get it at all. At six that evening Julie called, hysterical.

"Oh my god! I've just finished the book. How are we going to discuss what it's like for six men to survive on the blood of one tortoise while we're all sipping Sea Breezes?" cried Julie. "And the *placement's* driving me nuts. There's *nowhere* to put Jazz Conassey. She's slept with everyone's boyfriend or husband. Mimi can't talk to anyone unless they're pregnant, and Madeleine Kroft can't be around thin people or she flips out. Cynthia Kirk and Gwendolyn

Baines aren't speaking to each other because they're jointly chairing the American Ballet Theatre gala and they can't agree whose name should come first on the invitation. No one can sit next to anyone. And I'm so sleep-deprived I woke up this morning looking like Christina Ricci!!! Ee-oo-www . . ."

I couldn't totally focus on what Julie was saying. The real thing on my mind was Patrick Saxton. The conversation with Daphne had put things in perspective. Patrick was even more insidious than Eduardo or Zach: he was a professional playboy, a hopeless prospect for a girl like me. For a brief second I had an image of myself surrounded by ravenous, unreliable men on a sinking ship, but I shook myself out of it. Julie was the one who needed to be calmed down. I told her I was just leaving the house and would be with her in thirty minutes.

How many diamonds does it take to read a book? I asked myself as I scanned Julie's guests that night. Between the twelve girls at the book club, there must have been at least sixty carats of diamonds gathered in the library in Cartier stud earrings alone, maybe more. I mean, Shelley was wearing an ocean liner of a ring, a blue diamond that must have been ten carats at least. The only person who didn't look like she was off to a cocktail party was Julie. She was dressed as though for a weekend in Cape Cod in the Rogan jeans and a vintage sailor's smock. Her feet were bare and her toes were manicured a delicate shade of seaweed.

"I'm really worried about my girlfriends' minds. I don't

think any of them have gotten past page one," she whispered as I walked in. "I haven't improved them *at all*. I love my girls but their jewels are so . . . *tiresome*. Okay, let's sit."

The only thing that Julie usually found tiresome about jewels was not having enough new ones. Hopefully this was just a temporary lapse of her usual state of insanity.

Barclay had transformed the library into a glamorous take on a ship's cabin. Sea lanterns flickered as though there really were an ocean breeze blowing through the room. The table was spread with faded maps and antique logbooks. A waiter was handing out Blue Martinis and Mai Tais, plus cocktail napkins with corners so sharp a sailor could slit his throat with one. The girls were sitting in an oval. Henry was in a large armchair at one end. He was anxiously balancing a pile of books and notepads on his knee, nervously sipping his drink. Honestly, I think he would have been more comfortable in an electric chair.

Julie and I flopped onto the sofa. It would be good to forget everything and discuss the whalers' tragedy, sad though it was. A hush descended and Henry began.

"Well . . . here we are! W-w-welcome. This is a marvelous . . . um . . . book and I—excuse me—hope you all had time to read some of it . . . ," he said shyly.

Although I was of course concentrating *fully* on Henry's lecture, you could say 99.9 percent of the girls in the room were paying more attention to Henry's undeniable cuteness than his subject. Julie was literally mesmerized by him. Whispered snippets of conversation came into earshot.

"Do you think he's a *Hartnett* Hartnett?" hissed Jolene.

"Oh, go-o-d. As in the steel dynasty?" murmured Lara.

"Ye-e-e-s! They're like the Kennedys of the steel world.

You should marry him. One of us has to marry him," said Jolene in hushed tones.

Jolene hadn't remembered she was engaged for a really, really long time now. Henry was coming to the end of his talk. He turned to Jolene.

"So, um . . . Jolene? You seem to have a comment? Would you like to dive in, so to speak?" said Henry.

"Sure!" said Jolene enthusiastically. "Are you from the steel family?"

Henry shuffled his papers. He cleared his throat. He seemed embarrassed.

"It is the same branch of the family, yes. But we're not here to discuss that tonight. What would you like to talk about in the book?" he said.

"Well, in terms of *character analysis*," said Jolene *très* seriously, "and all that intellectual stuff, I'd just like to know whether, you know, when they make the movie of the book, do you think George Clooney or Brad Pitt should play Captain Pollard?"

"I'm not really, uh-hum, s-s-sure," said Henry. "Anyone else?"

Jazz Conassey waved from her seat.

"Hi. I'm Jazz-eee," she said flirtatiously. "I have a *proper* book question. You know that book, *A Heartbreaking Work of Staggering Genius*? Do you know if Dave Eggers, the author, is, like, single still?"

"Anyone else?" said Henry, perturbed.

"Could I ask a question about theme?" said Madeleine Kroft gravely. "Do you think you can lose weight by writing? Because it's like all those girl writers like Joan Didion and Zadie Smith and Donna Tartt are, like, skinnier than cigarettes."

Henry rubbed his forehead anxiously. There was a bleak silence.

"Henry, why don't you read a section of the book aloud? That might focus the discussion," said Julie.

"Excellent idea," said Henry. "If we could all turn to page 165."

He began to read:

> When the ship's carpenter died in the third week, one of the crew suggested that they use their shipmate's body for food—

"Shrimp puff, Henry?" said Jolene proffering a tray of delicate eats.

"No, no. Thank you. Shall I go on?"

"Oh, do," whispered Jolene. "Sorry. Sorry. Fascinating."

Henry continued:

> Captain Dean initially found the proposal to be "most grievous and shocking." Then, as they stood over the carpenter's dead body, a discussion ensued. "After abundance of mature thought and consultation about the lawfulness or sinfulness on the one hand, and the absolute necessity on the other," Dean wrote, "judgment, conscience, etc. were obliged to submit to the more prevailing arguments of our craving appetites—"

"Would you like to join my table at the American Ballet Theatre gala next week, Henry?" said Gwendolyn.

"I'm sorry, Henry's already taken," said Cynthia. "He's at my table. *Top* table."

"May we continue?" said Henry. He read on:

Dean, like most sailors forced to resort to cannibalism, began by removing the most obvious signs of the corpse's humanity—the head, hands, feet, and skin—

There was a loud thud from the other side of the table. Shelley had fainted, which wasn't much of a shock because she is always thinking of ingenious ways to attract attention.

"Oh my god!" shrieked Lara. "Quick! Someone call 911!"

Henry rushed over to the victim. He gently patted her face and she started to revive.

"I feel nauseous," said Gwendolyn, frantically fanning herself. "Can we get some air in here?"

"Shall we *all* go to the hospital?" said Jazz. "I've heard there are some really cute doctors in there."

Suddenly there wasn't a girl in the room who wasn't having some kind of anxiety attack or stomach disorder. Julie's book club had descended into chaos. It got so nuts in there I barely noticed my cell phone ringing. I grabbed it.

"Hello?" I said.

"This is Miriam Covington, I'm Gretchen Sallop-Saxton's personal assistant. I have Mrs. Saxton on the line. Putting you through."

I didn't get a chance to reply before Mrs. Saxton came on the line. She sounded clipped and stern.

"Hi. This is Gretchen Sallop-Saxton. You've been seeing my husband," she said.

"Nothing happened—" I said.

"Really. I can imagine. I hear Patrick's quite taken with you—this week. Just so you know, he dates a different actress or socialite or model every night. It's all completely meaningless to him. I hear you're husband-hunting. I want to make it completely clear: Patrick will never be anyone's husband but mine. At the end of the day, he's married to me."

There was a pause, as though Mrs. Saxton were reloading her gun with more ammunition. She continued, "Your boss is an extremely close personal friend of mine. She comes up to the house in Millbrook all the time. We often discuss staff changes. Jobs like yours are extremely precarious, aren't they?"

This was a clever move on Mrs. Saxton's part: my editor is allergic to New York girls who knowingly date married men. She won't have those sorts of girls in the office. You could say Mrs. Saxton had planted a land mine.

"Mrs. Saxton, I'm very sorry about the confusion," I said. "Patrick is just an acquaintance, that's all there is to it. Honestly. Please don't say anything to my boss."

"Stay away from him," she said coldly and hung up.

Mrs. Saxton had completely freaked me out. It definitely wasn't worth jeopardizing my job over Patrick Saxton. I had to get out of Julie's apartment and call him in private. This was serious. I didn't want anything more to do with him. I walked over to Julie, who was leaning over Shelley *à la* Florence Nightingale. Henry was looking on, concerned and rather impressed by Julie's nursing skills.

"Julie, I've got to go," I said.

"What's happened? You look terrible," she said.

"It's Mrs. Saxton. She's gone totally psycho on me. I've got to get hold of Patrick."

"You can't leave me here with these . . . *crazy* girls," whispered Julie, glancing around the room at her chaotic guests. "You need support. I'm coming with you. Why don't we go get a sneaky Bellini at Chip's first? That'll make you feel better."

"Julie, I can deal with this by myself," I said. "Look after your guests. Let's speak tomorrow."

I left the party and went straight home. There are some things in life that even a Bellini at Cipriani can't fix.

10

It's fair to say that Manhattan society girls are generally 100 percent allergic to the word *career*. It brings them out in a deep mauve rash, like anthrax or something. However, there is one career here to which they are positively addicted—if you could call it a career, that is—because it's the kind of career that doesn't involve much actual working, or ordering staples, or being handcuffed to a PC all day, or anything grim like that. The most coveted job here is to work as a "muse" to a fashion designer. The "chores" consist mainly of sitting home all day waiting for clothes to arrive by messenger and being photographed at glittering parties every night. This is what society girls do anyway, of course, but this way they can say, "It's really hard work" and no one can argue. Most muses favor party conversations that consist exclusively of the word "Great!" because you can smile prettily through one-syllable words which is *key* if you want to look your best in magazine pictures. The most professional muses stop talking completely to relax their face muscles when there's a photographer in the vicinity. Occasionally they get kidnapped and have to go live in Paris, like one poor American girl did recently for Mr. Ungaro. But it was worth it in the end because she got to be the official inspiration for Karl Lagerfeld, who, it is rumored, has a muse in every capital from Moscow to Madrid.

When Jazz Conassey called me a few days later to say she'd been asked to be a muse for Valentino, I wasn't surprised. I mean he hires a new one every five minutes. Still, I was thrilled for Jazz. She worships Valentino dresses more than life itself. Now she wouldn't have to pay retail for them. (Jazz's new career was secure, despite her entanglement with Patrick. Gretchen Sallop-Saxton would never harass the Conassey lumber heiress, which made me slightly envious—she'd certainly succeeded in rattling me. Anyway, Jazz was in such small need of work that she'd probably find Saxton-style threats little more than an amusing diversion from the daily grind as the Valentino girl.)

"I'll be at the bar at Plaza Athénée at ten o'clock tonight. Come and celebrate with me? Jolene and Lara are coming," said Jazz, who knew them from childhood vacations in Palm Beach. "I asked Julie but she can't make it. She's staying over in Connecticut and driving into town tomorrow morning."

"I don't know," I said listlessly.

The last few days didn't exactly make me feel like celebrating. Mrs. Sallop-Saxton had followed up her call with an attempt to destabilize my social life by trying to get me blacklisted from the Whitney after-party benefit committee, and spreading suggestive rumors about my trip to Cannes with Patrick. When I'd finally got hold of him after Julie's book group, he'd just laughed at his wife's behavior. He said she always made a fuss about his "friends," and that it meant nothing. He wanted us to meet again. Of course, I refused. It was very apparent to me that Patrick's "friends" were simply pawns in the power game being fought between him and his wife.

"Please don't call me again, Patrick," I said. "You're very nice but this is all way too complicated for me."

"Why don't you come to the Venice film festival with me this fall?" he said flirtatiously.

"Patrick! Jazz is going with you."

"I can chuck Jazz—she'd understand."

"Patrick! I'm not going anywhere with you. I can't."

"What about dinner tonight, at the Carlyle?"

"You have to leave me alone, okay?"

"Colorado for Christmas?"

"Patrick, I've gotta go," I said, hanging up.

I felt as though my protestations were falling on deaf ears, which worried me. Over the next few days I'd wondered what Gretchen Sallop-Saxton would do next, and how much Patrick was winding her up about me. I felt edgy and nervous, and slightly depressed. I just wanted the whole Patrick-Gretchen-*moi* thing to disappear.

"Pleeease come out tonight," persuaded Jazz. "It'll cheer you up. I told you, Patrick's just awful, but you can't take it too seriously. You've got to move on."

Maybe Jazz was right—a night with my friends might help. I didn't much want to go out that Sunday night, but I didn't want to stay home alone even more. Determined to cheer myself up, I told Jazz I would see her later. I threw on a black chiffon ruffled Zac Posen dress, pulled a lace shawl around my shoulders, and headed out.

With those heavenly leather chaises, old gilt mirrors, and yellow lamplight, the bar at the Plaza Athénée feels like a 1930s boudoir. Whenever I'm there I half expect to see Jean Harlow appear from behind a pillar smoking a bright purple Sobranie cigarette. Jolene, Lara, and Jazz—all in their "Vals" as they call their Valentino frocks—were sitting at a corner table like the chicest trio you can imagine when I arrived. Jazz looked spectacularly high-end in a simple black lace shift. It had a satin bow under the bust and splits at each side. Lara's and Jolene's dresses were pretty as well, but not a patch on Jazz's. It's protocol that the muse gets the best outfit and their friends have to look slightly less gorgeous, like ladies-in-waiting. They were all picking at the specialty of the house—miniature scoops of homemade ice cream. (Six weeks ago all New York girls thought ice cream would kill them. Now that everyone's into the Shore Club diet, it's suddenly slimming food.)

"Hey! Champagne cocktail? You look a-maaa-zing! How much do you *adore* my new bracelets?" said Jazz, jangling the gold bangles on her wrist. "Cartier. Next season. Aren't you loving them?"

"Loving," I said, sitting down next to her. "I'd adore some champagne right away."

That's the thing about reality. You can always block it out with a champagne cocktail and a detailed discussion about a Cartier bracelet if you really want to. You could say Gretchen Sallop-Saxton and the imminent end of my career and social life disappeared from my mind within minutes.

"Did Valentino send you a ton of free stuff?" asked Jolene.

"Well, *publicly,*" replied Jazz, "I'm saying no, because I don't want people to think I just took this job for the free clothes. But between us, I did get a *few* sneaky things. I'm loving the job, but *it's really hard work*. It makes me feel bad for all those girls on the Upper East Side who've got nothing to do but shop and go on vacation to St. Barths. It breaks my heart actually, because I used to be like that and I know how lonely it can be. I just want to help Mr. Valentino out. He's *so cute,* have you seen his hair?"

There is something surprisingly tiring about listening to a girl of leisure like Jazz examine the American work ethic. By midnight I decided to leave the three of them to it, and took a taxi home. They were going out dancing, but I felt too exhausted and fraught to join them. I really die over his frocks and everything, but I never wanted to hear the word *Valentino* again.

It was a relief to get back to my building. I couldn't wait to get inside, throw on my sweatpants, and curl up in bed. When I reached the door to my apartment I fumbled in my purse for my key. As I went to put it in the lock I noticed something strange. The door handle had come loose. It was barely hanging from its socket. Spooked, I looked closer. In the halflight, I could see that the lock had been pried away from the door. It was badly scratched and had a couple of small dents on the face. Someone had broken in.

Nervously, I peaked my head around the door. The whole place had been turned upside down. I quickly withdrew into the passage. Maybe someone was still inside, hiding. I couldn't risk going into the apartment. I pulled the door closed. Heading quickly back down the stairs, I fished in my little silver vintage purse for my cell—I had to call the police. Then, if I could reach Jazz and Co., I could sleep at one of their places. Damn, my cell wasn't in there! I must have left it at the bar. I rushed out into the street, anxiously looking behind me. I ran over to the phone booth on my corner and picked up the receiver. No dial tone. For a few seconds I stood there on the dark street wondering what I was going to do. I was panicked, desperate to be somewhere safe. New York can feel very threatening when no one's home and you've got nowhere to spend the night. A taxi turned into the street with its light on. I flagged it down. When I got in, I asked the driver to take me to the Mercer Hotel on the corner of Prince and Mercer Street. The police could wait until tomorrow. I was freaked out and tired, and all I wanted was to get to bed.

Listen, I didn't decide to check into the Mercer Hotel that night because of the four-hundred-thread-count pistachio-colored sheets, or because of the darling miniature margherita pizzas they do on room service, or because the busboys there are so hot it's beyond belief, or because everyone in the hotel has *that* look in their eye. None of that mattered: the issue was not luxury, it was security. I couldn't go to Julie's since she was outside the city, and the truth is there is nowhere more secure in downtown New York than the Mercer Hotel. I know that for a fact, because a lot of rap stars with major personal security issues, like Puff Daddy and Jay-Z, are always staying there and they feel *très* safe in that lobby.

It must have been after 1 AM by the time I reached the hotel. I love that the lobby's decorated like a huge, chic loft with whitewashed walls and all those Christian Liaigre sofas. You always see girls like Sofia Coppola or Chloë Sevigny just hanging there, as though it's their living room or something. Tonight the lobby was unusually quiet. The only people in there were a gamine young waitress—who will probably be a movie star one day—puffing up the cushions on the sofas and the concierge behind the reception desk.

"Good evening, miss. Can I help you?" said the concierge, who looked like he should be in a Tommy Hilfiger ad. He was so friendly I felt better already.

"I'd like a really quiet room, please," I said. "I need to get some sleep."

"Sure. How many nights will you be staying with us?"

"Just tonight." I sighed.

This had to be a one-night-only kind of thing. Twenty-four hours at the Mercer Hotel is a very expensive way to calm yourself down. The concierge tapped at his computer.

"You've got 607. You know, 606 and 607 are the sexiest suites in the hotel. You can have it at the regular double rate because it's so late. Calvin Klein lived up there for two years. It's the quietest room we have," he said. "Is this a fantastic night for you or what?!"

"Not really!" I said. "Can someone bring me up a cup of tea?"

"Room service is twenty-four hours. Any bags, miss?" asked the concierge.

"Just hand luggage," I said holding up my tiny silver vintage purse. "I travel light."

"Okay, here's your key." He handed me one of those high-tech plastic keys that look like a credit card. Then he said, "Why don't I order the tea for you now?"

"That would be so nice," I said.

I examined my face in the mirror as I was transported to the sixth floor in the elevator. God, I needed an Alpha-Beta peel, I thought. Even with the low lighting in there,

there were those traces of exhaustion around my eyes that you can't so much see as sense. I looked like I was over thirty-eight years old. My hair was limp. I pulled it back into a ponytail and regarded myself again. Frankly, there was zero improvement. God, I looked worse than Melanie Griffith does when she's caught without her makeup on.

When the elevator doors opened, I stepped out into that particular hush you only get in hotel corridors. There wasn't a sound, just the smooth quiet of sleep. The long corridor was lit by a soporific orange glow. I tiptoed right to the end, past room 606. Room 607 was the last door along. Bliss! Sleep was imminent. A minibar was also imminent, and those always make me feel better.

I pushed my plastic key into the slot under the handle on the door of room 607 and turned the handle. The door wouldn't open. I tried again. The door was defiantly rigid. God, maybe the hotel had made a mistake and Calvin Klein had never left or something. I'd have to go back down to the lobby. I turned and saw someone approaching. As he came closer, I could see it was a busboy with a silver tray. My tea! Heaven!

"Room 607?" said the busboy when he arrived.

"Yeah. I can't get in though. Can you unlock it for me?" I asked.

"Sure."

He pulled out his card and fed it into the slot and pushed on the handle. It didn't move. He frowned, sighing, "Sorry. I can't get in. I'll have to go get hotel security. I'll be back in five minutes."

He left the tray on the little side table outside the door and disappeared down the corridor. I looked at my watch: 2 AM. Tired and weak, I sank to the floor. I poured myself a cup of tea to kill the time. I took a sip. Ugh! It was tepid. There's something indescribably dismal about being all alone with a cup of cold tea in a deathly quiet hotel corridor. Where were those security guys? I would have to go back downstairs and track them down myself.

I placed my cup back on the tray and hauled myself off the floor. *Crash!* There was an almighty clatter of china as the tray and its contents hurtled to the floor. I heard a muffled noise from behind the door of 606. God, I thought, I hope I haven't disturbed whoever's having a very sexy time in that very sexy room.

I leaned down to clean up. The front of my dress pulled and I heard a loud rip: one of those stupid ruffles had gotten caught on the corner of the tray. The front of the dress was torn and the poor ruffle was dangling by a thread from its seam. (Those are chiffon frocks for you—invariably they're wrecked on the first wearing, which is why most New York girls don't count on them for the long term.) I unhooked myself and noticed that a damp patch of tea was spreading across my waist. Droplets of milk were trickling down my right thigh.

"Fuck fuck fuck fuck fuck!" I yelled, stamping my foot and kicking the lousy tray. I never swear, but when I do I really mean it.

Ooh, that felt really good. I kicked the tray again and collapsed on the floor in a horrible moody huff in the manner of Courtney Love. A tear rolled down my cheek and hit my lip. I hate tantrums, I really do. They're great fun at the beginning but they invariably end badly.

Can I admit something, very much on the d-l? I used to think that being somewhere chic with lots of room service and Christian Liaigre furniture makes you happy. It doesn't.

Honestly, if you're miserable, you're miserable, four-hundred-thread-count sheets or not. That's why you see all those paparazzi pics of celebrities hanging out on the backs of yachts, or leaving the lobbies of gorgeous apartment blocks looking like they're off to commit suicide or something. The fact is that when you're down, it doesn't matter how many Bellinis and ball gowns you have, it doesn't make a jot of difference. Chloé jeans and Alpha-Beta peels don't make the nasty things go away. You have to live with the nasty things forever, like Liza Minnelli does. To make matters worse, I was about to spend the night in the sexiest suite in the Mercer Hotel *on my own.* God, maybe life is more like *Fargo* than *High Society,* I thought. (I hope not though. I mean, I couldn't cope with all that snow and those bad clothes 24-7.)

I guess I was a few minutes into my major crying session when I heard a click from the next room. I stared with horror as the door of 606 inched open. No! It was two in the morning or something, I had probably disturbed someone's wedding night, or sexy affair, and I would never be allowed back. The door stopped moving when it was just ajar. There was no light on and I couldn't see inside. A sleepy voice emerged from behind the door, whispering, "Could you be quiet out there? I'm trying to sleep."

"Sorry," I whispered. "There's been a minor accident and I'm totally evacuating the area."

Then something odd happened. A chuckle came from inside the room.

"Hold on, I'm coming out," said the voice.

A nasty, niggling fear was creeping up on me: that voice sounded familiar. It sounded awfully like Charlie Dunlain. But it couldn't be. No. I heard some rustling, then a light came on and a head popped around the door. Eew. Just as I suspected, it was him. This was *so* not happening to me.

"Do I detect tears?" he asked.

His hair was disheveled from sleep and he blinked at the light. He seemed dozy but amused, and was dressed in a white terry robe and fuzzy hotel slippers. Actually, he looked adorable, but then everyone does in a hotel robe. Even if I was a little embarrassed that he'd shown up like a white knight in a white terry robe, I was sort of relieved it was Charlie and not some random rap star. I mean, he had a room, and no doubt he'd figure out how to get me into mine.

"No!" I hiccuped, hurriedly drying my eyes and wiping my nose.

"What's going on?" said Charlie.

"I'm waiting for security to let me into my room," I said.

"Why? Why aren't you home?"

"Why aren't *you* at home?" I retorted.

"I'm working here for a few days," he said. "But you live here. What are you staying in a hotel for?"

"Someone broke into the apartment. I was too scared to spend the night there and now I can't get into this damn room."

"You wanna come inside?" said Charlie, gazing down at me.

Unless I am very much mistaken, I could have sworn Charlie had *that* look in his eye.

My blood sugar dropped a mile, literally, just like it had when I'd seen Charlie at Nice airport. And then, the really weird thing was, I think, but I can't really remember exactly how or why, which is what happens to me on occasions like this, but I think *I* had *that* look in my eye too!

And I think he saw! And then out of nowhere I got *that* feeling, by which I mean the *do-you-have-condoms-because-I-want-to-go-to-Brazil-with-you-right-now* kind of feeling. (And I will even if you don't have condoms because I'm terrible like that. Don't tell a soul I said that or they'll all start harassing me about STDs.) Almost immediately I'd had the condom feeling I was hit by the *but-my-god-I-shouldn't-be-thinking-this-he's-my-b.f.'s-boyfriend-but-that-makes-it-all-the-more-insanely-tempting* feeling. If you've never had either feeling, I highly recommend them. The fact is, every girl should have one night they know they're really going to regret. It's always delicious, until the regret bit starts.

"Are you coming in?" he said again.

"Yes," I answered, melting quicker than a box of chocolates.

"I'll call down to reception and sort everything out," said Charlie, putting an arm around my shoulders.

If it's possible for a box of chocolates to melt twice in the space of ten minutes, then this one did.

"Okay," I whispered.

Once inside Charlie called reception. They told him security should be up "soon." Charlie's suite was super-cool. An airy bedroom opened onto a cavernous sitting room with huge arched windows that looked right onto Prince Street.

"Can I wash my face?" I said to Charlie.

"Sure," he replied.

I wandered into the bathroom. Lit by a single candle, it was spacious, with a square tub so large it was clear it had been specifically designed with regretful behavior in mind. I mean, why else make it the size of a small swimming pool? What was I thinking, I thought suddenly. I needed to pull myself together. Tonight must *not* be a night of regret, or Julie would strangle me with the chain of her Chanel purse, and then I'd regret a lot more than tonight. I flicked the light on. On the edge of the sink was a small white box with the words OVERNIGHT KIT written on it. I opened it. Inside was a packet of breath fresheners and a box of LifeStyle Ultra Sensitive condoms. I snapped it shut. God, no wonder everyone here has *that* look in their eye.

I found some soap and washed my face with cold water. I glanced at my reflection in the mirror. I didn't look as bad as I'd thought. In fact, I mused, there's something semi-glamorous about a ripped Zac Posen party dress. As I patted my face dry, I decided I would handle the situation in a very adult way. Charlie was like a fierce older brother who criticized everything I did. He was dating my best friend. Some things just aren't worth the regret.

I walked back into the room. Charlie was lying in bed watching TV. He looked outrageously cute. It wasn't safe to go near him. I went and sat on the sofa.

"Come over here. You look worn out. Let's watch a DVD until they sort out next door. I've got *Moulin Rouge*," he said.

I was safe. Charlie was gay. No straight man I know will watch *Moulin Rouge*, which, by the way, is one of my favorite movies of all time. Thank goodness there was no danger of any regret after all, even if I had been up for some.

"Okay," I said, curling up on the bed. "I love that film."

"I can't really handle it," said Charlie. "But I thought you'd like it."

Maybe I wasn't safe after all. He pressed PLAY on the remote.

"Hey, come here," said Charlie. "You need a snuggle."

I turned to face him. He put his arms around me. I don't think we watched any of *Moulin Rouge*.

❦

It's super-considerate of the Mercer Hotel to so thoughtfully provide guests with that gorgeous little Overnight Kit. The only trouble is, it inevitably precipitates *that* sort of night. (I blame hotel security—they never showed up.) I awoke early on the Monday to the lilac light of a Mercer morning. It was the beginning of a major Shame Attack. Last night I had knowingly broken the Two Commandments, the guiding principles by which all girls govern their love life:

#1. Thou shalt not sleep with someone on the first night (Having sex too early ruins a relationship.)
#2. Thou shalt not do #1 with thy best friend's boyfriend (Ruins three relationships.)

This was too icky for words. There I was, wildly underdressed, in bed with someone I shouldn't be. I must depart immediately, in the manner of Ingrid Bergman in the last scene of *Casablanca*. But, ooh! he looked so adorable asleep. Charlie has the longest eyelashes, yards of them. And his hair looks super-cute when he's slept on it. It actually looks better like that. I must remind him not to change it when he's awake. His eyes cracked half-open.

"Hi," he smiled at me.

He looked really, really amused, as usual. How men can be so lighthearted when they are conducting a highly illegal affair amazes me. Charlie obviously had some issues to deal with.

"Charlie—"

I was cut short by a very long kiss. The thing about kissing Charlie is that I completely forget whatever I am doing when the kissing starts because I get a fever of over 104 degrees. He's that good. The first time I kissed him last night (which was actually right during the credits for *Moulin Rouge* if I'm being totally honest), it felt like my body temperature would never get back down to 98.6. The thing about Charlie's particular way of kissing, if you want to get into the real detail, the fine print of it, which most of the girls I know generally do, is that each kiss lasts at least 125 seconds. You can imagine how exhausted I was the next morning. And that was just the kissing. The *really* regrettable stuff was a whole other story.

After about 450 seconds—that was a little too long, if I'm honest, I mean we all need oxygen—Charlie finally let me go. He lay back on the pillows.

"What were you saying?" he asked.

"I was saying . . ."

What do you say when you discover your best friend's boyfriend is cheating on her? With you.

"Charlie! You're Julie's boyfriend!" I yelled, jumping out of bed. "You're sleeping with someone else. I'm going to have to tell her. This is the worst!"

"What?" said Charlie, looking confused.

"You're cheating on her, you're an absolute hideous cheat. If Julie or I ever suspect our boyfriends are seeing someone else we tell each other. It's a pact."

Like United Nations resolutions, best-friend treaties

rarely allow for every eventuality. We hadn't decided what to do if the "someone else" was one of us. Even Kofi Annan couldn't have mediated this one.

"Julie and I broke up in Paris. You knew that. Come on," said Charlie. He seemed slightly annoyed.

"You *broke up* there? She e-mailed me from Paris saying, I think it was something like, how brilliantly it was all going with you. And then when I saw you at Nice airport you said you were with her."

"If I recall," said Charlie, "I think I said we figured it out. I assumed you knew we hadn't been seeing each other since Paris."

I was silent. What was I going to do? Even if Charlie wasn't officially dating Julie anymore this was still icky beyond belief. Clause (i) of the Second Commandment states that thou shalt not touch former boyfriends unless official permission has been granted.

"What am I going to say to Julie?" I cried.

"Nothing," said Charlie.

That's the wonderful thing about nights of regret. You both regret them so much no one else ever gets to know about them.

"Okay," I said.

"Now, get back in bed and let's order breakfast."

Two croissants, two café lattes, two hundred kisses, and an absolute minimum of two very regrettable orgasms later, we were well entrenched into the bed in 606. I felt giddy with happiness. An orgasm really is the answer to almost every problem in life. I honestly believe that if everyone was having orgasms regularly, there wouldn't be a Palestinian conflict. Seriously, no one would ever get out of bed in time for it.

By ten o'clock I was starting to worry that if I didn't get up soon, a night of regret, which was turning into a morning of regret, might turn into a day of regret, and then I'd *really* regret it. I had a lot to organize that morning—I had to contact the police about the break-in, clear up the mess, get the locks changed, and ages ago I'd promised Julie I'd go to a lunch with her. On top of that, Dad's birthday party was only a few days away and I had to prepare to go away the following Friday night.

As I was getting dressed—which took forever because I kept being interrupted by those 450-second kisses I told you about—Charlie's cell phone rang. He had just gone into the bathroom to shave.

"Shall I get that for you?" I called out.

"Please," he replied.

I picked up the phone.

"Hello?" I said.

"Hey, that's weird. Is that you?" It was Julie.

I froze. Why was Julie calling Charlie if they'd broken up?

"Julie?" I said.

"Yeah. What are you doing answering Charlie's phone?"

"Mmm . . . this isn't Charlie's phone. You called my phone by mistake."

"Oh, okay. See you at Sotheby's later?"

"Totally," I said, snapping the phone shut.

Almost immediately the phone rang again. An international number flashed up on caller ID: I didn't recognize it. I answered the call.

"Hello?" I said.

"Who's this?" said a low, husky female voice.

"I'm a friend of Charlie's."

"I need to speak to him."

"Can I tell him who's calling?" I asked.

"It's Caroline," she said.

"Let me go find him."

I went into the bathroom. Charlie had shaving foam all over his face. I put my hand over the phone and whispered to him, "It's a woman called Caroline wanting you."

"Oh . . . can you take a message?" he mumbled.

"Can I take a message," I said, "and he'll call you back."

I hung up. I know it was none of my business, but who on earth was Caroline? That's the trouble with having croissants in bed with someone fabulous: if another female's existence is even mentioned, you want to die on the spot.

Weeks ago Julie had press-ganged me into accepting an invitation to a "luncheon" at Sotheby's that day. It was being held to celebrate an upcoming auction of the Duchess of Windsor's jewelry collection. Sotheby's manages to find something, *anything,* once belonging to the Duchess to auction off every three months or so—furs, furniture, watercolors, hairpins, even her monogrammed Egyptian cotton handkerchiefs have made a sale. The auction house entices New York's wealthiest young girls to bid by inviting them to an exclusive private viewing over a lobster lunch. Someone in the Private Clients Department had brainwashed Julie into believing that not owning a piece of the Duchess's Cartier would be a regrettable tragedy from which she might never recover.

It was after midmorning by the time I'd gotten home from the Mercer, located my lost cell phone, spoken to the police, and sorted out the mess in the apartment. As far as I could tell, only one thing had been taken from the apartment—the chinchilla coat. It was disastrous—it wasn't even mine. Valentino would never lend me anything again after this. I'd read about couture burglaries in *New York* magazine, where thieves steal to order. Apparently it had happened to Diane Sawyer, who's famously chic, and now everyone on the Best Dressed List was terrified that their closets were going to be targeted too. I only had a few minutes to change for the lunch. I threw on a nipped-in linen jacket and a vintage lace skirt and by 12:45 I was in a taxi whizzing up to Sotheby's on York Avenue.

Just as I'd suspected, anxiety hit me hard as we swerved round the corner of Sixth Avenue and Twenty-third Street. Oh, the guilt after a night of regret! It's almost unbearable. Julie could never, ever find out about my one-night stand with Charlie. She was highly possessive about ex-boyfriends. I suspected Julie's revenge could be worse than Gretchen Sallop-Saxton's. When K. K. Adams ended up marrying a guy Julie dated for three days in eighth grade, Julie banned her from the salon at Bergdorf's for life. It was like the spa version of death row. Her hair never looked good after that, which was a terrible shame for K. K. If Julie ever found out about me and Charlie, she'd never speak to me again and I wouldn't get any of my clothes back I'd lent her. The only thing I could console myself with was the knowledge that last night would never ever be repeated. That's the good thing about one-night stands: by definition they're over immediately. Eventually, it's like it never happened at all. Strictly *entre nous*, I've had a few and I can't recall a thing about any of them.

❧

The Chanel pastel mafia were out in force at the lunch. There must have been twenty-five girls in the dining room seated at large round tables, which were groaning with floral center pieces decorated with pink diamonds, black pearls, and dark rubies. It is the custom at such lunches to drape the room in jewels, in the manner of Elizabeth Taylor's bedroom. I slipped into my seat next to Julie. She was wearing flip-flops, bright red Juicy sweat pants, and a pink Taavo T-shirt that read I AM NEW YORK in red glittery letters.

"This is so dull," she mouthed at me.

Our table wasn't exactly party central. The other four girls—Kimberley Guest, Amanda Fairchild, Sally Wentworth, and Lala Lucasini (I think she's a P.A.P. by way of Spain) were intently discussing the "torture" of getting out to Southampton on the L.I.E. with the summer traffic. Sometimes I feel really sorry for those girls; I mean, they're very sweet and all, but a lot of the time it's like they've forgotten they're not their mothers.

Julie turned to me and drew her finger across her throat. She doesn't understand why everyone freaks out about the Long Island Expressway when they could just take a helicopter like she does. She whispered, "I wish someone would do something crazy, like start a fight."

I laughed. Then she said, "So, I'm hooking up with Charlie this afternoon. He's so adorable!"

"*What?*" I said, incredulous.

"He's in town, we spoke earlier."

"But Julie, I thought you and Charlie had broken up."

"*What?*" she gasped. Now it was her turn to look incredulous.

"He told me he broke up with you in Paris."

"I don't believe it!" she said. "When did you speak to him?"

Without thinking, I said, "Last night."

Julie turned scarlet.

"It *was* you on his phone, wasn't it? You were with him this morning. I don't believe it!"

"What?" I said. There was a silence.

"You didn't," she said slowly.

"No!" I said, blushing furiously.

"You did. I can tell," said Julie. "You look exhausted and you've got The Glow."

Was it that obvious I'd had a 450-second kiss with someone of the opposite sex that morning? Julie is the queen of intuition. I would be too if I spent that much money on psychics. It's impossible to hide anything from her, particularly affairs of the heart.

"Did what?" asked Amanda politely.

"Nothing," I said.

"Slept with *my boyfriend*!" shrieked Julie.

Sally and Kimberly's forks, poised to plop a delicate slice of lobster into their mouths, jolted to a dramatic halt just in front of their lips. Their mouths were paralyzed wide open like two immaculate little black holes.

"Julie—" I said.

"How could you?" said Julie, furious. "I am never, ever speaking to you again. Or lending you any of my diamonds."

She stood up, slapped her napkin loudly on the table, and dramatically drew in a long breath. Then she announced, "Sally, Amanda, Lala, Kimberley. I'm leaving."

As Julie marched toward the exit all four girls rose and abandoned the table. The chatter in the room hushed. All eyes were fixed on Julie. As she reached the door, she turned and looked right at me, saying, "And by the way, you owe me my Versace pantsuit back."

This was weird, because it was actually my Versace pantsuit all along, it was just Julie really liked it and borrowed it all the time. I'd only just got it back from her. How could Charlie have been so dishonorable? How could I have been such a fool? Mind you, with my recent history with boyfriends I suppose I shouldn't have been too surprised.

"I'm just going . . . to the restroom," I said to no one in particular as I left the table.

The minute I was outside in the corridor I heard a crescendo of female babble explode. Julie was right. Now that someone had started a fight, the party was much more interesting.

I called Charlie at the Mercer the minute I was out of the building.

"Charlie!" I said when he picked up. "Why did you lie to me? Why did you say you'd broken up with Julie when you haven't? How *could* you!" I cried.

"Hey, calm down. I *have* broken up with Julie," he laughed.

Why did he find everything so funny all the time? It was sick.

"What are you talking about? Julie says you haven't broken up," I cried. I was furious with Charlie and even more furious with *moi*.

"You wanna know exactly what happened?" said Charlie.

"Yes, I do."

"In Paris, I told Julie that I didn't think we were very well suited, that Todd was more her thing, and we should just continue as friends. So she said no, she couldn't accept that. I think she said she wasn't allowing me to call it off, or something crazy like that. So I guess I said fine, but I am still calling it off and she said she wasn't. I didn't think she was serious; that's nutty behavior."

Admittedly that scenario sounded highly likely. The only person who does any breaking up around Julie is Julie. I don't recall anyone ever following through on an attempt to leave her. It's not worth the aggravation. Julie can be *très Fatal Attraction* when she puts her mind to it. Even if Charlie had broken up with her, Julie would never admit it to herself or anyone else. In Julie's mind Charlie was still her boyfriend, regardless of the fact that he didn't think she was his girlfriend any longer. That's what happens when you always get your own way like Julie: when you don't, you just pretend you have anyway, and it becomes reality. Although I felt Charlie's version of events was probably the real one, it was almost irrelevant whether the two of them were officially broken up or not: by Julie's reckoning, I had broken Commandment #2, which was unforgivable.

"She says she's never going to speak to me again," I said.

"She'll get over it. I can't understand why you told her anyway. She called me earlier and I didn't say a thing," said Charlie.

"She guessed. She said I looked exhausted."

"Do you fancy dinner?" asked Charlie. "It might be nice to get to know each other a little better. I only ever see you in, well, sort of *extreme* situations."

I knew what he meant. The idea was appealing. It felt safe and sexy at the same time, which was rather novel.

"I can't," I said immediately.

If you are going to turn down dinner with someone as adorable as Charlie, you have to do it right away, before you lose your nerve. And anyway, didn't Charlie understand that it's procedure that when a one-night stand is done, both parties are supposed to carry on as though nothing ever happened, regardless of any feelings? Dinner the following evening was not part of the arrangement—sadly.

"Well, I hope you change your mind. I'll be at the hotel all evening working. I'll be waiting for you."

I called Julie's apartment early that evening from home. I'd had a miserable afternoon, and I wanted my best friend back. I had to apologize. The housekeeper picked up the phone.

"Can I speak to Julie, please?" I asked.

"No, miss."

"It's really urgent. Is she there?"

"Yes, miss, but she told me that if you called, I had to tell you to return her suede Hogan bag."

"Oh, I see," I said sadly. I mean, I'd gotten really attached to that bag after all this time. "Could you tell her I called anyway?"

I collapsed on my bed, bleak. I'd been such an idiot and now I was paying for it. I was desperate for someone to talk to, but I couldn't face calling Lara or Jolene. They probably wouldn't speak to me anyway. No one was ever going to speak to me again when they found out what I'd done.

Everyone probably knew already anyway. A Sotheby's lunch is a more effective way of spreading gossip on the Upper East Side than a mass e-mail. I felt like I had nothing to look forward to, except possibly being friends with Madeleine Kroft, if she'd have me. I'm not a self-destructive person, but I was starting to feel like that demented Elizabeth Wurtzel from *Prozac Nation*.

The thing is, as I lay there on my bed, I started to wonder if one night of regret were to become two nights of regret, would it really be that much more regrettable than one night? Listen, I'd already broken the Second Commandment and there was no going back. It wasn't like I had any more best friends to lose, or could shock the Sotheby's crowd more than I already had at lunch. Things couldn't get worse, whatever I did. But I guess if I had to admit the real, truthful, serious reason I decided to surprise Charlie at the Mercer tonight, it was because last night had been the best sex of my life. I know Dr. Fensler had said that was a terrible omen and everything, but it's very, very hard to turn down dinner with the best sex of your life. In fact, the more dangerous it is, the less likely you are to reject it. And anyway, I was never, ever going to do it again, with him, after tonight, I swear it. I just really needed to cheer myself up.

I looked at my watch: 8 PM. I got up from the bed and browsed my closet. I selected the perfect Regrettable Night #2 Look—a red sundress by Cynthia Rowley. It's *très* appropriate for dinner with the best sex of your life because it comes off in less than three seconds, honestly. I slipped my feet into little white flip-flops, threw my hair in a ponytail, brushed my teeth, and left the apartment.

"Could you tell Charlie Dunlain that I'm here?" I said to the concierge when I arrived at the Mercer a little later. "He's in room 606."

"606?" said the concierge, tapping at his computer. "Ah . . . Mr. Dunlain. He's checked out."

Checked out? How could he do this to me? Didn't Charlie know that when a girl says no to dinner she means maybe, which means yes? Then I thought, *Caroline.* The girl who'd called earlier. My stomach felt like it had fallen thirty-six floors down an elevator shaft. I couldn't take another rejection now.

"Are you sure?" I asked. "He's meant to be working in his room. He asked me to meet him here."

"I checked him out myself. He left for Europe this afternoon."

"Is there a note?"

"I'm afraid not."

11

I knew I hadn't imagined my Mercer Hotel epiphany when I suddenly found myself turning down a ride on a PJ for absolutely no good reason. A few days later, just before I was due to fly to London for my dad's birthday, Patrick Saxton called. I had barely said hello before he was trying his G-V trick on me again.

"I'm going over to London tomorrow for the weekend," he said. "Why don't you come? No strings attached."

My general rule is that when you hear "no strings attached" it means ropes will be. Even though, as you know, turning down a ride on a PJ has historically been impossible for me, I went right ahead and did it. A ride on a private plane was not going to console me after the last few days.

"You know I can't, but thanks for the invitation," I said breezily. The night at the Mercer had changed everything.

"Don't you want to go to London? It's great over there," said Patrick.

"I'm already going to London tomorrow night, for my father's fiftieth."

"So, you go to the party, then you hang in my suite at Claridges. Then I'm popping down to Saint Tropez to check out a boat. I'm thinking of buying a Magnum 50. Apparently you can get ten supermodels *and* their legs in the back. Don't you fancy a spin along the Côte d'Azur? Then maybe we'll pop down to the Scalinatella, in Capri. It's my favorite hotel. Let me take you."

"I can't, I'm flying with someone else."

"Who?" said Patrick.

"American Airlines," I said proudly.

Even I was shocked by how easy it was to refuse Patrick's offer. I mean, I seemed to be a thoroughly reformed character already.

"You'd rather fly *commercial* than go with me?" said Patrick, alarmed.

"It's just it's better if I make my own way," I replied. I'm an independent girl, I thought—I don't need anything from a playboy like Patrick Saxton. "Hey, flying coach to London isn't the end of the world," I added.

Inside, the past few days had made me feel end of the world-ish, if you want to know the truth. The trouble with nights of regret is that the aftermath invariably consists of many days of regret, only minus the fun bits, like the best Brazil of your life and so on. What was strange was that I felt let down in a way I never did with other cute guys. It was like I'd found someone who I had the greatest Brazil with but who felt as cozy as my oldest friend. I didn't hear a peep from Charlie, which was slightly mortifying. I'd always thought Charlie had good manners.

Still, if he didn't care to call me, I decided, then I didn't care to call him.

Meanwhile, Julie didn't return my messages. Jolene said I shouldn't take it personally. She reported that Julie had disappeared off on a romantic trip, was madly in love, and wasn't telling anyone who he was. She wasn't returning anyone's calls, even her dermatologist's, which was a first for Julie. I didn't believe Jolene. The fact was, I had been a lousy friend to Julie and deserved every bit of punishment I got.

Mom called later that night after I'd spoken to Patrick. It was late and I was tired. It must have been three in the morning in England but Mom sounded wide awake. Even though I was looking forward to the visit, the call set me on edge.

"Darling!" she cried excitedly when I picked up. "I hope you haven't forgotten your father's birthday. I've left Julie Bergdorf three messages inviting her—you know how Daddy adores her—and she still hasn't called back. Is she coming?"

"I've no idea, Mom," I replied.

"What is the matter with you? How long are you staying?"

"I get in Saturday and I have to leave Monday. I've got a story next week."

"Only three days! If you keep on working like this you are going to turn into Barry Diller! A career isn't everything, you know. Anyway I have the most marvelous sheets for you in the spare bedroom. Irish linen puts Pratesi to shame. Americans simply do not understand linen like us—"

"Mom, you are an American," I reminded her.

"I'm an English lady trapped in an American woman's

body, like a transsexual, that's what my yoga teacher says. Now, I've heard the family is back, which is such good timing, isn't it?"

"What family, Mom?"

"The Swyres, dear. I thought you might want to meet up with Little Earl while you're over. Everyone says he's *charmant* and more handsome than Prince William and Prince Harry put together."

Sometimes I wonder if I can get a divorce from Mom. I could cite irreconcilable differences over relations with our neighbor. Apparently Drew Barrymore did that and she turned out really well.

"Mom, we're not exactly b.f.'s with the Swyres, remember?"

"Darling, I do not want you missing your chance with him again."

"There are other things in life apart from finding a man to think about," I said, exasperated. (Like most other girls in New York, I have to confess on the very, very q-t that it is *all* we think about 95 percent of the time. We just don't admit it in public. It's way more acceptable to say you worry about your career all the time. Although I generally find the more career a girl has, the more man she thinks about.)

"I'm doing a tent in the garden, like Jackie Kennedy used to do on the White House lawn. Lord and Lady Finoulla have accepted, so I'm thrilled to bits. The forecast's for rain but it's always wrong."

Mom is the queen of denial. It's rained every year for my dad's birthday. It always pours on everyone's birthday in England, even the Queen's.

"Okay, Mom. See you Saturday night. I'm renting a car

at Heathrow and I'll drive straight down. I guess I'll be with you mid-afternoon."

"Wonderful. And please do wear makeup for the party—that nice foundation I got you from Lancôme that Isabella Rossellini likes. Dad will be so disappointed otherwise."

"I'll try," I lied. Mom still hasn't realized that the only person apart from her who still wears foundation in the day is Joan Collins.

The next morning as I packed my bag for England I realized I had to pull myself together. However lousy things seemed, I couldn't show up at Dad's party in a depressed sulk. It was too selfish. I mean, that's the kind of thing Naomi Campbell does but she can get away with it because she's got a size-2-body. I'd behaved rashly that night in the Mercer, driven by desperation, insecurity, and a total lack of recent orgasms. Now I had to pay for it. I had somehow contrived to date one brute, one congenital liar, and a professional lothario with a Glenn Close wife. Then to top it all off, I'd slept with my best friend's ex-boyfriend, who had promptly vanished into thin air. I was destined for the solitary life—well, for the next week or so. I tried to be positive. Hopefully, Julie and I would make up soon—she'd want to borrow that Versace pantsuit again one day, I was sure of it. As I rode out to JFK to catch my plane that Friday evening, I resolved to be cheerful about what I had, rather than miserable about what I didn't. I mean, most girls would die to own as much Marc Jacobs as me.

There is nothing like being stuck in line at security at JFK Airport at ten in the evening behind a man who is inexplicably travelling with four laptop computers—each of which has to be unzipped, placed in a separate plastic tray, scanned, investigated, and then repacked—to really send your spirits plummeting. Moments like this can make a girl wish she hadn't reformed herself after all. If you are going to reform yourself, be selective: there are some bad habits that, for purely practical reasons, should be hung on to. Turning down rides on private planes is *très* foolish. Take it from me, one should never do it.

I arrived at Heathrow at 11 AM the next morning. Before I went to the Hertz desk to pick up my rental car, I snuck into the restroom to change. I wasn't planning on showing up at home looking as rejected as I felt inside. Paying attention to personal grooming while you are recovering from a one-night stand can improve things immensely. I mean, look at Elizabeth Hurley, her eyebrows get more genius with every breakup. She always looks her best when arriving at English countryside locations for pointless high-profile events like polo games or cricket matches starring Hugh Grant. Inspired by her, I locked myself into a stall and changed into a superfine cashmere orange tee (DKNY) and skinny cream pants (Joie). Accessorized with a tan leather belt, plain gold drop earrings, pale turquoise Jimmy Choo sandals with a delicate gold kitten heel, and a squashy canvas zebra stripe shoulder bag, I thought the look exuded casual, Liz-ish glamour. No one would know I'd obsessed about it for three whole days back in New York.

The clothes weren't exactly 100 percent practical for the English countryside, but then I wasn't planning on actually setting foot in the English countryside while I was in it. The only danger to my shoes, which was negligible, would be the short walk from my rental car to the house. Mom had

Tarmac'd the drive in front of The Old Rectory years ago when she had realized that even if gravel driveways were *très* English and all that, and considered way classier than Tarmac ones by her peers, they were murder on her favorite tan-and-cream Chanel pumps.

❦

There is nothing in the world—even the infinity pool at the Hotel du Cap—that compares with England on a warm summer's day. Except perhaps Macaroni Beach in Mustique, but that's a whole other scenario.

Two hours later I found myself heading off the motorway in my tiny rented Renault Clio toward our village, Stibbly, which is accessible only by narrow, winding lanes. They were wildly overgrown with cow parsley and bramble bushes, which brushed against my side-view mirrors. The British are not into anything manicured—their hedgerows or their nails. I drove past crumbling farm walls and into little villages with thatched cottages, each with a more impressive herbaceous border than the last. Herbaceous borders are an English obsession. They devote whole sections of Sunday newspapers to them, honestly. The only thing that wasn't picturesque along the drive was the occasional notice reading PUBLIC TOILETS with an arrow pointing towards a grubby portapotty.

By two o'clock in the afternoon I was about fifteen miles from home. A roadside sign read WELCOME TO THE PARISH OF STIBBLY-ON-THE-WOLD. The countryside looked wonderfully pretty, as ever, except for a familiar gloomy, run-down building that was once a Victorian hospital marring the view. A board on the gate stated ST. AGNES'

REFUGE FOR WOMEN. The place has been used as a safe house for battered wives and single moms for years. When I was a kid I'd see the girls drifting aimlessly around the village. Easy targets, they were unfairly blamed for every ill that befell Stibbly, even the weather vane falling off the church spire.

A couple of miles on I slowed down while I took a particularly sharp bend in the lane. The Renault Clio juddered and suddenly stalled. I put on the handbrake, set the car in neutral, and turned the key in the ignition. The engine turned over and over, but it wouldn't start. I tried again. Same thing. I think I must have tried to get moving for at least the next ten minutes, to no avail.

Defeated, I let the car roll as far as it could onto the grass verge. I got out and sat slumped on the hood in a moody, Kelly Osbourne–style huff. How was I going to get home? My cell phone didn't work here (*God I must get Tri-Band,* I thought, irritated) and I couldn't see a house or any sign of life in any direction. The only sound was the rustle of the fields of wheat as it swayed gently in the wind. It's at moments like this that a girl can really regret *not* being squashed between two supermodels on the back of Patrick Saxton's Magnum speedboat, even if the supermodels are the annoying kind who keep going on about how "fat" they are. Still, I reminded myself, I'd turned over a new leaf: I guess I'd have to start walking.

I put on my sunglasses, grabbed my bag from the front seat, locked the car, and started to stomp down the hill. *God I bet Elizabeth Hurley never breaks down in the English countryside,* I thought as I walked. You don't get to be the face of Estée Lauder by being the kind of idiot who relies on Hertz for important transportation. She probably gets to the English countryside in ten seconds by helicopter. I had gone only a few yards when I heard the sound of an engine. An old tractor was chugging slowly down the hill pulling a trailer loaded with livestock. A young guy was driving. Maybe I could persuade him to drive me home. As he approached I flagged him down. The vehicle came to a creaky halt beside me. I noticed it had a layer of dust and bits of hay covering its flaky blue paint.

"A'right there?" said the boy.

God he was cute. He had dark curly hair and was wearing a red T-shirt, muddy jeans, and old hiking boots. He was totally giving Orlando Bloom. My Kelly Osbourne huff disappeared *immediately,* you can imagine.

"I'm good," I said, smiling. I couldn't think of anything to say.

"Broken down?"

"Yeah," I said, twisting my hair. I know Mr. Farmhand couldn't have been more than nineteen, but I couldn't resist having a light flirt with him. (As opposed to a heavy flirt, when you know something's going to happen, and you've had the Brazilian bikini wax in advance and everything.)

"Need help?" he said. God I adore English boys who talk in two word sentences. It reminds me of Heathcliff or something.

"Could you give me a ride home?"

"Where to?"

"The Old Rectory. It's in Stibbly."

"Bit far. The heifers," he said, gesturing at the trailer. "But I can drop you by the farm. They'll let you use the phone."

"Okay," I said. I guess Dad could come and pick me up.

Orlando—whose actual real name was Dave, but I prefer to think of him as Orlando—put out his hand and helped me up onto the tractor seat beside him. He lit a roll up, turned the engine on, and we chugged off. All I can say is this: thank goodness for Hertz and their useless rental cars. I was so happy sitting there next to him that I barely noticed that my lovely cream pants now had an oily smudge across them where Dave had pulled me up onto the tractor, or that my feet were resting on a bale of hay, covering my gorgeous shoes in dust.

A couple of miles on Dave pulled up in front of a stile. A footpath wiggled away from it up a little hill. Absolutely no mention of a farm. The only sign of life was a herd of sheep grazing in the meadow.

"Farm's up there," said Dave, nodding his head in the direction of the hill. "Five hundred yards."

"Eew," I said. Dave obviously had no idea about Jimmy Choos. You can walk five yards in them, not five hundred.

"A'right?"

"Sure," I said reluctantly, slipping down from the tractor seat. "Thanks."

Dave drove off, and I clambered over the stile. As I dropped over the other side, there was a squelching sound. I looked down. My darling shoes had a rim of black, peaty mush around the edge of the soles. That's the thing Americans don't realize about England. Even on a hot day, there are invisible bogs everywhere. It's like the place looks really cute, but in reality it's a minefield for shoes. The fact is it's a lot more like *Wuthering Heights* there than *Emma* most of the time. *God,* I thought as I puffed up the hill, *I take it back, I really do, about how the English countryside is better than the du Cap. It isn't.* I never wanted to set foot in it again.

At the top I came to a wooden gate and a fork in the

path. Below me a river snaked its way through a little valley speckled with copses and woolly clusters of sheep. In the distance to the right I could make out barns and farm outbuildings. To my left a large house sat nestled in a green stretch of parkland. Swyre Castle, I thought. The adjoining farm must be part of the estate. I have to say, the place was totally giving *Gosford Park*. I mean, it was way better than I remembered it as a kid. Of course, it doesn't look much like a castle at all, it looks like a regular mansion, but that's the thing about England. No one just calls their house a house, it has to be hall, park, palace, castle. I think they do it to confuse foreigners.

Swyre Castle was so pretty, I could *almost* imagine losing my country-house phobia over it. Built of honey-colored stone, it's one of those immaculate eighteenth-century Palladian English houses—you know, the ones that look like a perfect giant doll's house, only with two large wings attached. In the distance I could make out a lake and formal gardens. You know what? For the few minutes I stood gazing at the castle, I could almost sympathize with the Brown Signers. (There's still a ton of them in New York and Paris, it's just now they mainly pose as fashion designers for Louis Vuitton. It's really good cover.)

Mom and Dad must have been wondering where I was by now. I looked back at the farm buildings again. They looked a little nearer than the castle, but for a girl like me, if it's a choice between a muddy farmyard and a castle, I'll always take the castle. Despite the fact that Mom had bored me about the place for twenty years, I guess I was still curious. I could ask to use the phone there and, while I was waiting for Dad to pick me up, have a sneak peak. No one had to know I was me, I mean in that I didn't have to let on that I was the daughter of the neighbor with the dodgy Chippendales from all that time ago.

I turned and walked down the little dirt track toward the castle. Maybe I'll bump into the Little Earl, I thought. I didn't care anymore. He was probably balding and wore those awful bright pink cords and polka dot socks so beloved of the toff crowd. The path soon joined the gravel drive, and I crunched my way up it, navigating a cattle grid on the way (*très* difficult in Jimmy Choos, but doable, in case you were wondering). The grounds were gorgeous. God I totally worship English parks by Capability Brown, don't you?

When I reached the main entrance of the house I noticed a coat of arms painted above it in gold and blue. That's the thing about the British upper classes. Just in case you aren't intimidated enough already, they go and do the coat of arms thing just to really freak you out. No wonder no one in England has any self-esteem. I grabbed the gargoyle-shaped iron knocker and rapped nervously on the front door.

I stood there for a few minutes with the gargoyle glaring at me. No one came. Maybe no one was home. There were no cars in the driveway, though that didn't mean anything—Brits obsessively hide their cars in stable blocks and barns, even the really nice ones like Audis, so as not to be accused of either a) marring the view or b) showing off. I knocked again, louder this time. Still, no one came.

I couldn't deal with the idea of walking over to the farm now. As usual, my Jimmy Choos had completely cut off the blood supply to my feet and I could barely feel them anymore. I grabbed the door handle and turned it. I wasn't surprised when it opened. Toffs always leave the front door unlocked, like they're living on Cape Cod or something.

I walked into a cavernous hall. The room was thick with moldings and cornicing. I felt like I was inside a wedding cake. God, I thought, keeping this place clean would drive Martha Stewart out of her mind with worry.

"Hello?" I called out. "Anyone home?"

While I waited I kicked off my shoes. The stone floor felt deliciously cool against my swollen feet. The only sound was the sharp tick of a gold clock above the fireplace. No one appeared. I guess the house was so large and must have had so many entrances and exits that, even if anyone was home, the Swyres wouldn't necessarily know who was coming in and out. It must be a bit like living on the Syrian border, only with less terrorists.

Maybe I could find a phone by myself. And get a private tour. I opened a paneled door to the left of the hall into an ornate dining room. The walls were lined with family portraits. The faces, porcelain white, loomed like ghosts, they were so pale. They really needed a fake bake. Sometimes I wonder how those girls survived the deprivations of the eighteenth century. I mean, how did women cope without Bobbi Brown bronzer and Lancôme's Juicy Tubes for lips in twelve shades? The only sign that I wasn't in 1760 was the overhead projector and screen at one end of the room—this must have been the "conference center."

I was getting sidetracked. I needed to find a telephone. I went back into the hall. A red cord was hung across the staircase with a sign reading PRIVATE on it, I guess to keep the conference people out. You know me. If I see a velvet rope I have to be on the right side of it. I slipped underneath and zipped up the stairs. Maybe there would be a study up there with a phone.

On the landing I was faced with a long corridor of doors.

I opened the first one. Inside was a four-poster bed draped with fringed Chinese silks. I snuck inside. Hidden behind the bed's drapes was a small painting of a flower-strewn maiden. It looked exactly like the Fragonards in the Frick. It was probably real, I thought. Sleeping under your Old Master is exactly the sort of thing a rich British Lord would do.

The last room along the passage was a grand library. I slipped inside. There was bound to be a telephone in here, I thought. I wanted to get home now. The back wall was lined with shelves of leather-bound books, and a huge marble fireplace at one end had an Italian landscape painting hanging above it. Underneath was a little gold tag reading *Canaletto*. I don't get it, I really don't. English people go on and on about how over the top Americans are, when all along they're secretly living like they're at the Bellagio in Las Vegas or something.

At the other end of the room a grand piano was covered in old black-and-white family photographs, and a large walnut desk was piled high with papers. I could see an old-fashioned black telephone peeking out from under the mess. I walked over to the desk and picked up the phone.

As I dialed Mom and Dad's number, a little oval-shaped gold pillbox on a side table caught my eye. An English battle scene was painted on the enameled top in tiny detail. I picked it up, examining the jeweled clasp. The table was covered with at least a dozen other little jeweled pots and ornaments. I'm telling you, British people have the best tchotchkes, no argument. The phone rang and rang. Why wasn't anyone picking up?

"Can I help you?" said an English voice from behind me.

I jumped and dropped the receiver. A stooped old man stepped before me. His face was so riven with lines he looked more antiquated than anything in the house. He was wearing a shabby black jacket and pinstriped pants. It's good to know there are some people J. Crew will never reach. I didn't want him to see the little box in my hand. I slipped it into my pocket. I could put it back later.

"Oh, hello," I gasped breathlessly. "Who are you?"

"I'm butler to the Swyre family. What exactly are you doing?" He looked me up and down suspiciously, staring disapprovingly at my filthy bare feet.

"Gosh, well, my car's broken down in the lane and I was looking for a telephone," I said, nervously picking up the receiver from the floor. "My mom and dad live at The Old Rectory."

"I must inform Lord Swyre. Wait here," he said and swiftly exited the room.

As he shut the door, I heard a key turn in the lock. My god, he thought I was stealing or something. I grabbed the phone and dialed home again. This time someone picked up on the first ring.

"Mom?" I said.

"*Hey boo!* How are ya, dude?"

"Julie?" I asked.

"It's so cute being in the British countryside but the English people I met in London are real scary. Those people have no idea who Barbara Walters is or anything. Can you imagine, I'm at your folks' place?"

What about our argument? And Julie's secret romance?

"You came for my dad's party?" I asked, amazed.

"Well, I didn't *only* come for the party. You're never gonna believe it. I came for a wedding-dress fitting! With Alexander McQueen *himself*. Then your mom called and persuaded me to come to your dad's freaking party."

"You're getting married? Who to?"

"Henry Hartnett. You'll never guess what happened. He took me for a Bellini after the book club, and we've been together ever since. I've dropped all the other boyfriends, even Todd, poor thing. Henry's so cute and so rich, it's beyond—he's Hartnett Steel but he's real shy about it. He thinks I'm the funniest thing ever. You've no idea how much we've got in common. Where the hell are you? We're all waiting. By the way, I'm talking to you again. I totally forgive you for everything."

I'll say this for Julie. She can be amazingly graceful about her friends' misdemeanors, considering how spoiled she is. That's the sweet thing about her. Her ADD is so bad she's physically incapable of holding a grudge longer than a few days.

"Congratulations! Tell Dad I'm at the castle and he needs to come and get me."

"You're at that place next door? Oh god, I'm so jealous. Is the interior decoration awesome? Or is it totally icky like Buckingham Palace? I heard the royal family has the worst taste."

"Julie! Just get Dad here. My car's conked out and I broke in here to make a phone call and now they think I'm robbing them."

"Have they got Delft china everywhere and footmen?"

"Julie!"

"Okay dude, whatever. I'll tell him. By the way, the wedding's next summer—June 14. You have to be my maid of honor."

I put the phone down. Julie was engaged? With a wedding date? Don't engaged people know that it's bad enough for the unengaged among us, without them *immediately* announcing a wedding just to really pile on the agony? This was all very sudden. I hoped she was doing the right thing. I went over to the locked door and twisted hopelessly at the handle. Eventually I gave up and sat on the little tapestried ottoman by the door. I tensed and put my ear to the keyhole. I could only make out a few words from the butler: ". . . says her car's broken down . . . looks like a gypsy . . . terrible dirty clothes, probably one of those battered single mothers from the Refuge . . . not even shoes on her feet . . ."

I looked down at my grimy clothes and my filthy bare feet. It was sad, really. I mean, I was quite glamorous once. Liz Hurley would never let herself go like this during one trip to the countryside.

". . . she must have broken in . . . I've called the police. I'm sorry, sir."

The police? I started rapping at the door.

"Hey! Let me out!" I yelled.

After a couple of minutes a key turned in the lock. Honestly, I swear you are not going to believe what happened next. It's like Michael Jackson denying he's had plastic surgery or something. In walks the butler and—I promise I am not making this up—Charlie Dunlain strolls in right behind him. That's the thing about one-night stands, you think you want to see them again but when you do it's always icky beyond belief, particularly if the last time you spoke to them properly they had their head in the same place Chad did all that time ago. What made it even ickier was that Charlie still looked really, really cute. He was in his LA uniform of beaten-up cords and a T-shirt. My blood sugar dropped three miles, I'm sure. I felt like I was having an attack of hypoglycemia or something. When Charlie saw me, he looked as shocked as I was.

"What the hell happened to your clothes?" he said.

For a moment I was speechless. Every time I saw Charlie I was somehow at a disadvantage. And what on earth was he doing at the Swyres'? I had never felt so foolish in my life. But this time I was irate.

"What would you care?" I retorted. "Disappearing off like that and not even saying good-bye. You obviously have no manners at all."

"You know the young lady?" asked the butler.

"Yeah, I do," said Charlie, never taking his eyes off me.

I looked away. I mean, I felt like I was going to melt, or cry, I wasn't sure which. Just to really confuse things I also found myself wondering if they have Overnight Kits in Britain. There was a tense silence, interrupted by the butler asking, "Can I offer your friend a sherry?"

"Actually, I'd *adore* a Bellini," I said optimistically.

"She'll have a cup of tea," said Charlie.

I don't want to get all analytical or anything, but the fact is people never change. Charlie was as fervently opposed to Bellinis now as ever.

"Certainly," said the butler, scooting from the library.

"Well, we do seem to meet in the oddest places. Perhaps you'd like to tell me what you're doing here," said Charlie, propping himself up against the mantelpiece in front of the Canaletto.

God he looked cute, but who wouldn't with Canaletto as a backdrop? Still, I was *très* annoyed. Why did I always feel like a schoolgirl being admonished by a head prefect whenever Charlie was around?

"My parents live down the road. I'm here for my dad's fiftieth and my stupid car broke down. I was trying to call home. But what the hell are *you* doing at the Swyres'? Do you know the Earl?"

There was a pause, then Charlie said, "I am the Earl."

"Excuse me?"

"It's a long story, but the reason I left New York in such a hurry on Monday was because I'd just heard that my father died. My mother, Caroline, reached me as soon as she could—don't you remember when she called? I took the first flight. I've inherited the title."

It all took a little while to sink in. The mysterious Caroline was Charlie's estranged mom. There was no other girl, I thought, somewhat relieved.

"Oh my god, I'm so sorry," I said.

I felt terrible. There I was, sulking about the one-night stand, being rude to Charlie, breaking into his place, and it turned out that his dad had died. The last few days must have been a nightmare for him.

"Charlie, are you okay?" I said.

"I'm fine. My dad was a funny old bird—quite peculiar—and we weren't really that close. But it's sad."

"But why didn't you ever say anything?"

"We lived in America. My dad never told anyone he was an Earl. He just used Dunlain, the family name. You don't go around in LA advertising you've got some crazy English title. And then, this place, I vaguely knew Dad still had it but he was pretty secretive about it. When he died I found I'd inherited this estate I've never thought about or had any real connection to. I haven't been here since I was six. It's all rather a shock."

Why do one-night stands always end up being way more complicated than you ever could have imagined? If I'd gotten the story correct, Mr. Overnight Kit here was the Little Earl, the Boy Next Door of Mom's fantasies. There I was thinking Charlie was just some nice, normal guy, and all along he was a total secret silver spoon, completely tricking me about who he was. And he'd called me spoiled! I preferred Charlie before, when he was just some struggling movie director from LA.

There was the tap of heels and an attractive older woman walked into the library. She was wearing skin-tight navy riding breeches, muddy hunting boots, and a man's white shirt. Her brown hair was in a net at the nape of her neck. She was a walking Ralph Lauren ad, only chicer.

"I'm Caroline, Charlie's mother. You must be the lady from the halfway house?" she said, looking at me.

Suddenly I remembered Mom's old feud with Charlie's mom, a.k.a. the Countess of Swyre. It had never been resolved. Oh god, I thought, this could be awkward.

"Mom!" said Charlie. "She's a friend of mine from the States. Her parents live at The Old Rectory."

I froze. The Countess tensed. She knew that I knew that she knew that I was the daughter of the Chair Affair guy.

"What's wrong?" asked Charlie.

"Ugh, whoever said being in the country was a quiet life! I've never been so worked off my feet," said the Countess, speedily changing the subject. She sat down opposite me in a Louis chair, looking piqued. "It takes me half an hour to get anywhere in the house."

There was a knock on the open door. The butler walked in carrying a silver tray laden with tea things.

"Your mother's here, miss, to take you home," he said, setting the tray in front of Caroline.

"Darling! I insisted *I'd* come and get you," trilled Mom,

walking jauntily into the room with Julie following. "Dad had to go into town and pick up the wine for the party tomorrow, otherwise he would have come."

Mom was dressed in her favorite hot pink dress. Worryingly, she had her opal brooch at the neck. She only wears her opal brooch for special occasions, like Princess Anne's birthday. She came over to me and suffocated me with a hug. Although I was pleased to see her, I was worried this was not the best scenario for a liability like Mom to walk into.

"Oh goodness! Look at you! You look like one of those underprivileged wives from the loony bin. Please, *do* wear shoes for Dad's party tomorrow. Ah, Little Earl!" she said, turning to Charlie. "I am so sorry about your father. Awful, everyone in the village is thinking of you. I'm your neighbor, Brooke," she said, holding out her hand to Charlie and curtsying. (I swear she curtsied, she really did. I wanted to die.)

"Thank you," said Charlie, looking bemused.

"Ah, Countess, how lovely to see you after all this time," Mom continued, turning to Caroline, who barely acknowledged her. "And this is Julie Bergdorf—"

"Hey honey!" Julie interrupted, rushing over to hug me. She was sporting a glowing Southampton tan, a flashy engagement ring with a diamond that was princess-cut (of course), and a flowing lilac dress that I didn't recognize at all. "Vintage. Prada, 1994. Don't you love it?"

Julie had changed dramatically since I last saw her. It's the general consensus among Park Avenue Princesses that you'll catch a contagious disease from thrift store clothes. I remember one time we were in Alice's Underground on Broadway she wouldn't touch me for days after I tried on a pair of 1970s men's Levi's in case they had hepatitis B.

"Love it!" I said, kissing Julie on the cheek. As I did so I whispered in her ear, "He says he's the Earl and that this is his place. It's *so* weird."

"No!" she murmured. Then she dashed over to Charlie crying, "Ooh, *loverboy*!"

She kissed him full on the lips. After about five seconds she pulled back, her eyes transfixed by the painting behind his head.

"Charlie, you never said you had secret Canalettos!" she exclaimed. "Wow, this place would be worth like a hundred million dollars if it were on Gin Lane. Have you thought of just selling the whole lot and buying Ibiza or something?"

"Hi, Julie," said Charlie when she released him.

"You know each other?" asked Mom, surprised.

"Very well," said Julie flirtatiously.

"Now, have you met my *lovely* daughter?" said Mom, dragging me toward Charlie. "She doesn't always look like this, you know. She can look very pretty, if she wears foundation and pressed powder."

"Mom!" I said.

"We're old friends, actually," said Charlie, slightly embarrassed.

"Friends! You two! Well, how thrilling!!!" said Mom.

"You've *no idea* how well these two know each other," said Julie, winking at Mom. "Better than you can imagine, Brooke."

"Oh goodness me! What a lovely pair they make. Didn't I always say it was all about the *boy next door,* darling?" said Mom, her cheeks reddening with excitement. She glanced knowingly from Charlie to me and back to Charlie. "And ooh, so handsome. Tell me, have you inherited *everything*?"

"Mom!" I said. "Don't."

Mom really needs to go to Dr. Fensler. She could get an Alpha-Beta peel and a personality makeover all in one go. I looked over at Charlie. For someone who is never unhappy, you could say he'd undergone a dramatic personality change. His face was expressionless, glazed with disbelief, as if to say, *Who is this ghastly woman?* I had to get Mom out of there before she did any more damage.

"Charlie, do you really own half of Scotland like Brooke says? I think that's totally cool. You're a dude," said Julie.

"We should be going, Mom," I said firmly.

"Now, Little Earl, I would be honored if you'd come to my husband Peter's fiftieth birthday lunch tomorrow," said Mom, completely ignoring me.

"Charlie's busy tomorrow," said Caroline abruptly. "He's spending the day with me before I go home to Switzerland on Monday."

"Well, you must come too, Countess," said Mom. "How delightful it would be for our families to spend some time together."

"Our families have nothing to say to each other," said Caroline coldly. She turned away and poured herself some tea.

Suddenly the atmosphere in the room was frostier than the Arctic. Caroline and my mom both froze over like icebergs.

"What is it?" said Charlie.

"Nothing important. It's all in the past," said Mom, looking a little flustered.

"No, tell me, I want to know," insisted Charlie.

"This is the worst family in the village, Charlie. They're a totally untrustworthy, dishonest bunch," said the Countess unemotionally. "I don't want you going anywhere near them."

"Countess!" gasped Mom.

"I feel like I'm in an episode of *The Forsyte Saga*!" said Julie, enthralled by the drama.

I had to step in before things got any worse. I said, "About two hundred years ago, Charlie, my father sold your father some fake Chippendale chairs. My dad admitted the mistake but there was a rift. The two families stopped speaking to each other completely." There, it was out. How silly it all seemed now.

"Is that it?" said Charlie, looking bemused and slightly relieved.

"Yes. Now can we please forget the chairs? It was a ridiculous misunderstanding," chipped in Mom. Then just for good measure she glared at the Countess and added, "Your mother turned it into a scandal. It was simply dreadful for me."

"That's not entirely true, but it hardly matters since we have nothing more to discuss," responded the Countess icily.

There was an uncomfortable silence, and Charlie looked anxiously between his mother and mine. I couldn't tell who he believed. Maybe the light was dawning and he was recalling distant family history. No one said a thing or moved. As the seconds ticked by, the silence became increasingly awkward. Then Mom threw in a real gem: "Well, now everything's out in the open, why don't you *both* come to the party tomorrow? I've got the dearest little mini pita breads in from Waitrose." She paused and you could see the cogs turning in her brain. "Gosh, this place would be lovely for a wedding, darling, wouldn't it? Vera Wang could do the dress."

That was the final straw.

"Mom, stop it!" I burst out at her. "There isn't going to be a wedding. The idea of me marrying Charlie is the last thing on anyone's mind, except yours. His mom can't stand you. The Countess thinks she's way too classy for us. What she says is true. Charlie and I have nothing to say to each other. Zero. Nothing. You know what? I don't even like Charlie very much. He can be really mean and patronizing. The Swyres don't want to come to your party tomorrow, and they're not impressed by mini pitas." Then I turned to Charlie and said, "Charlie, I'm truly sorry about your father and everything, but this is a total nightmare. How can I ever trust you when you didn't even tell me you were the Earl? I've got to go. You can all sort it out by yourselves."

Flushed with embarrassment and on the verge of tears, I fled from the library, shoes in hand. I dashed down the stairs, out into the driveway and straight into the arms of a man in uniform.

"The young lady from the Refuge?" said the policeman.

"That's me," I gasped. I didn't care anymore. "Can you take me home, please?"

12

The most noticeable thing about The Old Rectory is that it's not old at all. Much to Mom's irritation, there is no getting away from the fact that it dates from 1965, not 1665. It's a very comfortable, faux-Victorian, redbrick, four-bedroom house. Still, that hasn't stopped Mom from investing in climbing roses, wisteria, and ivy, trained to grow abundantly around the front door and windows in an effort to make it look way cuter and more authentic than it really is.

No one was home when I got back. P. C. Lyle, the policeman I'd bumped into outside the castle, had kindly towed my rental car home with us. I went around to the back door and let myself in through the kitchen, lugging my suitcase with me. God, I thought as I climbed up the back stairs to the spare bedroom, what on earth had I just done at the castle? I suddenly regretted the things I'd said far more than I'd thought I would. I felt irritated and bothered but I couldn't quite figure out why. Maybe I was just jet-lagged. I was so tired after this afternoon, I just wanted to collapse for an hour on my bed.

For a woman afflicted with migraines, Mom's choice of wallpaper is 100 percent inexplicable. Every inch of the spare bedroom, including the ceiling, was covered with wallpaper of climbing yellow roses, with matching duvets and lamp shades. There were even yellow towels and dressing gowns. Honestly, when I saw it all I thought I was going to die of a headache. The rest of the room was covered with Julie's stuff, as though she'd just walked in and emptied three suitcases over the bed and the floor (she probably had). There were jewel pouches and wash bags, piles of makeup, two cell phones, an iPod, and brand-new clothes and shoes everywhere. There were even Diptyque candles and a couple of framed photographs of Julie and her dad tossed on the mounds of stuff. Julie always travels as though she is moving house because she read in *Paris Match* that Margherita Missoni, the young beautiful Missoni kid, always "personalizes" her hotel rooms with things from home to make her feel more relaxed.

I dumped my case and zebra bag in the middle of the floor and collapsed on top of Julie's clothes on one of the beds. Desperate to distract myself from recent events, I picked up the phone off the side table by my bed and called Jolene.

"He-ey!" she said when she picked up. "Can you believe it about Julie and Henry? I always said one of us would snag him. But I've got an issue, with the wedding, and I was wondering if you could influence things?"

"What's happened?"

"Julie's asked Zac Posen to make her bridal gown. Vera Wang's so gutted she's threatening to retire from bridal all together. Can you persuade her to drop Zac and go with

Vera? If Vera retires before I get married, I'll die. What on earth would I wear?"

"She said Alexander McQueen was making the dress."

"Oh god, don't tell me she's asked him too!"

Weddings always bring out the worst in the Park Avenue set. Their friends' weddings make them obsess about one thing: their own. But Jolene had a point. If Vera Wang retired, it would devastate the entire unmarried Park Avenue female demographic. Just then I heard a cell phone ringing. It must be Julie's Tri-Band.

"I'll try," I said. "I gotta go. Julie's cell is ringing. I better get it."

"Okay. But don't forget about Vera, and my dress!"

I picked up Julie's cell. It was Jazz. She sounded even more frazzled than Jolene.

"Where's Julie?" she wailed.

"She's not here right now," I said.

"Oh nooo! I need to speak with her about Mr. Valentino. He's desperate to make her wedding dress. Any chance you can drag her back from the Zac Posen abyss? *No pressure,* but I'm really worried about losing my muse job if I don't secure the Bergdorf bride, plus entourage."

"Jazz, I don't know." This was not a fashion fiasco I cared to be involved with.

"Plee-eease. Valentino will gift you *big time.* I'm with him on his boat in the Aegean. Why don't you come down? It's lovely here. God, what am I going to say to him tonight at dinner?"

One minute Jazz was another innocent lumber heiress, the next she was a ruthless satellite of the Valentino fashion empire. It's shocking really, when you see your close friends resort to bribery. I would have no part of it, however gorgeous an outfit Valentino might flatter me with.

"Jazz, I gotta go," I said.

"Are you all right?" she asked.

"I'm fine," I said. "Speak soon, okay?"

Right now Jazz's career problems seemed very superficial to me. She'd have to sort them out herself. Concerned about my party outfit being horribly creased for tomorrow, I hauled myself off the bed and started to unpack. I hung my new Balenciaga minidress (very hot, very now, very likely to be underappreciated in Stibbly) on the front of the armoire. I laid out my shoes, sweater, and lingerie. But where were my gorgeous pavé diamond hoops? Strictly speaking, they weren't exactly mine, they were Julie's. She'd forgotten about them, but I swear I've been planning to give them back to her for ages (over nine months now), and I've almost gone through with it several times.

I checked every inch of my little suitcase. Emptied my wash bag. Scrambled through my clothes. I grabbed my handbag and shook the entire contents out on the bed. Everything tumbled out. But there was no sign of the earrings. Hopelessly, I put my hands in my pockets and rifled around. I felt a hard little object in my right pocket. My heart sank as I remembered the enamel and gold box. Shoot! I'd totally forgotten to replace it after the butler found me. I pulled it out of my pocket and sat down cross-legged on the floor. I flicked open the top. The inside was lined with smooth gold. On the roof of the lid was an inscription: *Presented to the Earl of Swyre, for bravery in the battle of Waterloo, 1815.*

Oh, no. Not only was the box a beautiful object, it was of historic significance to the Swyres. It was probably worth thousands of dollars. Somehow, I had to get the box back to the Swyres without Charlie's finding out I'd taken it. As if Charlie didn't disapprove of me enough already, this was going to make it worse. Not that I cared; I mean, I was never going to see him again. If he offered me another night of regret I wouldn't even be tempted. I'd had quite enough of him. I couldn't wait until tomorrow was over and I could go back to New York and have a regular one-night stand with someone I was never going to see again, who wouldn't turn out to be the son of the man next door whose family had been feuding with mine for a generation.

I heard a door slam downstairs and voices. Everyone was back. I hurriedly hid the little box in my zebra handbag. Feet sprinted up the stairs and suddenly Mom, Dad, and Julie were crowding in at the door.

"Are you all right, dear?" said Mom. "Why are you lying on Julie's clothes?"

"I'm just really jet-lagged," I said, not getting up. "Sorry about today, Mom, I didn't mean it about the party."

"I'm sure most people would rather be stuck in traffic than come to one of your mother's parties," said Dad. "Aawwggghhh!" he howled as Mom clipped him smartly on the back of the head.

"Peter, it's *your* party."

"Well, I wish you'd let me invite some of my friends then."

"Mom, I'm sure everyone's going to love it," I said.

"We had a lovely chat with Caroline after you left. That Charlie is a very sensible boy, you know. Convinced his mother that she was being melodramatic about the chairs. We've made up. After all these years! The Countess is coming to the party, with Charlie. Isn't that *sensational* news?"

No, I thought. *Maybe if I called Patrick Saxton he'd send a helicopter for me. I wonder if there's anywhere it could land in the garden of The Old Rectory?*

"I thought I'd wear my Caroline Charles cream suit. What do you think?"

"Who's Caroline Charles?" said Julie.

"She's Princess Anne's favorite designer."

If only Mom would face up to the fact she's American and wear Bill Blass like everyone else's moms, she'd look a whole lot better.

"Do you know how the father managed to disappear like that, in America?" asked Mom.

"They never used the title. Charlie told me," I replied.

"Title*s* darling, plural. Dunlain is the family name and the titles are the Earl of Swyre and Viscount Strathan. If you've got that many names and you move countries, I suppose no one ever knows who you really are. I don't understand the British, covering up those wonderful titles! It's criminal. By the way, the Finnoullas are bringing their daughter Agatha tomorrow. She's a lesbian, darling, but we all have to pretend we don't know."

Rest was impossible that night. Maybe Julie *would* look more glam in Valentino than Zac Posen, I thought as I lay in my bed in the spare room not sleeping. Anything to distract my mind from the day's events. I mean, yes, Zac P. is the trendiest designer in the world this second, no argument, but does a girl really want to look like Chloë Sevigny on her wedding day? I swear this is *nothing* to do with wanting a free Valentino outfit, but I suddenly felt compelled to stop Julie from ruining her wedding day by dressing as an indie actress.

"Julie," I whispered. "Are you awake still?"

"Sort of. What is it?"

"What about Valentino, for the dress? I mean, when Debra Messing wore him to the Golden Globes she went from no-name TV girl to fashion star overnight. Maybe Zac's too avant-garde."

"I'm asking a lot of designers to make me something. I'm just trying to keep everyone happy. Then I'll decide on the day. I always change my mind a million times about what I want to wear when I go out so I'm figuring I need multiple options on my wedding day."

"You can't do that."

"I so can. Wow, can you believe Charlie has that incredible place? And all that antique stuff. I wonder if he'll ever invite me to stay after I was so mean dating Todd in Paris. Eew, the triple-dating I used to do!"

Henry had really had an effect on Julie. I mean, she never even used to be conscious she was triple-dating, let alone show any remorse.

"Julie, can I ask you something?"

"Sure."

"Did Charlie break up with you in Paris?"

"Eew! Okay, yeah, I guess he did."

"Why did you say you were still together?"

"Duh. Because, historically, no one *ever* leaves Julie Bergdorf. I don't know why you let so many men break up with you. Do you think Charlie would sell off any of those paintings? I really dig that Canaletto in the library. It would look so much cuter in my bedroom at The Pierre though."

"I don't think people sell off their family heirlooms here," I said.

"Shame. Everyone thinks you're madly in love with each other. And he's got that house and everything! You two would be so cute together."

God, Julie was turning into my mom.

"Julie, stop it!"

"He wouldn't be a bad person to date. At least we know now he could afford a driver. He's a *terrific* catch. Mind you, after your incredible tantrum this afternoon and being so rude to Charlie—"

"Oh god, was I terribly rude?" It was starting to dawn on me how unforgivably ill-mannered I'd been today.

"How *weren't* you rude?"

Coming from the reigning queen of bad manners herself, this was a bit much. Still, Julie was right. I mean, I'd broken into Charlie's house, stolen a beautiful tchotchke—though since he didn't know about that it didn't really count—had a meltdown in front of him, insulted Charlie, his mom, and mine, and all right after a death in the family. Looking back on it, I realized how embarrassed and cross I was about the whole Little Earl business, thinking Charlie was trying to trick me. Now, lying there in the dark, I felt foolish. Maybe I'd overreacted. Charlie was probably a perfectly decent human being—even if he'd taken terrible advantage of me during that weak moment at the Mercer—who'd actually been pretty sweet to me on several unhappy occasions. He hadn't tried to mislead me about being the Earl, he just wasn't a big fat show-off, unlike some of my other dates, Eduardo and Patrick to name but two. I mean, English toffs have some crazy code of honor where they never say anything that might be considered even the teensiest bit show-offy. The fact was, I regretfully admitted to myself, Charlie had impeccable manners, and I had shown myself to have less than perfect ones today.

"Julie, god, I feel like such a jerk. Do you think if I apologize to him at the party tomorrow he'll forgive me?"

And I could return the pillbox, I thought. That would be almost as hard as apologizing. It was so divine I was getting totally attached to it. It would be so much nicer for my Tylenol to live in there than in their paper carton.

"Yeah, you should. Then we can all enjoy the party, and maybe you can get laid."

"Julie, stop it! Have you got an Ambien?" I asked. I'd never get to sleep without a chemical boost.

"Sure," said Julie, rifling around on the floor. She found a little plastic jar, popped it open, and handed me a tiny pale orange tablet.

I slipped it in my mouth and washed it down with a sip of water. Bliss, I thought as I lay back on Mom's crisp Irish linen pillow. If only I could take another Ambien when I woke up tomorrow morning.

"Wear this," commanded Julie the next day, handing me a pale pink silk dress trimmed with lace. It had a sexy split up one side. It was completely inappropriate for an English garden party.

"I'm wearing the Balenciaga dress," I protested.

"You can't! That dress has been so *done*. Kate Hudson wore it to the Golden Globes, then there was a shot of Charlize Theron at Cannes in it. Next thing you know it'll turn up on Rebecca Romijn-Stamos at the MTV awards, and then it'll really be over," sighed Julie. "I'm concerned that a preppy white dress is not the best get-the-guy-with-the-castle number."

Since I wasn't planning on getting the guy with the castle anyway, I didn't really care. But it did occur to me that maybe Charlie wouldn't be quite so cross with me when I gave him back his golden pillbox if I was looking really adorable and showing a bit of leg. I mean, if you can distract a man from his real purpose with fashion, do, I always say. I took the silk dress and slipped it on. It was almost one o'clock and we needed to join the party.

"You look delicious," said Julie, who looked pretty delicious herself in a pistachio Narciso shift and too many pearls.

"Thanks, Julie," I said, surreptitiously grabbing the pillbox from my zebra bag and stuffing it inside my clutch. "Let's go down. Mom's gonna be going nuts."

"Darling! Yooooo-hooooo! Over here!"

Mom was beckoning Julie and me from a shady corner of the tent at the bottom of the garden. Dad's party was in full swing, the perfect picture of English country life. Guests were milling about sipping Pimm's on the lawn at the back of the house. I had to hand it to Mom, she'd done a great job. She'd gone totally Thomas Hardy with the décor (one of her favorite themes). There were little wooden benches for guests to sit on, and glass jars filled with cottage garden flowers—lupins, sweetpeas, cornflowers—on the tables. Dad was in his element, dressed in his favorite striped seersucker suit, surrounded by a gaggle of his friends' leggy teenage daughters. As Mom had predicted, the sun was beating down as though we were on South Beach. If only I wasn't feeling so tense, I thought, I might be able to really enjoy myself.

Julie and I each grabbed a Pimm's off a tray and wandered over to Mom. She was wearing the aforementioned cream suit and hat. (Any chance to wear a hat and Mom is in one. You can imagine.) She looked somewhat overdressed, as did Julie and I: most of the guests were dressed in tatty straw hats and ancient tea dresses, as is the custom of the British upper classes at garden parties.

"My god, haven't these people heard of fashion?" asked Julie as we crossed the lawn.

"Julie, British people think fashion's tacky," I explained.

"That's really sad," she said, a tragic look on her face.

"Darling, are you wearing foundation?" said Mom.

"Actually, Mom, no. It's too hot," I replied.

"Julie, you look wonderful, who made that sensational dress?" asked Mom. Before Julie could answer, Mom looked over my shoulder and said, "Ah *Countess-sss*." I tensed. This was going to be humiliating, I thought. "How marvelous to see you. Pimm's?"

Julie and I turned to see Caroline approaching. She looked 100 percent chic in that undone English way. She was wearing men's pants with a sheer Indian shawl thrown elegantly over her shoulders.

"Brooke, call me Caroline, please."

"Caroline. Pimm's?" said Mom, beaming.

"Hello girls," said Caroline. "What lovely outfits."

"Thank you. You look totally hot, too," said Julie.

"Julie, do tell us about your wedding. Who's making your dress?" said Mom.

I couldn't focus on the small talk at all. Where was Charlie?

"Well it changes every day—obviously—but right now it's Oscar de la Renta, Valentino, McQueen, and Zac Posen. I guess I'll decide on the day," said Julie.

"Won't someone get upset?" asked Caroline.

Smiling sweetly Julie replied, "Yeah, probably, but you know, I'm really spoiled, and very rich and exceptionally pretty, so I get to do exactly what I want." Seeing Caroline's expression of shock, Julie added, "It's okay, you don't have to feel sorry for me. I like me like this."

"So, where's the birthday boy?" asked Caroline.

"Peter is smoking with the *teenage* girls," said Mom. "Where is your little boy? On his way I hope."

"He sends his regards, Brooke, but he wanted me to let you all know he's so terribly sorry not to be here today. He had to go back to Los Angeles this morning."

"So soon after the funeral?" said Mom, unable to hide her disappointment.

"He's just directed a film and it seems someone wants to talk to him about doing another one. Had to go today, he said. You know what Americans are like when it comes to business. Very pushy, aren't they?" said Caroline pointedly.

Charlie wasn't coming? This was a disaster, from the apology perspective. I suddenly felt anxious and edgy.

"Julie, shall we go in and get some Bucks Fizz?" I said, making a let's-get-out-of-here expression.

"What is it?" said Julie.

"Back in a minute, Mom," I said, taking Julie's hand and leading her out of the tent.

I snuck off with Julie into the kitchen. It was fearfully hot in there because Mom insists on having an Aga, which is like a rich English person's stove. It's like they all absolutely have to have one, like Americans have to have a Sub-Zero fridge if they're anyone who's anyone. The problem with Agas is they're on all the time, even in summer. It was like a furnace in there but at least we were alone.

"Oh god, Julie, what am I going to do?" I said, agitated

"What are you talking about? Why are you hyperventilating?" said Julie, looking concerned.

"He's not here!"

"Who?"

"Charlie."

"So?"

"But what about apologizing to him? Saying I'm sorry for being so rude and everything."

Even though I had actually been dreading seeing him after yesterday, I suddenly really minded that Charlie wasn't here after all.

"Send him an e-mail," suggested Julie.

"That would be so rude. You have to apologize in person if it's going to mean anything," I replied.

"You're completely obsessed with him."

"I'm not! What am I going to do?" I wailed, pacing around the kitchen.

"Why are you so desperate to apologize in person? Are you totally in love with him or something?"

"Oh Julie, it's not that. I just feel terrible for being such an idiot yesterday. I want him to see that I can be responsible, and grown up, and that I'm a good person and everything."

"Who are you kidding?! You're nuts about him."

"Julie! It's much worse than you think. I stole something out of that library last night."

"No! Did you take a piece of family jewelry?"

"No, I took a pillbox."

"Eew," said Julie, looking slightly disappointed. "What's the big deal about that?"

I rifled in my clutch bag and took out the little enamel box and set it on the kitchen table. I opened the lid and showed the inscription to Julie.

"God, how beautiful! I think you should keep it as a souvenir," said Julie.

"I can't," I said.

"Okay, so we'll just sneak out and go put it back and no one will ever know the difference. Come on, darling, let's get in the car and go now."

❧

Whenever Julie hits Europe she always rents a snappy BMW to allow her to take advantage of the liberal speed limits. The lanes to the castle, with their blind corners and steep dips, were no obstacle to this—Julie took them as though she were driving the Monaco Grand Prix.

"Julie, slow down!" I yelled as we took another curve at speed.

"Oh god, sorry," she said, braking dramatically. "I just find driving slowly so uncool."

She slowed to a more manageable pace. As we passed

a cornfield dotted with wild red poppies Julie said, "I can't believe we haven't discussed it yet, but what do you think of my engagement ring?" She flashed it in the sunlight. The stone was so large it could support its own solar system.

"It's really incredible," I said.

"Well you know what they say. The bigger the diamond, the longer the relationship lasts."

Frankly I'm a little concerned about Julie's understanding of marriage. She hadn't matured nearly as much as I'd thought since her engagement.

"He owns half of Connecticut, more or less. And you know I love it there."

Julie was definitely in love. She's been allergic to Connecticut forever. She always says that the huge number of married women there driving aimlessly around in Range Rovers, wearing identical vanilla-colored, thirty-thousand-ply cashmere turtlenecks by Loro Piana and solitaire diamonds makes her feel suicidal.

"Do you want me to come in with you?" asked Julie fifteen minutes later as we pulled up outside the castle door.

"No, you just wait here in the getaway car. I'll be five minutes," I said, putting the enamel box back in my clutch and getting out of the car.

"Okay, dude! Don't get caught."

God, I thought to myself as I slipped in through the main entrance, *this could be icky if I see that butler guy again.* Sneaking up the stairs and along the corridor to the library, I felt uncomfortable when I remembered my tantrum from the day before. I just wanted to put the little box back and be out of there. Even if I was never going to be able to apologize to Charlie in person, the least I could do was redeem myself by returning the box I'd taken. Not that anyone would necessarily know that I'd redeemed myself, since no one knew I'd taken the little box in the first place.

Just as I was coming to the library, I heard a door to my left being opened. I froze. What if that was the butler? I couldn't face being almost arrested twice in twenty-four hours. I looked around. I didn't dare go on, but I couldn't go back either. I pulled back into a dark alcove, with a stuffed stag's head hanging above me. Tense, I watched as the door opened and a figure appeared. I gasped. It was Charlie. What was he doing here? Wasn't he supposed to be on his way to LA?

He looked right at me. He seemed even more shocked than I was. Oh god, I thought, now I'll have to apologize face to face, and admit I have his box and be all grown up and honest about everything. Now that I had the chance, I didn't fancy it at all. But for once Charlie was speechless. Not only that, I detected a slightly shy, embarrassed look on his face. God, I couldn't believe it, Charlie was actually blushing. There was an awkward silence.

"I thought you'd gone to LA. What are you doing here?" I said eventually.

"Um . . ." Charlie looked more uncomfortable than ever.

"Yes?" I said.

"Frankly, I just couldn't face the party, after yesterday."

"I see," I said. How rude, I thought, after everything that had happened.

"I didn't want to upset you any more than I already have. I'm not leaving for LA till tomorrow night. God, I'm totally busted, aren't I?" he said sheepishly.

The tables had turned. For the first time ever, Charlie was apologizing to me. Strictly *entre nous*, I loved it.

"Very busted *indeed*," I said, unable to resist a grin. He smiled back, a little reassured.

"I'm sorry. I didn't mean to offend you, really. That's a nice dress," he said.

See. It had worked. I'd completely distracted him from the robbery I was about to put right with Julie's outfit.

"Thanks," I said.

He took a step closer, looking at me inquisitively.

"So, are you planning on making a habit of breaking into this place?"

"No!" Drat. Maybe the tables hadn't turned after all.

"Well, what are you doing here then?"

"Well, okay . . ."

God, he's still *très* cute, I thought, even without the Canaletto as a backdrop. He was wearing a navy shirt and pants and looked ridiculously handsome. What a drag he'd caught me. I mean, there'd be no chance of any more regret when he found out I was a thief.

"Okay what?" he said, coming and leaning against the wall next to me.

I had to pull myself together. I was not here to engineer another regrettable scenario with Charlie.

"Well, god, I'm so embarrassed about yesterday," I said eventually. Now it was my turn to blush. "I'm really sorry,

Charlie, for what I said. I don't think your mom's a snob, and I didn't mean it about you trying to trick me, and I do like you—"

"I don't think we'll ever be able to see each other again," said Charlie.

"Really?"

"It's doubtful," he said. "You are a dreadful girl."

"I'm sorry," I said sadly. I looked up at him. If I wasn't mistaken there was a very mischievous look in his eye. "You're kidding me!" I said, laughing. "Do you think you can ever forgive someone as dreadful as me?"

"Of course I forgive you. How could I not in that dress?"

That's the nice thing about Charlie. He forgives me everything almost immediately. I really admire that. Most people I know, like me, take forever to forgive even a tiny thing like Julie stealing my favorite Cosabella thong. Eew, now I'd have to tell him about the pillbox.

"Don't look so worried!" he said, seeing my anxious face. "What is it?"

"Well, actually, there's something else." That little gold box could ruin our *détente,* I thought unhappily.

"I can take it," he said, looking me straight in the eye.

For a split second, I stared right back. I swear I'm not exaggerating when I say this, but the whole universe was in that look. Everything. The past, the future, the sun, the sky, every pair of shoes Marc Jacobs ever designed, every Bellini, every ball gown, every trip to Rio I'd ever taken. God, I thought to myself, how could I have let Charlie slip through my fingers like that? He's the real deal. Kind, adorable, the cutest thing ever—and that's not even including how good he is in bed, or his lovely castle or anything (not that I was influenced by that at all, of course). What a dingbat I'd been! No one had cared more about me these past few months than Charlie. True, I'd been beyond annoyed when he'd saved my life in Paris and everything, but when you really think about it, it's a very enchanting thing to do. When he put me on that plane from Nice to New York, even though I could have murdered him at the time, afterwards I secretly thought it was sweet beyond belief.

"What was it you had to tell me?" said Charlie, taking my hand.

What did I have to tell him? Literally, I couldn't speak. When Charlie touched me my blood sugar dropped fifteen miles. The fact was, I realized now, I didn't have hypoglycemia, at all. I'll try and explain it better. If you only get hypoglycemia around one person, the chances are actually much greater that you might be falling in love than that you have suddenly contracted a nasty sugar condition.

"The thing is, Charlie, I've got to admit something bad," I said, starting to open my purse.

God I could murder Julie sometimes. The fact is, she was totally right about everything. I was *très, très* in love with Charlie, in love and infatuated beyond belief, and here he was off to LA tomorrow! Maybe I had to take my chance and tell him, for real, how I really felt, come what may and all that. Seriously, I had to do it. I mean, if I told him about the pillbox and then immediately made up for it with a really romantic, very regrettable afternoon, surely he wouldn't be so cross with me? To quote Julia Roberts in *Pretty Woman,* I wanted the fairy tale. She told Richard

Gere how she felt about him and it all worked out fine and it's not like she's got that huge an advantage over me, except for the smile. I mean she was a hooker in that movie and Richard didn't mind *at all.*

"Admit what?" said Charlie.

He turned toward me and traced his finger along my nose and over my lips. God, maybe I was in for some regret after all. Maybe I shouldn't admit to the box quite yet. There was the possibility of a very romantic moment on the way and it seemed foolish to ruin it. Charlie was still looking at me expectantly. I had to say something.

"Charlie, I have to admit . . . I thought it was sweet of you to take care of me that time in Nice airport. Sorry I was so ungrateful."

"How could I resist?" sighed Charlie. "You're exasperating."

"Oh," I said, disappointed. Maybe I wasn't Julia Roberts after all. Maybe I was just *moi.*

"Don't look so heartbroken! You're adorable, even if you do drive me crazy."

"Crazy?"

"Yeah, but you're not like those other girls in New York. You're funny and you don't even know you're funny. It's sweet. Sometimes I think you were made especially for me," said Charlie, kissing me on the lips.

I swear I'm not exaggerating but this kiss was beyond. Seriously, it was the kiss to end all the others, the one that makes you think you never want to kiss anyone else ever again. I mean, you can have all the Bellinis and ball gowns in the world, you can be invited on PJs and be given Harry Winston diamonds and Fred Leighton pearls, you can have six Marc Jacobs stores on your doorstep and go to movie premieres and gala dinners every night, but when you get a kiss like that, Marc Jacobs stores don't seem important at all. In actual fact you feel like you might never want to shop again, which is really saying something.

"Dudes! Hey, my god, romance alert! Let's all dial 911-LOVE!"

I looked up from the kiss of my life to see Julie standing at the top of the stairs. I'd completely forgotten about her waiting outside in the car.

"Julie, I'm so sorry!" I laughed.

"You two are so cute! You look like an Eternity ad! Why am I always right about everything? Didn't I say you two were madly in love with each other? Listen, I gotta get back to the party."

"Do I have to come with you?" I wailed.

I mean, I love my dad and everything, but I had the feeling I was on the verge of some extremely regrettable regret and you know me, when faced by a choice between another glass of Pimm's or a trip to Brazil, I'll always take Brazil.

"No," said Julie. "Stay here. When I tell your mom you've been making out with 'Little Earl' all afternoon she'll totally forgive you for missing your dad's birthday."

"Julie, you can't! I'll have to go back," I said, turning to Charlie.

"I don't think so," said Charlie, holding me firmly by the hand. "You're staying with me."

"Right on, dudes. I'll keep the moms away. See you two tomorrow!" said Julie. Just before she got to the staircase she turned and added, "By the way, Charlie, I know you're a terrific catch with half of Scotland and all those Canalettos, but she's the real catch."

The minute Julie had left, we snuck into the gorgeous room with the four-poster bed draped in Chinese silk, which was honestly as comfortable as the beds in the Four Seasons everyone's always going on about. I think the next thing that occurred was that Charlie said something *très* romantic about how he'd had extraordinarily low blood sugar from the absolute second he'd met me and that he'd often felt rather dizzy around me too, in a good way. I'm sorry, you know, because I can't recall the precise, beautiful words he used because it wasn't exactly the moment for historical accuracy. But one thing I can say for definite is that he kissed me for well over 976 seconds in six different regions.

Anyway, the kissing was so delicious that I forgot to breathe—you know how you do with really professional kissing—and you know, when your brain's deprived of oxygen for prolonged periods like that, everything goes kind of hazy and you can't really remember intimate details very brilliantly. So I'm not sure specifically what happened after the kissing, but I think it was pretty regrettable, like if it had been a movie it wouldn't have been allowed to be shown anywhere in America. Seriously, it was way beyond the Brazil I thought I knew so well, if you get my meaning. Honestly, I thought I knew everything there was to know about Rio and Latin America, but now I know that I know nothing. Anyway, after all that regret, which, incidentally, I don't regret at all, you can imagine, I was exhausted.

"Can I get you anything?" said Charlie, smiling at me as though I were Christmas or something. God, he looked cute with that Fragonard above his head. Everyone should get to make love under a French oil painting once in their lives, shouldn't they? "Anything you want."

"Anything?" I said.

"Whatever you want."

"I'd *adore* a Bellini."

THE END
(Almost)

A few things I want to take back:

1. I didn't mean it about four-poster beds, really. They're 100 percent awesome after all. (The little gold box is under the pillow, in case you were wondering what happened to it.)

2. Never reform yourself too much. That whole thing about never going on a PJ again was just dumb.

3. Jolene is married, though that fact regularly escapes her notice.

4. The police tracked the chinchilla to a resale store on the Upper West Side. Valentino was very confused when I sent it back: apparently none of the actresses or social girls ever return the good stuff.

5. Muffy is still thirty-eight. She turns thirty-seven next week.

6. Julie has extended her engagement indefinitely, enjoying changing her mind about the blooms too much to let it come to an end.

7. Vera Wang didn't retire. Due to unprecedented unity among the unmarried Park Avenue Princesses, Julie has promised Vera she can do her dress.

8. Lara is still *très* traumatized about the Van Cleef sample sale because they didn't invite her for the second year running.

9. Patrick Saxton has left Jazz Conassey voice mail messages at six separate numbers. She hasn't returned them, obviously.

10. Charlie lent the castle to the Refuge Moms indefinitely. Now everyone in the village is their New Best Friend, including Mom, who is trying to get Dad to leave her so she can move in. Meanwhile I've got my eye on a gorgeous apartment in Soho for the two of us.

11. I have hypoglycemia almost all the time now. It's a permanent condition. I highly recommend it.

THE END

(for definite)

Acknowledgments

There would be no *Bergdorf Blondes* without the help of a great many people. I wish to thank Anna Wintour, whose support during my career at American *Vogue* and while writing this book has been invaluable; my editors, Jonathan Burnham at Miramax Books and Juliet Annan at Viking Books, for their skilled editing and dedication; and Elizabeth Sheinkman, for being a great agent.

I am lucky to have friends and colleagues in New York who were always on hand to answer a question, whether it was the thread count of the Mercer's sheets, or the details of the du Cap diet. Thank you so much to Dr. Steven Victor, Marina Rust, Andre Balazs, Anthony Todd, Bill Tansy, Samantha Gregory, Sandy Golinkin, Pamela Gross, Holly Peterson, David Netto, Julie Daniels-Janklow, Alexandra Kotur, Lara Shriftman, Elizabeth Saltzman, Stephanie Winston Wolkoff, Kadee Robbins, Miranda Brooks, Hamish Bowles.

To those friends who saw me through the writing and editing—Katie Collins, Miranda Rock, GKP, Helen James,

Kara Baker, Allie Esiri, Bay and Daisy Garnett, Sean Ellis, Rita Konig, Richard Mason, Bryan Adams, Alan Watson, Matthew Williamson, Vicky Ward, Susan Block, Lucy Sykes, Alice Sykes, Tom Sykes, Fred Sykes, Josh Sykes, Valerie Sykes, and Toby Rowland—sorry for all the moaning and whining. We can talk about something else now.